The Origin of Sin

Also available from Bloomsbury

Ancient Persia and the Book of Esther, Lloyd Llewellyn-Jones
Ecology and Theology in the Ancient World, Ailsa Hunt and Hilary Marlow
The Devil: A Guide for the Perplexed, Derek R. Brown

The Origin of Sin

Greece and Rome, Early Judaism and Christianity

David Konstan

BLOOMSBURY ACADEMIC
LONDON • NEW YORK • OXFORD • NEW DELHI • SYDNEY

BLOOMSBURY ACADEMIC
Bloomsbury Publishing Plc
50 Bedford Square, London, WC1B 3DP, UK
1385 Broadway, New York, NY 10018, USA
29 Earlsfort Terrace, Dublin 2, Ireland

BLOOMSBURY, BLOOMSBURY ACADEMIC and the Diana logo are trademarks of Bloomsbury Publishing Plc

First published in Great Britain 2022

Copyright © David Konstan, 2022

David Konstan has asserted his right under the Copyright, Designs and Patents Act, 1988, to be identified as Author of this work.

For legal purposes the Acknowledgments on pp. xiv–xv constitute an extension of this copyright page.

Cover design: Terry Woodley
Cover images © PeskyMonkey/iStock and Martin Barraud/Getty

All rights reserved. No part of this publication may be reproduced or transmitted in any form or by any means, electronic or mechanical, including photocopying, recording, or any information storage or retrieval system, without prior permission in writing from the publishers.

Bloomsbury Publishing Plc does not have any control over, or responsibility for, any third-party websites referred to or in this book. All internet addresses given in this book were correct at the time of going to press. The author and publisher regret any inconvenience caused if addresses have changed or sites have ceased to exist, but can accept no responsibility for any such changes.

A catalogue record for this book is available from the British Library.

Library of Congress Cataloging-in-Publication Data
Names: Konstan, David, author.
Title: The origin of sin : from Graeco-Roman antiquity to early Christianity / David Konstan.
Description: New York : Bloomsbury Academic, 2022. |
Includes bibliographical references and index.
Identifiers: LCCN 2021033214 (print) | LCCN 2021033215 (ebook) |
ISBN 9781350278585 (hardback) | ISBN 9781350278592 (paperback) |
ISBN 9781350278608 (ebook) | ISBN 9781350278615 (epub)
Subjects: LCSH: Sin. | Sin–Biblical teaching. | Sin–Christianity–History of doctrines.
Classification: LCC BL475.7 .K66 2022 (print) | LCC BL475.7 (ebook) | DDC 241/.3—dc23
LC record available at https://lccn.loc.gov/2021033214
LC ebook record available at https://lccn.loc.gov/2021033215

ISBN:	HB:	978-1-3502-7858-5
	PB:	978-1-3502-7859-2
	ePDF:	978-1-3502-7860-8
	eBook:	978-1-3502-7861-5

Typeset by RefineCatch Limited, Bungay, Suffolk

To find out more about our authors and books visit www.bloomsbury.com and sign up for our newsletters.

For my family on both sides of the Atlantic, and to the newest member, my godson Alejandro.

Contents

Preface		viii
Acknowledgments		xiv
1	The Greco-Roman World: The Unwritten Laws of the Gods	1
2	The Hebrew Bible: Chasing after Foreign Gods	33
3	The New Testament: Jesus' Sense of Sin	77
4	The Church Fathers and the Rabbis: The Transformation of Sin	123
A Final Word		159
Notes		161
References		179
Index		193

Preface

The argument of this short book is easy to state: sin begins with the Bible. And, in one sense, it ends there. There is no comparable concept in the surrounding Greek and Roman world—that non-Jewish, non-Christian world that we conventionally label pagan, although it embraced myriad forms of religion of very different sorts, from the worship of the Olympian gods to mystery cults such as Orphism. Ordinarily, the word "pagan" is too broad and fudges over the immense variety of religious life in classical antiquity. But for our purposes it is a serviceable term, because I mean to demonstrate that the idea of sin is restricted precisely to the Bible, both the Hebrew Bible or Tanakh and the New Testament, and that this Biblical sense was not a feature of any of the many beliefs and practices that we may, for convenience, call pagan. This may not seem like a great discovery; however, as we shall see, the usual definitions of sin do not succeed in discriminating Biblical usage from Greek and Roman conceptions of wrongdoing. If by sin we mean something like violating the law of God (and this is the most common definition), then the idea of sin is certainly present in classical texts as well as in the Bible. In itself, of course, that is not surprising or unwelcome: why should there not be intimations of sin in pagan literature and religion? But the fact is that there is a sense of sin that is specific to the Bible, both the Hebrew scriptures and (in a somewhat different form) the New Testament, although it has not been recognized in modern definitions and interpretations. For that matter, it was already obscure even in antiquity, in the Talmudic tradition and the writings of the Church Fathers, which is partly why scholars and theologians have failed to identify it today. Yet this conception of sin is fundamental to the Bible, and not a mere nuance or marginal notion. Thus, the project of recovering the original meaning of sin, as I hope to do in this book, obviously has large implications for Judaism and Christianity alike.

Let me outline here the plan of the book. In the first chapter, I illustrate how sin is defined in modern dictionaries and Biblical handbooks, and show that this sense of sin is clearly present in pagan texts. I then turn to the Hebrew

Bible, and examine the passages in which sin is mentioned. By tracing the term for sin over the course of Tanakh, I show how it acquires a distinct meaning that is specific to this tradition. Rather than denoting just any offense against divine injunctions, sin refers more narrowly to the violation of the covenant, which takes the form of chasing after foreign gods. As such, it pertains above all to the Israelites, who alone are parties to the covenant. Those who have fallen away can earn forgiveness by repenting of their error and confessing before God—a paradigmatic script for sin and its remission that is entirely absent from the Greco-Roman tradition. When I speak of the term for sin, however, I am already engaged in interpretation. There are many words indicating evil, iniquity, injustice, wrongdoing, and the like, in Hebrew as well as in Greek and Latin, and in English and other modern languages too, of course. In singling out just one of these words as bearing the sense of "sin," namely the Hebrew ḥaṭaʾ, I am assuming that the vocabulary of the Bible is highly precise, and that this word is endowed with a meaning that separates it from other terms for moral error or wickedness. As we shall see, this is indeed the case: the term in question does have a special usage and bears just that significance that is unparalleled in classical religious thought and diction. In other words, the Hebrew Bible reserved a word, which may otherwise have had a broader set of connotations, for a special concept that is unique to its theology. The only way to demonstrate this is to track its uses and make manifest how they differ from those of other, apparently similar terms, and to exhibit the larger import of this technical expression. What follows is, therefore, of the nature of a philological investigation, treating passage after passage to elicit the exact sense of this or that word. Luckily, the texts themselves are fascinating and well known, and so the operation of casting a new light on them is interesting in its own right. Questions such as whether Adam and Eve can be said to have sinned (in the relevant sense of the term), whether pagans can sin, the extent to which sin can be forgiven, and what actions are labeled as sinful, are at stake, and the answers are often surprising.

The next chapter examines the idea of sin in the New Testament, with special attention to the Gospels and the Acts of the Apostles. Here we switch from Hebrew to Greek, the language of the New Testament as we have it, and here again I will be arguing that there is a particular word that carries the special sense of sin, as opposed to a wide vocabulary for wickedness and similar ideas. The term employed for "sin" is not a new coinage of the Bible, unlike some other words, such as *agapê*, for example, that are not found in classical texts (with some few, late exceptions) but are characteristic of Christian Greek. Rather, the authors of the Gospels and other books appropriated a word, *hamartia*, that was in common use. But this raises a problem of its own: how do we know that the term bears the specific sense of "sin" in the Bible, as opposed to its meaning in other Greek texts? And does it carry this special significance everywhere in the New Testament, or only in some passages, whereas in others it bears what we may call a secular meaning? Because so much contemporary Greek literature survives, it is possible to contrast the use of this word in the Bible with the ordinary language of the time, and thus to demonstrate clearly, I propose, that "sin" is indeed endowed with special sense in the New Testament. Here again, as we shall see, there is a tripartite structure to the sin pattern: an offense, a change of heart, and salvation. But despite this resemblance to the sin paradigm in the Hebrew Bible, the two conceptions of sin are not precisely the same. Rather, sin in the New Testament, and above all in the Gospels, constitutes a new twist on the Hebrew concept, adapted to the epochal change in the nature of the old religion inaugurated by Jesus' presence on earth. For sin is now not a falling away from God, but rather a failure to turn to Jesus, in the trust or confidence, inspired by his miracles, that he is indeed the Messiah and the Son of God. Confession and repentance give way, in the Gospels, to the idea of conversion.

The final chapter looks at how the Biblical idea of sin was interpreted and largely transformed by later commentators in the early Jewish and the Christian traditions (this is what I meant when I said that sin, in a certain sense, ends as well as begins with the Bible). The primary focus, however, will be on the Church Fathers, since they go further in reinterpreting the Biblical sense of sin. For here, sin begins to assume the lineaments familiar to us from daily usage as well as learned definition, that is, a violation of any divinely sanctioned prohibition, such as murder, adultery, incest, and the like. The reasons for this transformation in the meaning of sin are various. Christianity was evolving from the face-to-face encounters with Jesus and the direct oral transmission of his message recorded in the Gospels to a complex institution, with its own hierarchy and doctrines, responsible for guiding and often governing the lives of worshippers. In the process, it was necessary to develop the message of the

Bible in such a way as to serve the needs of a great Church, one that would become the official religion of the entire Roman Empire. Christianity itself was divided into various tendencies, and conflict between them was intense on a doctrinal level and often physically as well. New forms of monasticism also had an impact on how the Bible was interpreted, and these had a major influence on Christianity generally. With all this, it is not surprising that the notion of sin too would undergo some changes. One of the consequences of these developments, however, was that the original sense of the term in the New Testament was obscured or even lost. This book is an attempt to recuperate that sense of sin in its original Biblical contexts.

One further word on the nature of this book. When it comes to the Bible, commentaries and interpretations abound, even more than for classical Greek and Roman texts and rabbinical and patristic literature. On the many passages discussed in the chapters that follow, one could cite not hundreds but thousands of works that offer exegeses. Just recently, there have appeared several books on sin, such as Gary Anderson's *Sin: A History* (2009), Paula Fredriksen's *Sin: The Early History of an Idea* (2012), David Lambert's *How Repentance Became Biblical* (2016), and Joseph Lam's *Patterns of Sin in the Hebrew Bible* (2016), to name but a few. Nevertheless, I have provided only limited references to this scholarly literature, much of it excellent in its own right. The reason is simple: none of these works focuses on the terms that, as I argue, constitute the special sense of sin in the Bible, and so their interpretations of sin do not coincide, in this respect, with the one I am proposing. The reader may find that my own explanation of one or another passage in the Bible or in other texts is less than convincing, or even that, despite the abundance of episodes that I examine, the overall weight of the evidence I cite falls short of establishing my thesis. I have, to the extent possible, tried to allow the texts to speak for themselves, but texts never do so unambiguously. If one wishes to see alternative interpretations, they are easily found in virtually any commentary on the Bible.

There is one further potential problem with the hermeneutical approach that I have adopted in this book, and that concerns the very nature of the texts that constitute what we think of as the Bible, or rather, *the* Bible. The Bible is not a single work in the modern sense, like a novel, but rather a collection of materials, composed, edited, and re-edited over a period of centuries, by redactors who often had very different conceptions, among themselves, of

God's message. Scholars have discriminated different hands within a single book or even passage, positing, for example, that the Torah (the first five books of the Hebrew Bible) was compiled out of three or four (or sometimes more) originally independent documents, sometimes identified as the Jahwist, Elohist, Deuteronomist, and Priestly sources (abbreviated as J, E, D, and P). These separate sources are dated as early as the reign of Solomon (tenth century) to the fifth century (the time of Ezra), and all were subject to redactions and combinations at different times. One need only note the apparent doublets in the Bible, for example the two accounts of the creation in Genesis or the twin genealogies of Seth, to see why critics would have arrived at such a theory, reinforced further by more subtle variations in style. The details remain controversial, and no single reconstruction has won universal agreement. Nevertheless, these analyses might seem to call into question the procedure followed in this book, in which the books of the Bible are by and large examined in the traditional order in which they appear in modern editions, without regard to possible chronological disparities within and among the several tracts. A similar question can be raised concerning the books in the New Testament as well, which were composed at different times (the earliest being the authentic letters of Paul), and do not necessarily represent a single, coherent point of view, whether on the nature of sin or such related topics as faith and forgiveness. In fact, some notice is taken, in the pages that follow, of apparent discrepancies in the use of the primary terms for sin, *ḥaṭaʾ* and *hamartia*, within the Bible, and not just between the Bible and later exegeses. Nevertheless, on the whole I have indeed treated the Hebrew Bible and the New Testament as fundamentally coherent in their treatment of sin. The reason is again uncomplicated: my study of these privileged terms has, I believe, shown that there is an overall continuity in their uses. I say "overall," because there are some exceptions and discrepancies, to be expected, no doubt, over so large a range of materials of sometimes disparate provenience. These may be thought to undercut my argument, and perhaps to some extent they do. Nevertheless, I do not try to palm them off on one or another redactor, in an attempt thereby to recover an ostensibly authentic uniformity. There was no national Academy to legislate the use of the terms, no dictionaries that defined their meanings once and for all. It is remarkable that a reasonably consistent picture emerges at all. That it in fact does testifies, I argue, to an implicit but pervasive understanding of sin that is both coherent and peculiar to the Bible.

Although, as I have said, the method I have adopted is philological, my conclusions obviously have consequences for theology as well. If the word that I have rendered as "sin" in the Hebrew Bible is associated primarily with the worship of foreign gods (or idols), and if the corresponding term in the Gospels signifies lack of trust or faith in Jesus, despite his manifestly superhuman powers, does it follow that everything else is permitted, no matter how it contradicts the law? No, not at all. As I have indicated, there are many words for evil, and the acts covered by those terms are roundly condemned. Then why not call such actions sin? In principle, there is no objection, and clearly such behavior conforms to the modern definitions of sin. But if there is a particular term in Hebrew and in Greek, within the semantic sphere of words like "bad," "evil," "iniquity," and the like, that is more closely associated than the rest both with repentance or conversion and with forgiveness, then this tells us something important about how the Bible conceives of humanity's relation to God. It is, I believe, a special conception, absent, as I have said, from the pagan Greco-Roman tradition, and unremarked in much of later Jewish and Christian thought. Readers of this book have likely not encountered it before. If they find the analyses offered here to be plausible interpretations of the passages under consideration, they may be encouraged to reflect on the further implications of this special usage. And that is the purpose of the book.

Acknowledgments

This book benefited enormously from two fellowships that I was privileged to be awarded: the first was at the Swedish Collegium for Advanced Study, from September 1 to December 16, 2016; the second was at the Paris Institute for Advanced Studies (France), with the financial support of the French State managed by the Agence Nationale de la Recherche, program "Investissements d'avenir" (ANR-11-LABX-0027-01 Labex RFIEA+), during the period February 1 to June 30, 2017. I am also grateful to New York University for the leave granted me during that same year, and the constant exchanges with my colleagues in the Classics and Philosophy Departments.

Over the course of the past four years or so, I have written several articles and delivered a fair number of lectures on the topic of sin, where I invariably benefited greatly from the comments of members of the audience. Among earlier publications, I may refer the reader to Konstan 2017, 2019a, and 2021. I delivered my first lecture on sin at the Swedish Collegium for Advanced Study, and co-organized (with Renaud Gagné) a colloquium on the topic at the Institut d'Études Avancées de Paris. Other talks were presented at the Society of Biblical Literature, George Washington University in Saint Louis (at a special conference in honor of John and Penelope Biggs), Notre Dame University in Indiana, the University of Melbourne (Australia), the Universidad de Salamanca (Spain), the Universidad de Almería (Spain), the Union Club of the City of New York, a Colloquium in memory of Vincent J. Rosivach (Fairfield University), and at the workshop, A Invenção do Pecado: Paixâo, Pecado e Civilizaçâo no Mundo Greco-Romano Antigo (Universidade de Campinas, Brazil). I am deeply grateful to members of the audience at all these occasions for wise comments and suggestions.

It is a special pleasure to thank friends and colleagues who have commented at one or another time on the ideas presented here. I may single out Nathan Howard, who graciously read various early drafts, and also my dear friend

Stavroula Kiritsi, who helped in countless ways. Julia Annas kindly read the manuscript as well, and Maren Niehoff, Aldo Setaioli and Renaud Gagné offered generous advice and encouragement. My wife Pura was a constant stimulus to reflection on sin and many other matters.

1

The Greco-Roman World: The Unwritten Laws of the Gods

What is sin? In the concrete sense, in which we may speak of "a sin" or "sins," it denotes a wrongful action. More abstractly, it may connote a guilty state or condition. What is more, the word normally carries religious overtones. Modern accounts of sin (or of the comparable word in other languages) join these two aspects. Take, for example, the definition in the *Oxford English Dictionary*: "An immoral act considered to be a transgression against divine law." Or again, this from the *Merriam Webster Dictionary*: "an offense against religious or moral law..., transgression of the law of God." The *King James Version Dictionary*, keyed to the King James Bible, is even more specific: "The voluntary departure of a moral agent from a known rule of rectitude or duty, prescribed by God; any voluntary transgression of the divine law, or violation of a divine command; a wicked act; iniquity." Foreign lexica offer similar descriptions. In German, for instance, the word *Sünde* is defined as "a breach in the relationship with God by human beings."[1] Therese Fuhrer in turn observes: "The German concept of 'Sünde' – like the corresponding concepts in other modern Western European languages – designates a reprehensible act by which a person consciously contravenes a divine law or commandment and thereby turns away from God."[2] The last clause adds a dimension to sin that goes back to the early commentators on the Bible. Finally, Hermut Löhr, commenting on the Letter to the Hebrews, states simply: "Sin is *per se* sin against God."[3]

To be sure, the word "sin" is also used in an informal way to indicate any kind of offense, though usually one considered serious. Thus, the *Oxford English Dictionary*, in addition to the primary definition, notes: "An act regarded as a serious or regrettable fault, offense, or omission"; and the *Merriam-Webster* lexicon likewise adds: "an action that is or is felt to be highly reprehensible..., an often serious shortcoming: fault." Indeed, in Italian the exclamation *peccato*! means little more than "what a pity" or "too bad." Is the religious sense, however, as defined above, in fact specific to the Bible, or was a comparable idea current in the pagan environment of the Greco-Roman world? As it will turn out, there is indeed ample evidence of such a conception of sin in classical Greece and Rome, which on the surface falsifies the claim that sin in the rich, religious sense is somehow exclusively a feature of the Judeo-Christian tradition. The task of this chapter is to lay out the evidence, but it is not, as I indicated in the Preface, my intention to show that, in the final analysis, sin was simply part of the shared heritage of the Mediterranean World and beyond, and that it bears no special significance when we encounter it in the Bible. I mean only to show that sin, as commonly defined in the lexica and handbooks, extends beyond the Biblical texts and may be found in pagan thought as well. When we come to a discussion, in the following chapters, of the Hebrew scripture and the New Testament, we will see that sin has a more particular meaning that in fact is unique to those writings and is not found elsewhere, or at least not in the Greek and Roman texts that have come down to us. To be absolutely sure that sin, as used in the Tanakh and the New Testament, is solely Biblical, it would of course be necessary to examine the religious or moral concepts of a wide variety of cultures, from Egypt and Babylon to regions further afield, like India and China and all the places where a god or gods were worshipped. This is a task beyond my competence, and I do not presume to affirm that nowhere in the world did some analogous conception arise. I will say, however, that I have not encountered an idea of sin in the Biblical sense elsewhere, and scholars learned in the religious thought of many of these rich cultures have assured me that it is not to be found in those traditions. Greece and Rome, then, represent a test case or sounding: they are enough to show, at the very least, that sin as defined in the dictionaries did exist as a religious idea outside the Bible. What is more, the absence of the more restricted notion of sin that we will explore in the following chapters suggests that there was something special about the Biblical concept. If sin even in this latter sense does turn out to have analogues in other societies, then further work will need to be done to explain how and why it arose there as well as in the Bible.

Let us turn, then, to the pagan tradition, and there is no better place to start than Homer's *Odyssey*, among the earliest works to survive from classical antiquity. The poem opens with a conversation among the gods on Mount Olympus, in which Zeus complains of the human tendency to blame the gods for their misfortunes: "for in his heart he thought of flawless Aegisthus, whom far-famed Orestes, Agamemnon's son, had slain. Thinking of him he spoke among the immortals, and said: 'It's astonishing how ready mortals are to blame the gods. It is from us, they say, that evils come, but they even by themselves, through their own blind folly, have sorrows beyond that which is ordained.'"[4] Zeus is upset that Aegisthus married Clytemnestra, Agamemnon's wife, and killed Agamemnon when he returned home from Troy, even though Zeus had sent Hermes to warn him precisely not to do this, or else Orestes, Agamemnon's son, would kill Aegisthus in turn—which is just what happened (1.29–43). Does Aegisthus' "blind folly," by which he ignored the specific instructions of Zeus, the chief deity of the Olympic pantheon, and murdered the legitimate ruler, count as a sin? The phrase "blind folly" in the translation represents the Greek word *atasthaliai*, the plural of *atasthalia*. The authoritative dictionary of ancient Greek into English, edited by Henry Liddell, Robert Scott, and Henry Stuart Jones and commonly abbreviated to *LSJ* (1966), defines *atasthalia* as "presumptuous sin, recklessness, wickedness," so sin has seemed at least a plausible translation of the term. We may note here that the great Greek-Spanish dictionary, the *Diccionario Griego-Epañol* (*DGE*), under the general editorship of Francisco Rodríguez Adrados, which so far has not got beyond the letter E, offers the more cautious Spanish equivalents "*orgullo insolente, arrogancia, insensatez culpable*" (that is, "insolent pride, arrogance, culpable stupidity"). Now, ancient grammarians connected the word *atasthalia* with *atê*, which means something like "ruin," "blind and criminal folly, infatuation," according to the dictionaries. However, that derivation is uncertain, and, as is almost always the case, it is best to interpret the meaning of *atasthalia* by the way it is used in context rather than rely on possible etymologies, even when they are not as fanciful as some of the ancient examples. In the present instance, then, why not translate *atasthaliai* as "sins"? After all, Zeus himself sent Hermes, his messenger, to warn Aegisthus not to murder Agamemnon, and Aegisthus ignored the command, to his sorrow. This would appear to be an act of sheer disobedience to a god, indeed the top god of all.

Aegisthus' fault seems similar to that of the Sodomites, according to the narrative of the destruction of Sodom and Gomorrah recounted in Genesis.

Having heard reports of the goings on in those towns, "the Lord said, 'The outcry against Sodom and Gomorrah is so great and their sins so grievous that I will go down and see if what they have done is as bad as the outcry that has reached me. If not, I will know'" (18:20–21). He sends some angels to investigate, who are entertained in the house of Lot; but when the inhabitants of Sodom seek to have intercourse with them, refusing even Lot's offer of his own daughters so as to avoid the greater crime of abusing guests, God wipes out the entire city. The behavior of the Sodomites bears a certain analogy to that of Aegisthus in killing the legitimate king in his own palace. There are differences, to be sure: in the Homeric passage, Aegisthus is punished by Orestes, Agamemnon's son, whereas in Genesis God acts himself to punish the Sodomites; we might add that the guilt of the Sodomites is collective rather than individual. Still, is the nature of their sins fundamentally different?

In the Septuagint—that is, the translation of the Hebrew Bible into Greek, begun during the third century BC and completed, in all likelihood, in the second—the word that is translated as "sins" is *hamartiai*, the plural form of the word *hamartia*. This word will turn out to be the key term for sin in the New Testament and later Christian literature, but in classical texts its meaning is not always so portentous, and may signify simply an error or mistake; the root meaning seems to have been missing the mark, as in archery or the cast of a spear. The Liddell-Scott-Jones dictionary, for example, defines the word as "a failure, fault," and more narrowly as an "error of judgement." In a secondary definition, they note that the term may bear the sense of "guilt" or "sin," but they restrict this significance to "Philosophy and Religion." As examples from Greek philosophy, the lexicon cites Plato's late dialogue, *Laws* (660C, etc.), along with Aristotle's *Nicomachean Ethics* (1148a3); a little later, we shall examine both these passages, which do not, I believe, conform to the current definition of sin at all, much less to the specialized sense that I will explore in subsequent chapters. The lexicon also offers Biblical passages which bear the sense of sin, beginning with the Septuagint version of Genesis 18:20, which is precisely the account of the destruction of Sodom and Gomorra, and also the Gospel of John (8:46). The Greek to Spanish dictionary that was mentioned above offers "*error, falta*" as the primary senses of the term, along with "*equivocacíon, fallo, delito*," and "*hecho ilegal o injusto*" ("an illegal or unjust act"). Again, it is only in the secondary definition that it gives as the equivalent word "*pecado*," the Spanish for "sin," but this sense of the word is restricted to "Judeo-Christian literature," and the first instance of this meaning cited in the dictionary is, again, the passage from Genesis under consideration here, along with a considerable list of other examples. We shall consider in greater detail the use of *hamartia* (and the Hebrew equivalent) in this connection in the following chapters; here, we may simply note that there is no fundamental divergence in the connotations of the words *hamartia* and *atasthalia*, as the latter is used in the proem to the *Odyssey*.

In the *Iliad*, Achilles, after slaying Hector in retaliation for the death of Patroclus, drags the Trojan hero's corpse behind his chariot, defiling it in the dust. His behavior is such as to offend even the gods, or most of them, but "Hera and Poseidon and the flashing-eyed maiden [i.e., Athena] ... continued even as when at the first sacred Ilios became hateful in their eyes and Priam and his folk, by reason of the sin of Alexander" (24.25–28).[5] "Sin," here, in Murray's archaizing translation, renders *atê*, a term that, as we noted earlier, means something like "*bewilderment, infatuation,* caused by *blindness* or *delusion* sent by the gods, mostly as the punishment of guilty rashness" (this is the first definition in *LSJ*), although the lexicon adds "reckless guilt or sin," as well as, in a passive sense, "bane, ruin," and, finally, "pest" or "abomination." The Spanish *DGE* is again more circumspect, offering as equivalents of *atê* "*desvarío, ofuscación*" (with ruinous consequences), of the sort inspired by a god or demon, or else by wine or passionate love (*erôs*), along with "*locura*" or "madness." In the passive sense, the dictionary gives "*ruina, calamidad, desastre*," and in the plural, "*desgracias, aflicciones, castigos*," with the further synonyms "*ruina, pérdida, perdición*," in reference to financial or other grave losses. It is noteworthy that here again, the *DGE* studiously avoids assigning the sense "*pecado*" or "sin" to *atê*, in line with the disposition, which we have already seen in connection with *hamartia*, to limit that concept, or at least that usage, to the Judeo-Christian tradition. In the present context, the offense in question is that of awarding the prize for beauty to Aphrodite rather than to Hera or Athena; the reference is to the Judgment of Paris, since in the *Iliad* Paris has the alternate name of Alexander, though why his decision should have irritated Poseidon as well is unclear (Poseidon had other motives for his hostility to Troy). Since Aphrodite promised that Paris would possess the most beautiful woman in the world if he voted for her, his judgment in the competition led to his abduction of Helen and hence to the entire war. One might plausibly render the word *atê* here simply as "foolishness" or "lack of prudence." It is certainly not "sin" in the sense of "An immoral act considered to be a transgression against divine law" or "an offense against religious or moral law," since Paris was obliged to pronounce some kind of verdict, and selecting one goddess over the other two does not run up against any kind of norm. One might reason that preferring the goddess of love and sexuality over Hera and Athena, who represented marriage and wisdom (among other things), was a sign that Paris or Alexander was ruled by passion rather than intellect, and that this can be considered a moral flaw. Nevertheless, there is no divine edict prohibiting human beings from acting on their passions, and had Paris voted for either of the other two goddesses in contention, it is, I suppose, equally likely that they would have harbored a grudge against Troy and plotted its destruction as well. The real lesson to be drawn from the Judgment of Paris, which is alluded to only here in the *Iliad*, is that in a polytheistic system like that of the Olympians, where each deity was out for herself or himself, there could not exist a single code that might guide a person's decision in such a case. Certainly, then, "sin" is not the appropriate translation of *atê* here, except perhaps in the looser sense of a "regrettable fault, offense, or omission."

In the passage from the *Odyssey*, however, there is no apparent dissension among the gods concerning Aegisthus' crime, and he might be said to have violated a divine consensus on what is lawful or not among human beings. In fact, the situation is not so clear, since at the divine assembly in which Zeus pronounces his somewhat petulant complaint about human irresponsibility (since the gods themselves are hardly models of upright behavior), one god is in fact missing, namely Poseidon. His absence is crucial to the plot, since all the gods are moved to pity Odysseus, who is now in the tenth year of his wanderings, far from home, a prisoner on the island of the goddess Calypso who is in love with him—all the gods, that is, except for Poseidon, who harbors a resentment against Odysseus for having blinded the Cyclops Polyphemus, Poseidon's own son. Athena takes Zeus' remark as the occasion to confirm that Aegisthus deserved his fate, as do all others like him (1.45–46), but Odysseus, on the contrary, has always performed the sacrifices due to the gods, which is a sign of his piety (1.60–61), and yet he is wasting away in captivity. Zeus pleads in excuse of this evident injustice Poseidon's resentment, but is prepared to initiate Odysseus' return home, in spite of his brother's anger. Here too, then, just as in the pity for Hector that all the gods save Athena, Hera, and Poseidon experience in the *Iliad*, there is division in the divine family. Still, there seems to be agreement about Aegisthus, and no reason to suppose that Poseidon would have dissented from that judgment had he been present on Olympus (although, as we shall see, there were other deities, the Furies in particular, who did not approve of Orestes' action).

Even if the gods do uniformly condemn certain kinds of behavior, however, there is another reason why we might hesitate to characterize Aegisthus' deed as a sin. Although the gods condemn his behavior, there is no indication that they are abiding by a set of rules or code of conduct that might be described as law. No doubt regicide was frowned upon in any monarchy and Aegisthus' act certainly would have contravened the norms that would have prevailed, if only implicitly, in such regimes (it was different in democracies, where tyrannicides such as Harmodius and Aristogeiton, in Athens, might achieve the status of heroes). The gods at the beginning of the *Odyssey* share this sentiment, out of respect for the institution of kingship (this is uncontroversial in the *Iliad*), but they do not do so on the basis of a legal code of their own; rather, they appear to serve as guarantors of human norms. To be sure, Aegisthus defied a direct command of Zeus, in much the way Adam and Eve do in Genesis (a narrative that will be discussed in its own right in the next chapter). But since there is no suggestion that Aegisthus' offense is in violation of legislation promulgated by the gods, it is reasonable to regard his act as a crime which the gods recognize as such, rather than as a sin in the prevailing religious sense of the word.

In Aeschylus' trilogy, *Oresteia*, performed in Athens in 458 BC, Orestes is indeed deemed to have committed an offense against divine regulations. Once again, however, the situation is complicated, since his action is condemned by one group of deities and condoned by another, which calls into question the coherence of divine law. In avenging the murder of his father, Orestes slays not only Aegisthus but also his mother, and so what is at stake in this tragic trilogy is not regicide but rather matricide. The Furies are represented as ancient goddesses who enforce an antique conception of kinship. It is true that Orestes killed his mother in return for her murder of her husband, Agamemnon. However, in the logic of the Furies, the blood relationship between mother and child outweighs the purely legal bond between spouses that results from marriage. Hence, it is not their responsibility to persecute Clytemnestra, who is represented as goading them on to avenge the crime; it is Orestes alone whom they must punish, since he violated the genetic relation that they uphold. Apollo, however, who authorized Orestes to perform the matricide, defends the act on the opposite grounds—that is, that only the father is the genuine parent, who must therefore be avenged, whereas the mother is merely the vessel in which the seed is planted. Thus, Orestes is innocent. The conflict comes to a head in the final play, the *Eumenides*, in which a human court adjudicates the matter. The twelve Athenian jurors are evenly divided, but Athena, who acts as judge, casts her vote in favor of Apollo on the grounds that she was born from the head of Zeus and no female played a role in her conception, thereby breaking the tie. In the finale, Athena wins over the resentful and outraged Furies by a mixture of veiled threat and persuasion; they accept their new role as The Kindly Ones (the meaning of the Greek word "Eumenides") and agree to settle in Athens and help protect the city. The trilogy thus pits two divinely sanctioned principles against one another: the patriarchal family, defended by the young Olympian deities, versus the mother-oriented conception of the family upheld by the Furies, for whom blood lineage trumps the civic marriage bond.

One might reasonably imagine that Orestes has sinned against the Furies (called in these plays by their Greek name, *Erinyes*), save that he was simultaneously fulfilling the commandment communicated to him via the Delphic oracle, which represents the view of Apollo and, by implication, of the Olympian gods. These latter gods are treated as newcomers to the divine corps, destined to usurp the authority of the older divinities, in much the way the generation of Zeus rebelled against and overthrew the previous dominion of his father Kronos and the other Titans. The tension, as Aeschylus presents it, is between two divine codes, one archaic, the other new, and conforming to the one entails violating the other, at least before the Furies have been domesticated and obliged to accept the new order, backed up by human institutions of justice embodied in the foundation of Athens' august homicide court, the Areopagus. Under this secular regime, it would appear, unjustified homicide will henceforward be punished as a crime, rather than as a sin against divine law. The classical Athenian tribunals, like the modern system of jurisprudence, condemned delicts; the gods castigate offenses against their governance, each according to his or her will.

In Sophocles' *Antigone*, however, there is a clear contrast between human decrees and "the unwritten and secure statutes of the gods" (*agrapta k'asphalê theôn nomima*, 454–55), and it is here that something very close to the modern definition of sin can be found. After Oedipus blinded himself, abandoned Thebes, and died in Athens, his two sons, Polynices and Eteocles, agreed to share the kingship by ruling in alternate years. When Eteocles refused to surrender the throne to his brother, Polynices raised an army with the help of Argos and attacked his native city. The assault failed, but the two brothers killed one another in face-to-face combat, with the result that Creon, Oedipus' brother-in-law, assumed royal power. In the aftermath of the war, he issued an edict honoring Eteocles and prohibiting the burial of Polynices, on the grounds that he was a traitor who had invited foreign troops to conquer Thebes. Oedipus' daughter, Antigone, decides to defy her uncle's decree by casting earth upon the body of her brother Polynices, and when brought before Creon to defend her action, she declares:

> It was not Zeus who decreed it [*ho kêruxas tade*], and not of that kind are the laws [νόμους] which Justice who dwells with the gods below [*tôn katô theôn*] established among men. Nor did I think that your decrees [*kêrugmata*] were of such force that a mortal could override the unwritten and secure statutes [*nomima*] of the gods. For their life is not of today or yesterday, but for all time, and no man knows when they were first put forth. Not for fear of any man's pride was I about to owe a penalty to the gods for breaking these.
> 450–60[6]

Antigone appeals to a higher law or laws (*nomoi, nomima*), the violation of which will not be merely a crime, like defying Creon's edict (here called a *kêrugma*), but might well be described as a sin—that is, a "transgression against divine law." There is no conflict over the validity of these norms, as there was in Aeschylus' *Oresteia*. The Olympian Zeus is allied with "the gods below," very possibly a reference to the Furies, who, we may imagine, would punish her failure to honor her brother's corpse as they did Orestes for murdering his mother, whether by driving her mad (like Orestes) or by some other god-sent affliction. Scholars have raised questions about the legal status of Creon's decree in contradistinction to the laws or *nomoi*—a technical term in Athens, where the tragedy was performed—established by the gods, and more particularly by the personification of Justice itself.[7] But Antigone's appeal to the overriding authority of divine laws or customs (for *nomos* may also signify "usage" or "traditional practice") clearly gives precedence to the norms laid down by the gods over human legislation of any kind, whether confirmed by the people or issued as a royal dictate. Failure to respect those immortal laws constitutes something more than a crime, and "sin," as it is commonly understood, would seem to be just the right word.

The contrast between divine rules and human legislation is not confined to poetry. The Athenian Xenophon, a soldier and disciple of Socrates, who among other things transcribed (whether accurately or not) various Socratic conversations, records an exchange between Socrates and the sophist Hippias over the nature of justice. Socrates affirms that what is lawful (*nomimon*) is identical to what is just (*to auto . . . nomimon kai dikaion einai, Recollections of Socrates* 4.4.18). He proceeds to inquire about the nature of "unwritten laws" (*agraphoi nomoi*). Hippias replies that these are laws that are observed in every land. Socrates then asks whether such laws were made by human beings, to which Hippias replies that this would be impossible, since people are widely dispersed and speak many different languages. Rather, he avers, they were established by the gods, and first and foremost among them is the duty to revere the immortals. Another such rule is respect for parents. But when it comes to incest, Hippias expresses a doubt, since, as he says, "some people commit it." To this, Socrates replies: "Yes, and they do many other things contrary to the laws. But those who transgress the laws [*nomoi*] established by the gods pay the penalty, which it is in no way possible for a human being to escape, although some do escape paying the penalty when they have transgressed laws [*nomoi*] established by human beings" (4.4.21). Socrates does not employ a special term to discriminate the violation of divine from human laws (he uses *parabainein*, "transgress," for both), and this is significant: the Greeks of Xenophon's time did not have a special vocabulary corresponding to the idea of "sin" as we understand it, with its predominantly religious as opposed to secular overtones. But "sin" seems perfectly apposite to the kind of offense against god-given laws that Xenophon describes.[8]

In a similar vein, Aristotle affirms that "there is a certain natural and universal right and wrong which all men intuit, even if they have no intercourse or covenant with each other; as the Antigone of Sophocles is found saying that, notwithstanding the interdict, it is right to bury Polynices."[9] So too, Thucydides has Pericles, in his famous funeral oration in praise of the Athenian national character, declare: "Although we associate as individuals in this tolerant spirit, in public affairs fear makes us the most severely law-abiding of people, obedient to whoever is in authority and to the laws, especially those established to help the victims of injustice and those laws which, though unwritten, carry the sanction of public disgrace."[10] Plato, too, refers to such unwritten laws, in his late dialogue that bears the title *Laws*; these laws, he says, "act as bonds in every constitution, forming a link between all its laws (both those already enacted in writing and those still to be enacted), exactly like ancestral customs of great antiquity" (793A–B).[11] The historian Polybius, who spent seventeen years as a hostage in Rome in the second century BC, describes in his *Histories* how Antigonus Doson of Macedon, together with the Achaean general Aratus, conquered the city of Mantinea and led its inhabitants off into slavery. Polybius finds this treatment entirely justified since the Mantineans had earlier slit the throats of the Achaeans in their midst, in violation, he says, of the customary treatment of enemies under what he calls "the laws common to mankind" (*kata tous koinous tôn anthrôpôn nomous*, 2.58.6; cf. 2.58.7, *ta koina tôn anthrôpôn dikaia*). Indeed, the Mantineans might even be said to have got off lightly. For being sold into slavery, Polybius explains, "is something that even those who have committed no impious act suffer, in accord with the norms or laws of war [*kata tous tou polemou nomous*]" (2.58.10), and so, Polybius says, the Mantineans deserved to endure an even greater punishment than this. Polybius, then, recognizes certain rules that govern conduct among peoples, employing the relatively rare expression, *hoi nomoi tôn anthrôpôn* or "the norms of human beings," without qualification.[12]

Polybius does not say that the laws common to human beings everywhere, whether written or not, have been established by the gods, any more than Thucydides, Plato, or Aristotle does. Correspondingly, it is not necessarily the case that local laws ascribed to the gods, or to some god, must have universal validity: unwritten rules or customs might differ in Athens and in Sparta, yet both might be supposed to have divine authority. But Sophocles and Xenophon (through his mouthpiece, Socrates) make the connection between universal and god-given laws, and it is reasonable to think that there was a felt distinction between the violation of these and of ordinary legislation, which, as Socrates and Hippias agree in Xenophon's dialogue, is subject to change and repeal.[13]

Nevertheless, the absence of a word that specifically designates sin may call into question the status of the idea for the ancient Greeks and Romans. According to the hypothesis associated with the names of the cultural anthropologists Edward Sapir and his student, Benjamin Lee Whorf, the vocabulary of a language not only influences but pretty much determines how its speakers perceive the world. Few would maintain the strong form of this kind of linguistic determinism today, which posits that people cannot conceive of a class of things that is not named in their own language.[14] Edward T. Jeremiah has recently offered what he calls a "milder version" of the thesis that should, he says, "be uncontroversial: what a culture does not have a word for is not important for them as an object of inquiry or socio-cultural signifier."[15] Even if we are right to note the difference that some Greek thinkers expressed between offenses against human and divine law and to label the latter "sin," since, strictly speaking, they conform to the definitions provided by our lexicographers and theologians, we may nonetheless affirm that sin as such was not a significant category of thought for them. What, then, of the passages by Plato and Aristotle that *LSJ*—that is, the dictionary edited by Liddell, Scott, and Jones—cites under the subheading "sin"? Might these two eminent philosophers have articulated the concept unambiguously?

We may begin by examining the passage in Plato's *Laws* that the great lexicon cites as an instance where *harmartia* is used in the sense of "sin." The anonymous Athenian who assumes in this dialogue the role that was earlier reserved for Socrates has just affirmed that "the good legislator will try to persuade the poet, or else force him, to portray men who are temperate, courageous, and good in all respects" (2.660A). He then corrects himself and says that he was not referring to contemporary poets: "To denounce things that are beyond remedy and far gone in error is a task that is by no means pleasant; but at times it is unavoidable." The phrase "far gone in error" is literally, in Greek, "having advanced far in *hamartia*," an expression that, in context, seems far removed from what we might think of as "sin." In the passage cited from the *Nicomachean Ethics* (7.4, 1148a3), in turn, Aristotle is discussing incontinence or *akrasia*—that is, lack of restraint or self-control, and he explains that incontinence in regard to bodily pleasures is blamed "not only as an error [*harmartia*] but also as a vice [*kakia*]." Clearly, the latter is the stronger term, and so this again is hardly a case in which we would employ the charged word "sin" as the equivalent for *hamartia*. It would seem, then, that the Greek-Spanish dictionary (*DGE*) is closer to the truth in reserving the sense "sin" for Judeo-Christian literature.

There is in classical Greek a related term, *hamartêma* (ἁμάρτημα), which in Jewish and Christian texts is sometimes used as a synonym of *harmartia* (it is rare, however, in the Greek Bible, occurring only four times, though more common in Philo and later writers). *LSJ* defines the word as "failure" or "fault," noting that it is frequent in Attic prose, whether oratory, history, or philosophy. The lexicon also renders the word as "sinful action," and cites several passages in Plato for this usage (*Statesman* 296B, *Apology* 22D, *Laws* 729E, *Gorgias* 479A). Here, too, we may doubt that "sin" is the right rendering. Aristotle, for example, affirms that *hamartêma* is "midway between *adikêma* and *atukhêma*"—that is, between a wrong or criminal act and a misfortune (*Nicomachean Ethics* 1135b18, *Rhetoric* 1374b7); this hardly assigns to it the charged sense that "sin" bears in English, and there is no reference at all to universal customs or to laws laid down by the gods.

There existed a type of offense in classical Greece and Rome that was specific to religious or cult practice, which took the form of rules for behavior in connection with temples or holy compounds. Such regulations, preserved mainly as inscriptions on stone, are sometimes referred to as *leges sacrae* or "sacred laws," although this label has been criticized for being too vague and blurring the various kinds of prohibition recorded on the stelae.[16] Violations of these rules had to be expiated by prescribed rituals or sacrifices. We may obtain an idea of the nature of these rites from a passage in the Hippocratic treatise *On the Sacred Disease*, that is, epilepsy, composed in the late fifth or early fourth century BC. The author denies that this ailment is any more divine than others, but rather has perfectly natural causes. He decries the tendency to resort to magic as a cure, affirming rather that "it is the divinity which purifies and sanctifies the greatest of offenses and the most wicked, and which proves our protection from them. And we mark out the boundaries of the temples and the groves of the gods, so that no one may pass them unless he be pure [*hagneuein*], and when we enter them we are sprinkled [*perirrainesthai*] with holy water, not as being polluted [*miainesthai*], but as being purified [*aphagnieisthai*] of any other pollution [*musos*] which we formerly had" (*On the Sacred Disease* 6).[17]

The so-called sacred laws specify the various kinds of impure condition that disqualify a person from entering the sanctuary in question, such as recent childbirth or abortion, menstruation (including anyone who comes in contact with a woman in either of these conditions), sexual intercourse (whether with one's spouse or someone else), consumption of certain foods, contact with a corpse, or acts of bloodshed. Also indicated is the time that must have elapsed before someone contaminated in any one of these ways may safely enter holy ground, and the requisite purificatory rites associated with the offense in question. Andreas Bendlin, from whom I have adapted the previous list, provides examples of such impure states: "a person claims to have entered a shrine in a state of impurity, being unaware of the locally prevailing purity regulations. A man with the name of Sosandros commits perjury and, thus polluted, nevertheless visits the temple. A man called Aurelius Soterichos has sexual intercourse with a woman in the sacred precinct. All three are duly punished by the gods. A slave owned by the sanctuary of some local deities even manages to have sexual intercourse with three different women on three different occasions before the gods stop him" (for the text, which derives from the so-called "confessional inscriptions" in Lydia, see below).[18] Another example, cited by Moshe Blidstein, derives from the city of Lindos on the island of Rhodes, and dates to the second century AD:

> For those who wish to enter the temple auspiciously.
> First and most important is to be sound and pure in hands
>   and thought, and not to
> have knowledge of dreadful [things].
> And the external things:
> After [eating] lentils, three days
> After [eating] goatmeat, three days
> After [eating] cheese, one day
> After abortions, 40 days
> After bereavement in the household, 40 days
> After lawful sexual relations, on the same day
> Following a sprinkling round [with water] and anointing
>   with olive oil
> After a virgin . . .[19]

Blidstein distinguishes between two types of impurity indicated by the inscription: internal, which involves purity of thought (<g>nômên) and conscience, and those that are explicitly characterized as external (*ta ektos*), involving various actions or circumstances, and which can be ritually washed away.[20]

Ought we to think of these ritual infractions as sins? No doubt, the rules are sanctioned, perhaps even regarded as having been laid down, by the god or gods of the precinct. Still, they are not general prohibitions, but pertain only to a sacralized space, deliberately set apart from ordinary life by precisely such injunctions. Outside these marked-off areas, sex, childbirth, burial, are perfectly natural activities, certainly not offenses against "the laws common to mankind" or "those unwritten laws which bring upon the transgressor of them the reprobation of the general sentiment," to quote Polybius and Thucydides. What is more, such violations are frequently involuntary, which sets them apart from crimes. Nor is the state of impurity noted in the temple inscriptions equatable with pollution or *miasma*; such conditions, as we have seen, involve everyday activities that bear no stigma in themselves and do not communicate contagion to others, which is one of the features that characterize pollution, as Robert Parker has observed in his exhaustive study of the topic.[21] A case in point is the fate of Philoctetes, dramatized by Sophocles in one of his late tragedies. Because he accidentally trod upon a sacred area, he was bitten in the leg by a poisonous serpent that dwelled there, perhaps to protect it from unwarranted intrusions. As a result, he was abandoned by his comrades en route to Troy on a deserted island, where he suffered for ten years. There is no suggestion that Philoctetes was at fault or that he deserved his miserable fate. Neither is Philoctetes defiled, and his affliction is not regarded as contagious.

But if the kind of impurity that prohibits entry onto sacred ground does not necessarily entail *miasma*, the condition of pollution may disqualify the bearer from contact with ritual spaces, although such restrictions are much more rare than one might suppose. As Blidstein points out, "Cult regulations rarely describe crimes as polluting: a sole regulation of the second century BCE prohibits the entrance of traitors and perhaps murderers."[22] But the deed that most typically entails pollution is undoubtedly manslaughter, and it too, like violations of temple rules, could be expiated by the performance of certain rituals. In Aeschylus' *Oresteia*, Orestes is, as we have seen, acquitted of the murder of his mother, for which the Furies persecuted him, in a court of law. However, prior to the trial, he was purified of the pollution or *miasma* attaching to the murder by Apollo, the very god who egged him on to the matricide. As Orestes explains:

> Schooled in misery, I know many purifications [*katharmoi*], and I know when it is justice [*dikê*] to speak and similarly when to be silent; and in this case, I have been ordered to speak by a wise teacher. For the blood slumbers and fades from my hand—the matricidal pollution [*mêtroktonon miasma*] is washed away; while the blood was still fresh, it was driven away at the hearth of the god Phoebus by purificatory [*katharmois*] sacrifices of pigs. It would be a long story to tell from the beginning, how many people I visited with no harm from the meeting. As time grows old, it purifies [*kathairei*] all things alike. So now with a pure [*hagnou*] mouth, speaking the right way, I invoke Athena, mistress of the land, to come to my aid. Without the spear, she will win me and my land and the Argive people justly [*dikaiôs*] as a faithful ally forever.[23]

There are two distinct processes here, ordered sequentially. First, Orestes must be purified of the stain or *miasma* caused by the blood guilt, and this is accomplished ritually in Delphi, where Apollo had his famous oracle. As a result, Orestes is not contagious, but can, as he says, associate with others without transmitting the stain. But this does not yet acquit Orestes of the crime of murder: for this, he appeals not to Apollo but to Athena, and trusts that she will redeem him "justly" (*dikaiôs*), which I take to be a charged expression intimating the forthcoming trial in an Athenian tribunal.

In Athens in historical times, a murderer was held to be impure and potentially contagious; hence, in certain trials a defendant charged with homicide was obliged to stand in a boat in order not to contaminate the land (see Demosthenes 23.77–78; Aristotle *Politics* 1300b29–30). It is tempting to regard such rituals as a primitive, pre-legal form of social control, later to be replaced by civic conceptions of law and justice, even if pollution remained as a vestige of the old order. But this notion of historical phases may well be a mirage, like the parallel hypothesis of a gift-giving stage of economic development preceding a fully developed form of exchange.[24] Indeed, Edward M. Harris has argued convincingly that *miasma*, as a feature of Athenian law, was in fact a self-conscious way of concentrating the power over death in the hands of the state. Now everyone, not just the affected party, would be concerned to bring the murderer to justice, since it would be seen to affect the entire community.[25]

We might distinguish, then, between two dimensions of the same offense: on the one hand, the infraction of the law, which may be called a crime, and, on the other hand, a transgression of a divine prohibition, which results in its own type of punishment, namely pollution. As Moshe Blidstein puts it: "In the case of crimes, these rituals acted in parallel to the legal process."[26] Might such ritual infractions be regarded as sins? We may note that the multiple causes of defilement or uncleanness in general, which, as we shall see in the subsequent chapter, have analogues in the Hebrew Bible, do not seem to have been associated with a special code of law, unless we single out homicide as a unique offense. The Furies afflict Orestes with madness for matricide, which violated the social arrangements that fell within their jurisdiction, as they perceived it. His pollution, however, is a separate matter, constituted independently of both the archaic code of the Erinyes and the novel ideology of Apollo, Athena, and the Olympian deities. Orestes' pollution does not seem to have been inflicted by a specific god; it is automatic, and may be communicated despite the will of the gods. It is possible to think of homicide as a double offense, both a crime and, in respect to *miasma*, a sin. Nevertheless, on the whole it seems preferable to separate the idea of impurity, with which contagious pollution is associated, although the two ideas are by no means synonymous, from that of sin proper, defined as "an immoral act considered to be a transgression against divine law" or "the voluntary departure of a moral agent from a known rule of rectitude or duty, prescribed by God."

There is another context in which purity is emphasized, and that is the various mystery cults, which, along with some philosophically disposed sects (e.g., Orphism, Empedocles), have various prohibitions and sometimes moral prescriptions for initiation and subsequent behavior. Conformity with these rules was believed to guarantee various blessings, often in the afterlife. The chorus of initiates into the cult of Demeter in Aristophanes' *Frogs* gives a sense of the reward for reverence: "Let's march to the flowery meadows, blooming with roses, revelling in our fashion with song and fairest dance which the blessed Fates array. We alone enjoy the sun and the light who have been initiated and followed the way of piety [*eusebê te diêgomen tropon*] towards strangers and laymen" (449–59).[27] Apuleius (second century AD) provides an insight into the initiatory experience in his novel, *Metamorphoses* (often called *The Golden Ass*), in which Lucius, the protagonist, is accidently turned into an ass when he tries a magic potion and is in the end rescued by the Egyptian goddess Isis, who enjoyed a popular cult in Rome and many Greek cities. The narrator recounts the experience:

> And now, diligent reader, you are no doubt keen to know what was said next, and what was done. I'd tell you, if to tell you were allowed; if you were allowed to hear then you might know, but ears and tongue would sin equally, the latter for its profane indiscretion, the former for their unbridled curiosity. Oh, I shall speak, since your desire to hear may be a matter of deep religious longing, and I would not torment you with further anguish, but I shall speak only of what can be revealed to the minds of the uninitiated without need for subsequent atonement, things which though you have heard them, you may well not understand. So listen, and believe in what is true. I reached the very gates of death and, treading Proserpine's threshold, yet passed through all the elements and returned. I have seen the sun at midnight shining brightly. I have entered the presence of the gods below and the presence of the gods above, and I have paid due reverence before them. When dawn came and the ceremony was complete, I emerged wearing twelve robes as a sign of consecration, sacred dress indeed though nothing stops me from speaking of it, since a host of people were there and saw me. As instructed, I stood on a wooden dais placed at the centre of the holy shrine, before the statue of the Goddess, conspicuous in my fine elaborately embroidered linen. The precious outer cloak hung from shoulder to ankle, so that I was wrapped around with creatures worked in various colours: here Indian serpents, there Hyperborean gryphons, winged lions of that distant region of the world. The priests call this garment the Olympian Stole. I held a burning torch in my right hand, and my head was gracefully garlanded with a wreath of gleaming palm leaves projecting outwards like rays of light. Adorned thus in the likeness of the Sun, and standing there like a statue, the curtains suddenly being opened, I was exposed to the gaze of the crowd who strayed around me. That day my initiation into the mysteries was marked, as a festive occasion, by a splendid feast among a convivial gathering. On the next day, the third, a similar ritual ceremony was performed, with a sacred breakfast bringing an official end to the proceedings.[28]

As in the Eleusinian mysteries, there is a vision of some sort that cannot be communicated (revealing the rites was punishable by death in Athens), and various formalities involving libations, dress, fasting, and the like. Purity of mind and heart was the essential qualification, as in the inscription from

Lindos quoted above. Without that, and failing due respect for the rituals, one could not join the blessed community of worshippers. The profane—the word literally means "outside or in front of the temple" (*fanum* is Latin for "shrine")—would miss out on the rewards promised for this life and the next, but this was not in itself an offense for which they were being punished. Here again, the condition of impurity, especially in connection with initiatory ceremonies, has little to do with transgressing divine law; the cult provided no generalized code of conduct for civic life or rituals for the atonement of such offenses, and hence no special vocabulary emerged to mark off sin from crimes or moral infractions more generally.

Plato, in his *Republic* (364B–65A), mentions that there are wandering priests who promise, by spells and incantations, to compel the gods to expiate crimes. They cite Phoenix's assertion in the *Iliad*, as he tries to persuade Achilles to accept Agamemnon's gifts and return to battle, that the gods themselves are moved by sacrifices and prayers when a person transgresses and errs (*hote ken tis huperbêêi kai hamartêi*, Iliad 9.497–500). These charlatans appeal also to the writings of Musaeus and Orpheus, claiming that there are "deliverances [*luseis*] and purifications for unjust acts [*katharmoi adikêmatôn*] by means of sacrifices and the pleasures of play for those who are alive, and there are also what they call rites [*teletai*] for those who have died, which deliver us from evils in that other world, whereas terrible things await those who have not sacrificed" (364E–365A). Such false magicians and prophets, satirized by Apuleius in his *Metamorphoses* (8.27–29, on the priests of Cybele who flagellate themselves in ecstatic frenzy) and by Lucian in his essay on the shenanigans of Alexander of Abonoteichus, a priest of Asclepius, were regarded with suspicion by philosophers. At the same time they were also potential rivals, like the "super apostles" (*hoi huperlian apostoloi*) against whom Paul sarcastically warns in 2 Corinthians 11:5. The promises of absolution and salvation are apocalyptic, but there is no clear indication that divine or universal laws have been transgressed, and the itinerant preachers to whom Plato refers resemble in a humble or popular key the priests who preside over initiatory rituals.

Although the body is the locus of impurity, along with the soul, in the ritual prescriptions surveyed above, it is not in itself a source of defilement or error. An early philosophical tradition did, however, inaugurate a radical depreciation of the body in relation to the soul, reflected in the Platonic formula, σῶμα σῆμα or "the body is a tomb" (Plato *Gorgias* 493A, cf. *Phaedo* 82E, 92A). Plato, moreover, attributes the view specifically to Orphism (*Cratylus* 400B), which flourished in various guises (often under the name of Pythagoras) in the Roman Empire and exerted a powerful influence on later views. The idea was congenial to ascetic practices of all sorts and was readily adopted by Christian writers, such as Clement of Alexandria (*Stromateis* 3.3.16.3) and Theodoret (*On the Passions* 5.13). Miguel Herrero de Jáuregui, who has examined the influence of Orphism on Christianity with exemplary learning and caution, observes: "The ascetic prescriptions believed to constitute the *orphikos bios*—that is to say, to refrain from shedding blood, eating certain foods, wearing certain clothes, and perhaps from sexual intercourse, along with a commitment to just behavior—are precisely the same ritual requirements inscribed upon temples for cultic practitioners before their approach to the deity. Orphism simply extends to the practitioner's entire life the ritual and/or moral purity that were only temporarily and momentarily necessary in cultic worship."[29] Might we then identify the body as the locus of sin? We may note first of all that there was nothing like a coherent body of Orphic doctrine. As Herrero de Jáuregui notes, there is little or no evidence for "ritual and ideological uniformity."[30] A case has, however, been made not just for the sinfulness of the body but for an Orphic doctrine of original sin. We may now examine the evidence for this claim.

Olympiodorus, a sixth-century AD commentator on Plato and Aristotle who was among the last pagans to teach philosophy in Alexandria, composed a commentary on Plato's *Phaedo*, in which he sought to explain the basis for Socrates' objection to suicide (62B). It is in this connection that Olympiodorus recounts an Orphic myth, according to which humanity arose from the ashes of the Titans. The Titans had been incinerated by Zeus's thunderbolts because they dismembered Dionysus and consumed his flesh. Olympiodorus reports:

> According to Orpheus there were four cosmic reigns. First was the reign of Uranus, then Cronus received the kingship, having cut off his father's genitals. Zeus ruled after Cronus, having cast his father into Tartarus. Next, Dionysus succeeded Zeus. They say that through Hera's treachery, the Titans who were around Dionysus tore him to pieces and ate his flesh. And Zeus, being angry at this, struck the Titans with thunderbolts, and from the soot of the vapors that arose from [the incinerated Titans] came the matter from

which humanity came into existence. Therefore, we must not commit suicide—not because, as [Socrates] seems to say, we are in our body as if in a prison, since that is obvious and [Socrates] would not call such an idea secret, but rather because our bodies are Dionysiac. We are, indeed, part of Dionysus if we are composed from the soot of the Titans who ate Dionysus' flesh.

Olympiodorus *On the Phaedo* 1.3 = 41 Westerink[31]

We must not, accordingly, destroy the divine portion of our constitution. Sarah Iles Johnston asks: "Why have many modern people also perceived the Orphic story as familiar, even in the midst of claiming that it is strange?" And she explains: "The answer lies in its broad thematic similarity to foundational Christian stories: a god dies and is revived; the human race carries within itself a stain that each individual member must expunge through rituals paid to that god or else risk eternal misery in the afterlife."[32] Later, Johnston observes that the filth from which initiates into the Orphic cult are cleansed is very likely "the ancestral blood-guilt that all humans inherited from the Titans."[33] In a similar vein, Alberto Bernabé and Ana Isabel Jiménez San Cristóbal explain that, thanks to initiation in the mysteries, "the soul has succeeded in liberating itself from its Titanic crime, the primordial guilt for which it has had to go through its sojourn in the mortal world. This expiation presupposes the soul's liberation from its corporeal bonds. This trial is surmounted by means of initiation, rites of purification, and the way of life to which the initiates are subject during their earthly existence. And it is the god Bacchus, Dionysus Lysios, the victim of the crime himself, who must ultimately approve this liberation."[34] Other scholars, however, have contested the notion that Olympiodorus is testifying that "the human race carries within itself a stain" and must be liberated from a "primordial guilt." Dwayne A. Meisner, for example, remarks that Olympiodorus "is talking about the opposite of original sin: because we have a Dionysiac nature, our bodies are partly divine."[35] It is this divine part of our nature, extending to our bodies, that renders suicide an evil. Claims have been made for the convergence of Orphic and Christian ideas of sin and redemption, and even for the influence of Orphic conceptions of the death and rebirth of a god on the fundamental Christian narrative. To be sure, the evidence for Orphic beliefs goes well beyond the passage from Olympiodorus, which is itself indebted to earlier sources, and includes prayers inscribed on gold leaves, Pindaric poetry, and more.[36] Cumulatively, however, these texts give the impression of a concern with holiness and initiatory purification rather than with transgressions of the law of God.

A remarkable set of inscriptions from Lydia and Phrygia, in what is now north-western Turkey, and dating to the second and third centuries AD, are unusual in indicating an offense that the dedicator of the stele has expiated through the performance of various rituals. The stelae are sometimes referred to as "confession inscriptions." However, although they commemorate the lifting of the punishment, which was atoned for by the sacrifices, they do not typically mention the confession as such but are rather a public declaration that the god has been appeased. Aslak Rostad, who has edited and translated a great number of these texts, refers to them more accurately as "reconciliation inscriptions." Because of the emphasis on wrongdoing and divine chastisement, some scholars have supposed that they reflect the influence of Christianity, although the inscriptions themselves do not refer to Christ or any other specifically Christian feature.[37] Is there any justification for describing the wrongs that are mentioned in these texts as sins? Let us examine some examples.[38]

> In the year 285 on the 30th of the month Panêmos. For the God Tarsios from whom no one may escape. Because Severus hindered cutting of wreaths the god examined the transgression. His foster daughters Asiateikê and Jouliané raised (this stele) in gratitude.[39]

The god is plainly not Christian, and there is no mention of confession, though evidently the offense was made public. It may be assumed that the penalty, whatever it was, was lifted, and this is the reason for his foster daughters' gratitude. The following inscription is more detailed:

> In the year 320, on the 12th of the month Panemos. In accordance with the fact that I was instructed by the gods, by Zeus and the great Mên Artemidoros: "I have punished Theodoros on his eyes according to the transgressions he committed." I had intercourse with Trophime, the slave of Haplokomas, wife of Eutykhes, in the *praetorium* (?). He removed the first transgression with a sheep, a partridge and a mole. The second transgression: Even though I was a slave of the gods in Nonu, I had intercourse with Ariagne, who was unmarried. He removed the transgression with a piglet and a tuna. At the third transgression I had intercourse with Arethusa, who was unmarried. He removed the

transgression with a hen (or cock), a sparrow and a pigeon; with a *kypros* of a blend of wheat and barley and one *prokhos* of wine. Being pure he gave a *kypros* of wheat to the priests and one *prokhos*. I took Zeus as intercessor. (He said): Behold! I hurt his sight because of his deeds, but now he has propitiated [*heilazomenou*] the gods and written down (the events) on a stele and paid for his transgressions. Asked by the council (the god proclaimed): I will be merciful, because my stele is raised on the day I appointed. You can open the prison; I will release the convict when one year and ten months has passed.[40]

The following inscription again records the successful propitiation of the offended deity:

> Polion (dedicates this stele) to Zeus Oreites and Mên Axiottenos, who rules Perkos (or: Perkon) as a king. When (the circumstances) were hidden for me, and I overstepped the border without permission, the gods punished him (= me).[41] In the year 323, on the 30th of the month Dystros. He removed (the transgression) with a triad consisting of a mole, a sparrow and a tuna. He also gave the means of atonement that by habit is due to the gods when the stele was raised: a modius of wheat and one *prokhos* of wine. As a meal to the priests he gave 1½ (?) *kypros* of wheat, 1½ (?) *prokhos* of wine, peas and salt. And I have propitiated the gods for the sake of my grand-children and the descendants of my descendants.[42]

In the next text, the dedicator again mentions his gratitude:

> Great is Zeus of the Twin Oaks. Stratoneikos son of Euangelos because of ignorance cut down one of the oaks belonging to Zeus Didymeites. And the god mobilized his own power because he (i.e. Stratoneikos) did not believe in him, and placed him ... in a deathlike condition. He was saved from great danger and raised the stele in gratitude. I declare that no one shall ever show contempt for his powers and cut down an oak. In the year 279, on the 18th of the month Panemos.[43]

The gratitude of the dedicator is emphasized once more in the following inscription:

> In the year 300, on the 12th day of the month Xandikos. Because of the transgression which they committed towards the god—and they stole (?) as well as other property—Melitê and Makedôn were punished by the god and their parents asked Apollo Axyros on their behalf. Having asked they raised (the ex-voto) in gratitude.[44]

To take one final example, the dedicator of the next stele does not state explicitly that he successfully propitiated the god, but it is clearly implied by the very fact of having erected and inscribed the stele:

> I, - - - mos, having been punished by the god, raised a stele to Apollôn Labênos (with an account) of how he punished me because of an oath, my awareness (of my guilt), and a defilement. I proclaim to all that nobody shall show contempt for the gods.[45]

It is evident that the rules that are said to have been violated resemble those documented in the temple regulations that are conventionally dubbed "sacred laws" or *leges sacrae*. The difference between the two classes of inscriptions is that the rules that are posted on the sanctuary grounds take the form of prohibitions issued by the temple authorities, whereas the reconciliation stelae represent the perspective of those who have violated the protocols, have been punished, and have propitiated the offended deity. Both kinds of infraction are restricted to particular times and places, and do not constitute or form part of a general law code sanctioned by a deity and governing daily life.

Clearly, the offender was obliged to acknowledge the fault, rather than deny responsibility and appeal to the god's pity for wrongfully inflicted suffering. As Aslak Rostad observes, these inscriptions "offered an opportunity for a person stigmatised by the allegation of impious behaviour to regain his or her former position." He adds: "Interestingly, this was not achieved by claiming and proving one's innocence, as may be seen in trials of impiety in classical Athens—even if this may have been one of the options tried before raising the reconciliation inscription—but by admitting the transgression and performing rituals of propitiation. Thereby, the transgressor could be redefined within the moral order and claim to be a pious person who was free of the binding spell. Despite the fact that the transgressor admits guilt, he or she can no longer be accused of being subjected to divine wrath."[46] Sometimes, however, the infraction that has been atoned does not involve guilt or responsibility in the moral sense but is simply the result of accident, as in the case of Philoctetes. The following inscription is a case in point:

> Great is Mêtêr who gave birth to Mên, great is Meis Uranios, Meis Artemidorou who rules Axiotta and his power. When P(h)osphoros, son of Artemas, a child six years old, was dressed in a garment stained with impurity,

the god investigated. A triad took (the transgression) away, and he (i.e. Phosphoros) wrote down the powers of the god on a stele. In the year 245 on the 12th of the month Panêmos.[47]

Clearly, a six-year-old boy cannot be deemed guilty of sinning against the god, or even of being negligent; one presumes that his parents too were unaware that the garment was ritually unclean. But even where responsibility or blameworthiness is admitted, it is not clear that confession is instrumental in atoning for the offense, as opposed to the sacrifices and other offerings that are enumerated. It is certainly not the element that is emphasized in the stelae, as opposed to the infraction itself, the retribution, and the lifting of the punishment or pollution, along with the expression of gratitude for the god's goodwill and the offender's reintegration into the community.

The marginal role of confession in these so-called "confession inscriptions" points to a larger absence, namely that of remorse for the misdeed. Although the standard definitions of sin that we have canvassed above do not mention remorse, it is frequently associated with sin, as in the definition offered by the *Oxford English Dictionary*: "a feeling of compunction, or of deep regret or repentance, for a sin or wrong committed." Remorse goes deeper than mere regret, which indicates dissatisfaction with the outcome of a previous action without necessarily involving a sense of wrongdoing. We may regret not having taken an umbrella when it begins unexpectedly to rain, but we would not speak of remorse in such a case. Contrariwise, we might feel remorse for having done serious harm to another person, for example in a fit of rage, whereas regret might suggest that, though we wish we had not done so, our reason is pragmatic rather than moral, involving a fear of reprisal or some other disagreeable consequence. When a king declares, "I am not sorry that I killed your son, but that I did not kill you as well" (Xenophon *Cyropedia* 5.3.6), we would hardly credit him with remorse, though the Greek word that he employs (μεταμέλει, *metmelei*; cf. μεταμέλεια, *metameleia*, 5.3.7) is frequently rendered as such. In a similar vein, the Roman biographer Suetonius records an episode in the Civil War that took place in the year 49 BC. Julius Caesar was negotiating the surrender of the opposing army in the Spanish town of Ilerda (today Lérida or, in Catalán, Lleida), which was under the command of the two legates, Lucius Afranius and Marcus Petreius. Then, "with a sudden change of mind" (*subita paenitentia*), the two ordered the slaughter of all the partisans of Caesar in their camp. Clearly, they were not feeling penitent, as the word *paenitentia* might suggest, but merely regretted their earlier decision to surrender, presumably in the belief that they could hold out against Caesar (Suetonius *Life of Julius Caesar*, 75).

True remorse or repentance, we suppose, involves a condemnation of one's own immoral conduct. Thus, the *Merriam-Webster Dictionary* offers as the first definition of "repent," "to turn from sin and dedicate oneself to the amendment of one's life." The *Oxford English Dictionary*, in turn, gives: "Feel or express sincere regret or remorse about one's wrongdoing or sin."[48] Such a change of heart is motivated not by fear of a negative outcome as such but by what we may think of as an attack of conscience, defined in the *Oxford English Dictionary* as "A person's moral sense of right and wrong, viewed as acting as a guide to one's behaviour." The *Merriam-Webster Dictionary* offers the more elaborate definition, "the sense or consciousness of the moral goodness or blameworthiness of one's own conduct, intentions, or character together with a feeling of obligation to do right or be good," and adds that the term may also signify "a faculty, power, or principle enjoining good acts." Characteristically, a guilty conscience produces a profound moral discomfort, frequently imagined as a biting (the root sense of "remorse," from the Latin *mordeo*) or stinging sensation.

It is doubtful, however, that such a notion of conscience had been formulated in classical Greece and Rome, although translations and dictionaries sometimes give the impression that there was indeed such a notion. Richard Sorabji, in his broad historical survey of the idea of conscience from antiquity to today, remarks that in classical Greek the word *sunoida*, which literally means something like "know," may be accompanied by a reflexive dative, as in the expression *sunoida moi* or "I know in myself." The compound phrase, Sorabji argues, signifies self-awareness (the corresponding noun, *suneidêsis*, is not found before the Hellenistic period).[49] This peculiar construction, according to Sorabji, connotes the act of sharing something—a secret or fault, for example— with oneself, and thus corresponds closely to the modern notion of conscience as the awareness of one's moral blameworthiness (compare definition V.2 in *LSJ*, "conscience," citing texts dating to the Roman Empire). The passages that Sorabji adduces, however, are subject to different interpretations. To take one instance (cited by Sorabji),[50] in Euripides' tragedy *Medea*, the heroine reproaches her husband Jason for violating his marriage vows. He must believe, she says, that the gods by whom he once swore are no longer in power or else that new laws exist among mortals, since, she says, "you know [σύνοισθά, *sunoistha*, from *sunoida*] that you have not respected your oath in regard to me" (495). Medea's point, however, would seem to be precisely the opposite, that Jason is fully aware of what he promised and that he is now acting inconsistently with his oath, but he is not conscience-stricken at all.

Another candidate that is often proposed for the sense "conscience" is the word *sunesis*, derived from the verb *suniêmi*, which literally means "to bring or set together," and hence, "to understand" (*LSJ*). The abstract noun *sunesis*, accordingly, signifies a "union," but also "sagacity" or "intelligence," and hence, the argument goes, "conscience." The Greek-English dictionary offers as the prime example of this use a much discussed passage in Euripides' tragedy, *Orestes*. Sorabji affirms that "*sunesis*, in Euripides' *Orestes* 396 and in Polybius 18.43.13 certainly refers to conscience, but might have the more general meaning of knowledge."[51] The context is this: Orestes' uncle, Menelaus, has just arrived in Argos, where Orestes is being tried in the Assembly for the murder of his mother, Clytemnestra. In the opening scene, Orestes is asleep, after an attack of madness induced by the Furies, who are punishing the matricide, as they did in Aeschylus' *Oresteia*. His illness takes the form of paranoid delusions: he is tormented by visions of the serpent-haired monsters, and when he awakens, he mistakes the chorus and his own sister, Electra, for Furies. He is still visibly shaken when Menelaus appears, and so asks his nephew: "What are you suffering from? What disease is destroying you?" To this, Orestes replies: "It is *sunesis*, because I know [*sunoida*] that I have done dreadful things" (vv. 395–96). Many modern translations of the *Orestes* render the word *sunesis* here as "conscience," and at first sight this seems like a reasonable enough choice. To be sure, Martin West, always cautious, renders *sunesis* as "intellect" in his edition and translation of the play. In the commentary, however, he remarks: "Greeks did not yet have a word for conscience …, but the concept was beginning to be familiar."[52] But let us look more closely at the exchange between uncle and nephew.

Throughout his self-defense, he expresses not so much guilt for his actions as an awareness of the terrible consequences of his deed, in the form precisely of the madness inflicted on him by the Furies. To begin with, Orestes has no thought of making amends for his action; on the contrary, he will soon try to kill Helen, whom he holds responsible for the war and hence, indirectly, for Agamemnon's murder at the hands of Clytemnestra (she and Helen are sisters), and he will attempt to kill Menelaus' daughter, Hermione, as well. Did he, then, believe that he was wrong to kill his mother, and that this was the cause of his present distress? Earlier, Menelaus had accused Orestes of having dared to do "terrible evils" (*deina kaka*, 376), and Orestes replies: "I willingly reveal my evils [*kaka*] to you" (381), and he goes on to beg his uncle for help, for, he says, he has arrived at the critical moment of his evils (*auton es kairon kakôn*, 384). Orestes has evidently twisted Menelaus's words around: Menelaus was referring to the awful crime that Orestes had committed, but Orestes speaks rather of his present misfortune, which is to say, his affliction. He goes on to say that even though he sees the light, he is no longer alive, because of the evils that beset him (386); here again, Orestes is thinking of his own condition, not the act of matricide, although he does allow that his deeds (*erga*) have disfigured him (388). Soon afterwards he exclaims that his fate has been rich in evils (394). It is precisely here that Menelaus asks Orestes about the disease that afflicts him, and Orestes replies that it is *sunesis* and, as he adds, his awareness of the dreadful things (*deina*) he has done (396). Is he manifesting here a sense of having done wrong? Scholars have observed that *deina*, the word I have rendered as "dreadful," has no necessary moral associations. Thus V. A. Rodgers observes that Orestes is conscious not of wrongdoing but rather "the full horror of the deed, a feeling which need have nothing to do with awareness of culpability or with moral guilt."[53] In sum, Orestes appears to have been concerned all along less about what he did than about the consequences of his act. Such an awareness, which has only recently dawned on him as a result of his madness, does not meet the conditions for "conscience" in the modern sense of the word.[54] Several centuries later, Plutarch will interpret this very verse in the *Orestes* in a way that does indeed come closer to what we think of as conscience. Amplifying Orestes' bald answer to Menelaus that what torments him "is *sunesis*, because I know that I have done dreadful things," Plutarch adds that this knowledge "leaves regret [*metameleia*] in the soul like a wound in the flesh, which forever draws blood and stings [*nussousan*]" (*Peri euthumias* or *De tranquillitate animi*, 19). But this is later exegesis.

The English word "conscience" is a compound of the Latin prefix *cum-* ("with") and *scientia*, "knowledge," and is thus analogous to the Greek *sunoida* (*sun-* means "with" and *oida*, "know"). What is more, Latin too combined the adjective *conscius* with the reflexive pronoun, yielding the phrase *conscius sibi*, occurrences of which are both frequent and early. An example is the following passage from Plautus' *Mostellaria*; here is the Loeb translation:

> Dear me, how scared I am, poor wretch that I am! Nothing's more wretched than a man's guilty conscience [*animus hominis conscius*], just as mine's torturing me [*me <male> habet*]. But no matter what's up, I'll carry on causing trouble: this situation demands it.
>
> vv. 543–46

The words are those of the slave Tranio, who is terrified that his plotting is about to be discovered by his master, Theopropides. The *Oxford Latin Dictionary*, the most authoritative Latin lexicon in the English language, cites this very passage in the entry on the adjective *conscius*, under the subheading, "Conscious of guilt, having a guilty conscience." But it hardly seems likely that Tranio has been suddenly struck with moral remorse on account of his previous plotting. If that had been the case, he would scarcely be announcing his intention to persist in causing trouble. Tranio is an unrepentant plotter, and it is far more likely that he is simply afraid that that his past actions are about to catch up with him, and that this is the torture to which he refers. He is anxiously aware of the danger of being whipped, not conscience-stricken for having done wrong.

There is a Latin passage dating to the first century BC, contemporary with Cicero and Julius Caesar, that seems to indicate something like remorse or a guilty conscience in the modern acceptation of the term. It comes from the hand of Lucretius, who composed a didactic poem in defense of Epicureanism. The Epicureans maintained that the highest good for human beings was tranquility of mind, and believed that the greatest source of mental perturbation was a belief in the afterlife and the possibility of posthumous punishment for one's misdeeds. Hence, they denied the immortality of the soul, insisting that the soul, like the body and all things in the universe, was composed of atoms and void, and that these atoms would disperse when the body perished and was no longer able to contain it. Among the proofs that Lucretius offers for the soul's mortality, in addition to those involving its physical constitution, is its vulnerability to various kinds of disturbance:

> For not to mention that it sickens along with bodily disease, something often comes that torments [*macerat*] it about the future, keeps it miserable in fear, wearies it with anxiety [*curis*], and, when there has been evil done in the past, its sins bring remorse [*peccata remordent*].
>
> 3.824–27[55]

Epicurus himself had counseled that, when we are in pain, we ought to recall past pleasures and anticipate future ones. Lucretius, however, in the present passage summons up rather the effects of anticipatory anxiety and retrospective anguish. But what is the source of this backward-looking distress? By rendering the Latin word *peccata* as "sins," a meaning it certainly bears in Christian texts, the Loeb translators import a notion which would seem foreign to the thought of Epicurus, who maintained that the gods are supremely happy and therefore must be entirely indifferent to human affairs, which could only cause them worry and pain.[56] Lucretius makes it clear that the reference is simply to "deeds wrongly committed in the past" (the Latin is *praeteritisque male admissis*); there is no implication of divine disapproval or the violation of divinely sanctioned rules of conduct, which is part and parcel of the definition of sin according to the standard dictionaries.

Nevertheless, the idea of sin does not seem entirely out of place in this context. The reason is the associated verb *remordent*, the source, as we have noted, of the English "remorse"; the word means "bite repeatedly" or "sting," or in the definition given in the *Oxford Latin Dictionary*, "vex persistently, gnaw, nag." Epicurus himself held that one should avoid wrongdoing because otherwise one would always be nervous about possible detection. His counsel was thus pragmatic: if one could be absolutely certain that a crime would never be brought to light, presumably there would be nothing to inhibit one from committing it. It is possible that some such practical consideration is implicit in Lucretius' view as well, but the phrasing suggests not so much the fear of future reprisal as a gnawing discomfort caused by the very fact of having done wrong. Such an inner moral sensibility, comparable to the modern notion of guilt, would not depend on the fear of detection and might even obviate the need for repressive legislation in the first place.

Lucretius would not have been inhospitable to such a view. In his discussion of the origin of laws, Lucretius affirms: "thence does fear of punishment tarnish the rewards of life" (*inde metus maculat poenarum praemia vitae*, 5.1151). In a similar vein, Lucretius' contemporary, the Epicurean Philodemus, whose writings have been recovered from the volcanic ash of Mount Vesuvius, wrote: "The many are rather led to right conduct by the laws which threaten with death, and with punishments coming from the gods, and with pains which are considered intolerable, and with the privation of things which are supposedly hard to procure. This is the case … partly because these things threaten men who are foolish and who cannot be persuaded by the true precepts; and the only thing that is achieved through them [sc. the laws] is deterrence for a short period of time."[57] Law is at best a second-best means of maintaining social order, and brings with it the kind of anxiety that Epicureanism was at pains to avoid. It may be, then, that Lucretius indeed had in mind something like the pangs of conscience and a notion of genuine moral regret.[58] It is nevertheless misleading to render *peccata* here as "sins," given the prevailing theological connotations of the word.

Clearly, there existed a notion of sin in the classical world, if by "sin" is meant "The voluntary departure of a moral agent from a known rule of rectitude or duty, prescribed by God" (*King James Version Dictionary*) or "a reprehensible act by which a person consciously contravenes a divine law or commandment."[59] The testimony of Sophocles' *Antigone* and related texts suffices to prove the point. If, however, we extend the idea of sin to include such concepts as guilt, conscience, and remorse, not to mention confession and divine forgiveness, which play so central a role, as we shall see, in the Judeo-Christian conception of sin, then we may doubt whether a comparable conception emerged in the pagan traditions.[60] Even the sense of a higher code of conduct, such as that invoked by Antigone, did not rise to the level of orthodoxy, as we may call it. Although the unwritten laws of the gods were associated with what were perceived as the universal condemnation of certain offenses, they were never embedded in a coherent religious doctrine. This is no surprise, given the variety of cults and beliefs in the pagan Greco-Roman world and the absence of a widely acknowledged sacred scripture. Ritual infractions might be expiated, and one might be cleansed of pollution or *miasma*, but such practices remained at the margins of that generalized conception of divine law to which Antigone and Xenophon's Socrates appealed.

In his didactic manual, *Works and Days*, the poet Hesiod, roughly contemporary with Homer, explains:

> the gods keep hidden from men the means of life. Else you would easily do work enough in a day to supply you for a full year even without working... But Zeus in the anger of his heart hid it, because Prometheus the crafty deceived him; therefore he planned sorrow and mischief against men. He hid fire; but that the noble son of Iapetus [i.e., Prometheus] stole again for men from Zeus the counsellor in a hollow fennel-stalk, so that Zeus who delights in thunder did not see it.
>
> vv. 42–52[61]

In his anger, Zeus created Pandora, the ancestress of all women (it seems) and a plague for men. According to Hesiod, "ere this the tribes of men lived on earth remote and free from ills and hard toil and heavy sickness which bring the Fates upon men; for in misery men grow old quickly" (90–93). Just why human beings should suffer as a result of Prometheus' theft is not entirely clear, but the story evidently connects the hardships under which mankind labors with an original offense that enrages the chief god of the Olympic pantheon, with the result that he takes vengeance both on the rebel who sympathized with mankind and on mortals themselves.[62] Ought we, then, to characterize Prometheus' purloining of fire as a sin? Certainly, he has controverted the will of Zeus, and he, along with those he sought to benefit, will be punished. There is missing, however, any suggestion of remorse on Prometheus' part. Zeus will later relent and free Prometheus from the chains in which he had been bound, implicitly suggesting his reconciliation with mankind as well (Aeschylus *Prometheus Bound*). Prometheus' rebellion is not precisely an infraction of a divine rule—he is himself a god of a previous generation—and mortals are not charged with insubordination. But the story bears evident analogies to the Biblical narrative of the Garden of Eden, to which we turn in the next chapter on sin in the Hebrew Bible.

2

The Hebrew Bible: Chasing after Foreign Gods

The biblical story of mankind begins with a sin—or does it? As we know, God placed Adam in the Garden of Eden, and commanded him: "You may freely eat of every tree of the garden; but of the tree of the knowledge of good and evil you shall not eat, for in the day that you eat of it you shall die" (Genesis 2:16–17). The serpent, however, persuades Eve that if she eats the fruit of the tree, she will not die but will rather gain the kind of knowledge that will make her God's equal. "You will not die," the serpent tells her; "for God knows that when you eat of it your eyes will be opened, and you will be like God, knowing good and evil" (Genesis 3:4–5). The form that their knowledge takes is the awareness of their nakedness (3:7), which they had been unconscious of previously (Genesis 2:25), like animals, one presumes. But their new moral sensibility must extend beyond simple sexual modesty: by eating of the tree of the knowledge of good and evil, they become fully ethical beings, in a way that other creatures that God placed under their dominion are not. God immediately punishes the serpent, Eve, and Adam for their defiance, with the result that all women will henceforth suffer in childbirth and be subservient to their husbands (evidently, Eve was not so in Eden), and all humans will eke out a bare living from the unfertile earth and return to the dust from which they were created. This may suggest that death is the consequence of Adam and Eve's disobedience, just as God had said (and the serpent had maliciously denied), but there follows a second concern. For God then says, "See, the man has become like one of us, knowing good and evil; and now, he might reach out his hand and take also from the tree of life, and eat, and live forever." It is now suggested that this is the reason why "the Lord God sent him forth from the garden of Eden, to till the ground from which he was taken" (Genesis 3:22–23). This scenario suggests that Adam and Eve did not become subject to death for eating the fruit of the tree of knowledge, but were created mortal.[1]

Whatever the cause of their mortality and that of the human race thereafter, however, they certainly defied God's command concerning the tree of knowledge and were punished for this offense. Their disobedience, moreover, is widely viewed as the paradigmatic instance of sin, interpreted in later Christian sources, indeed, as the original sin, tainting all their descendants who must not only earn their bread by the sweat of their brow but can only be absolved of their corrupt condition by God's grace. We shall return to the issue of original sin in the fourth chapter, when we examine the doctrines of the Church Fathers. Here, however, I wish to raise a different and more fundamental question: if, prior to eating the fruit, Adam and Eve did not know the difference between good and evil, or even what the terms meant, can they be said to have sinned? Is it possible to commit a sin, or indeed to be held responsible for a crime, when one is demonstrably ignorant of the nature of right and wrong? The condition of Adam and Eve prior to eating the fruit would appear to be that of a small child, who has not yet acquired moral awareness. It is true that they have disobeyed God's express order. We may discipline a small child (or even a pet animal) if it fails to heed instructions, but one would hardly say that the child or the pet has sinned.

The question is not just one that a modern reader, alert to fine points of the law, might raise. Irenaeus, a Christian writing in the late second century, argues that Adam was created with a childlike mind, which, he says, God would have allowed to mature: "as it certainly is in the power of a mother to give strong food to her infant [but she does not do so], as the child is not yet able to receive more substantial nourishment; so also it was possible for God himself to have made man perfect from the first, but man could not receive this [perfection], being as yet an infant" (*Against Heresies* 4.38.1).[2] Nevertheless, Irenaeus does not draw the conclusion that the still innocent Adam did not sin. But ought one to ascribe sin to a human being who is "as yet an infant" in respect to moral consciousness?

The brief account of the expulsion from Eden in Genesis leaves many questions unanswered. In the previous chapter, we considered the role of conscience in relation to sin, an awareness of one's own guilt that encourages confession and repentance. In the Hebrew Bible, as we shall see, these are crucial elements in the notion of sin. Genesis, however, gives no indication of repentance on the part of Adam and Eve, or whether their offense was pardoned by God. This gave room for Tatian, a Syrian whose life spanned the central decades of the second century and who converted to Christianity after a visit to Rome, to deny "the salvation of him who was first created," according to Irenaeus (1.28.1). So too, Eusebius reports in his *Church History* that the so-called Encratites, a sect later deemed heretical and said by some to have been founded by Tatian (though Eusebius traces it to Saturninus and Marcion), "preached celibacy, setting aside the original arrangement of God and tacitly censuring him who made male and female for the propagation of the human race. They introduced also abstinence from the things called by them animate, thus showing ingratitude to the God who made all things. And they deny the salvation of the first man" (4.29.2).[3] Eusebius adds that Tatian was the first to introduce this latter blasphemy. Irenaeus replies to Tatian's view at length, arguing that "inasmuch as mankind is saved, it is fitting that he who was created the original man should be saved. For it is too absurd to maintain that he who was so deeply injured by the enemy ... was not rescued by him who conquered the enemy, but that his children were" (3.23.2). As we shall see in the fourth chapter, Christian commentators of different stripes, concerned with the morality of their congregations and followers and engaged in intense polemics with those they regarded as heterodox, read the Bible variously, in accord with their understanding of the nature of sin and its consequences, among other things. Where there was sin, there must, they believed, be the possibility of forgiveness, even if it went unmentioned in the Scriptures.

And if there was forgiveness, there must also have been confession of guilt. There is a fascinating testimony to Adam's guilty conscience, and still more that of Eve, in a text of uncertain date and authorship that today goes under the name of *The Life of Adam and Eve* (it was formerly called *The Apocalypse of Moses*). Scholars are undecided even as to whether this text is Jewish or Christian in origin, since the earliest version, at least, contains no evident references to Christian themes. It has been dated as early as the first century BC (which would exclude a Christian provenance) and as late as the seventh century AD, and it survives in Greek, Syriac, Latin, Slavonic, Armenian, Georgian, and, in fragmentary state, Coptic versions, and was immensely popular in the Middle Ages, although it is little known today.[4] The narrative relates how Eve, after the expulsion from Eden, gave birth to Cain and Abel, and after the murder of Abel, to Seth. In broad strokes, the narrative runs like this: when Adam fell ill and was on the point of dying (he was 930 years old by then), he gathered round him his thirty sons and thirty daughters. Seth offers to fetch fruit from Paradise for Adam, but Adam replies that he is under the curse of death, since, at Eve's instigation, he ate the forbidden fruit, and so "God became angry at us" (8). Eve then says: "Adam, my lord, give me half your illness, and let me endure it, because this has happened to you on account of me, on account of me you are in such illness and pain" (9). Adam instructs Eve to seek out Paradise along with Seth, and to beg for God's pity. Eve exclaims: "Woe, woe, if I should come to the day of the resurrection, and all who have sinned will curse me, saying that Eve did not observe the commandment of God" (10). When Eve and Seth return, Eve, at Adam's behest, recites the story of the fall and God's terrible judgment. On the point of expiring, Adam begs Eve to pray to God, upon which she falls to the ground and wails: "I have sinned [*hêmarton*], God, I have sinned, Father of all, I have sinned against you, I have sinned against your chosen angels, I have sinned against the Cherubim, I have sinned against your unshakable throne, I have sinned, Lord, I have sinned greatly, I have sinned before you, and all sin in creation has arisen through me" (32). An angel approaches her and declares, "Arise, Eve, from your repentance [or change of heart: *metanoia*]" (32). He tells her that Adam has died, and reveals to her a vision of a chariot descending to Adam, and the angels begging the Lord to relent (33), since Adam is made in his image. God finally takes pity on his creation (37), and raises Adam to the third heaven, where he is to remain until the Day of Judgment when God will resurrect Adam and all mankind. Eve begs the Lord to bury her next to Adam, even though she is unworthy and sinful (*hamartôlon*, 42), and her wish is granted.

In addressing God, Eve acknowledges her error and is filled with remorse. She was, as she says, deceived by the serpent, but this is not to excuse her disobedience but rather to show that she now realizes that she was wrong and regrets her action. It is because Adam and Eve recognize and confess their guilt that God finally submits to the prayers of the angels and pardons them. The Genesis narrative, as we have observed, makes no mention of repentance and forgiveness; but neither does there occur in this context the Hebrew word for sin.[5] This point requires a philological excursus.

In the Tanakh, the word that is most commonly rendered as "sin" is *ḥaṭaʾ* (חטא, cf. the Arabic cognate, خطيئة). There are, to be sure, many Hebrew terms corresponding to wickedness, evil, iniquity, wrongdoing, and the various other words that are employed in rendering the Bible into English (and similarly for other languages). Why, then, should we single out one specific term as indicating "sin," when any of these other expressions for offensive behavior might equally imply sin or sinfulness? This question takes us to the heart of the argument of this book. The short answer is that the word *ḥaṭa'* is primarily reserved for special kinds of offenses that distinguish it from other words connoting evil more generally and that may be translated as "sin." The task of this chapter is to demonstrate that this is the case, by examining its uses throughout the Hebrew Bible and showing that they in fact manifest a distinct pattern (in the next chapter, I will attempt to show that the Greek word *hamartia*, which is the most common translation of *ḥaṭa'* in the Septuagint, also has a distinctive, though not identical, sense in the New Testament). To anticipate the conclusion, I propose that *ḥaṭa'* typically involves an offense against God's insistence on exclusive loyalty; he punishes any hint of regard for other gods, but is prepared to redeem those who have strayed, provided that they confess their sin and humbly acknowledge the justice of their punishment. Not all occurrences of *ḥaṭa'* conform to this pattern, and its uses evolve and are not uniform throughout the Tanakh. What is more, it is often paired with other expressions, such as iniquity (*'awon*), transgression (*pesha'*), trespass (*ma'al*), and other terms, especially in verse (the reasons for this will be indicated further on).[6] Nevertheless, the various Hebrew words signifying evil, wickedness, iniquity, and so forth do not intrinsically carry the core connection with idolatry or the pattern of atonement and remission that, I argue, sets *ḥaṭa'* apart. One consequence, it will emerge, of this special sense is that sin, as a falling away from fidelity to the one God, is more or less peculiar to the Israelites, God's chosen people with whom he has entered into a covenant. It is they who offend by chasing after foreign gods. Pagan tribes may worship idols, but those are their own, and hence not foreign. Nevertheless, for all their failings, God remains loyal to his people and is disposed to ease his anger despite their apostasy, provided that they repent. Since, as I claim (and hope to show), *ḥaṭa'* identifies a distinct type of wrongdoing that is specific to the Hebrew Bible, this is the term that is principally examined in what follows, though reference will be made to other terms for badness or wrongdoing as well, to indicate their more general uses.[7]

As we have seen, *ḥaṭa'* does not occur in the account of the fall or expulsion of Adam and Eve from Eden, conceivably because they were not aware of the nature of good and evil before they tasted the apple. The first occurrence of *ḥaṭa'* in the Tanakh is found in God's warning to Cain that sin lurks at his door and seeks to rule him (Genesis 4:7, translated as ἥμαρτες in Septuagint).[8] The sin is his intended murder of Abel; unlike his parents, Cain is fully aware that slaying his brother is wicked and indeed sinful, and there is no question of ignorance of good and evil. If Cain refrains from committing the deed, God affirms that he will be "accepted" or "uplifted" (*nasa'*, נָשָׂא), a word that is sometimes rendered as "forgiven,"[9] although since Cain will repent only of his intention and not of the deed itself, "forgiven" would seem to convey the wrong sense. Cain remains unrepentant even after the murder, although once he is banished he is in fear for his life until God plants on him the mark that will protect him from aggression. Still, there is perhaps a kind of anticipation here of the association between sin and remission that will become increasingly pronounced in subsequent books of the Bible.

By Noah's time evil is rampant in the world. The terms employed to describe this deteriorated moral condition are רַע (*ra'*), rendered as "wickedness" (Genesis 6:5; cf. 8:21); שָׁחַת, (*shachath*, 6:11, 12), translated as "corrupted" or "corruption"; and חָמָס (*chamac*, 6:11, 13), "violence" (later, the Amorites are cited for their depravity, עָוֹן or *'awon*, Genesis 15:16). These terms all represent profound faults, fully deserving of retribution. Indeed, God decides to destroy human beings altogether, save for the righteous Noah and his family, along with all land creatures and birds, saving only a remnant of each species (fish presumably survive the flood). But among the causes of this drastic action, which affects all humankind irrespective of their ethnicity or beliefs, we do not find the word *ḥaṭa'*. Perhaps the evil was of a generalized sort, sufficient to cause God almost to repent of having populated the earth but not of the sort specifically designated as "sin." More especially, no opportunity is given for confession and redemption; humanity is punished for its crimes by extermination, pure and simple. However this may be, the word *ḥaṭa'* first recurs in connection with Sodom and Gomorrah (Genesis 18:20). As we saw in Chapter 1, God declared that "The outcry against Sodom and Gomorrah is so great and their sin [*ḥaṭa'*; the Septuagint gives *hamartiai*, plural] so grievous that I will go down and see if what they have done is as bad as the outcry that has reached me" (18:20–21). Abraham, assuming the role so often played by the prophets, pleads with God to spare the cities if as few as ten righteous inhabitants can be found, so that they may not be destroyed along with the wicked (רָשָׁע, râshâ', 18:22); God consents, but evidently the dissoluteness was so widespread that even this number was lacking. By way of illustration of their depravity, the story has it that the Sodomites demanded that Lot surrender to them the angels whom God had sent to investigate the situation; the attempted abuse of Lot's guests is described simply as "evil" (Genesis 19:7), rather than as "sin." With this, the two cities are wiped out. It is possible that *ḥaṭa'* here is simply a synonym for wickedness generally, such as the Sodomites' abuse of the laws of hospitality and their perverse intention to violate Lot's guests, despite his offer to send out his own daughters to satisfy their lust. But it may be that the use of *ḥaṭa'* earlier was triggered by its connection with the intercession of the patriarch Abraham, to whom God confides his intention. There is at least the chance that the offenses may be pardoned, and this context elicits the idea of sin.

The case of Abimelech is something like the reverse of Cain's, with elements too of the story of Lot. When Abraham and Sarah came to Gerar, the king Abimelech sent for Sarah, presumably to make her part of his harem. However, God prevents Abimelech from committing the sin (*ḥaṭa'*, Genesis 20:6) against him of sleeping with a married woman by revealing to him in a dream that Sarah is Abraham's wife. Abimelech then asks Abraham how he had sinned against him, that he should lead his people into sin (20:9). Abraham explains that he was afraid that the local people might kill him on account of Sarah, and adds that she is in fact his half-sister, since they have the same father. "Then Abraham prayed to God; and God healed Abimelech, and also healed his wife and female slaves so that they bore children. For the Lord had closed fast all the wombs of the house of Abimelech because of Sarah, Abraham's wife" (20:17–18). Abimelech is exonerated, rather than forgiven, because in fact, as he affirms, he was innocent and acted in ignorance of Sarah's status, as God himself acknowledges. Unlike Cain, he had no evil intention and even an accidental offense, of the sort that God takes personally, is avoided. Nevertheless, the redactor felt the need to indicate that punishment was inflicted, and that it is lifted only thanks to Abraham's intercession. This alternative account, as it appears, situates sin in the context of what we may think of as a vicarious confession and the resultant remission, thus again prefiguring a paradigm that will emerge more clearly in later books.

After Jacob had labored for Laban for twenty years and realized that Laban would never part with his flocks or his daughters, he fled with the wives and cattle he had earned, and Laban pursued him. When he catches up with him, Laban protests: "Even though, you had to go because you longed greatly for your father's house, why did you steal my gods?" (Genesis 31:30). Now, Rachel, upon departing from her father's house, had in fact, unbeknownst to Jacob, taken with her the household gods (teraphim). But she concealed them successfully under a camel saddle upon which she sat, and so Laban, despite a thorough exploration, fails to find them. Jacob thus asks Laban what crime (פֶּשַׁע, pesha), what sin (ḥaṭaʾ) of his has caused Laban to pursue him so aggressively (31:36). "Sin" here may be used simply as a synonym for "crime" or "trespass"—that is, as a general term for an offense. But the offense he has in mind and which he is denying is specifically that of making off with the teraphim, for he believes he is wholly justified in taking the rest. Why Rachel carried off these objects is not made clear in the text.[10] Some have suggested that it was to prevent her father from worshipping idols, but this is unlikely, given that Jacob too regards their theft as wrong. It is more plausible that they were valuable religious tokens that Rachel wished to possess. Jacob's reference to sin, then, has to do with disrespect for divinity: it is stealing these objects, rather than escaping with Rachel, Leah, and the rest, that motivates the use of the term ḥaṭaʾ. That God himself intervened to warn Laban against doing any harm to Jacob once he overtook him further suggests that the teraphim were somehow under his jurisdiction.[11]

There is again a combination of sin with a term for evil in the tale of Potiphar's wife, where we may perhaps detect as well a distinction between the wickedness of an action in itself and an offense specifically in relation to God. When Potiphar's wife begs Joseph to sleep with her, Joseph declares: "How then could I do this great wickedness (rāʿāh), and sin (ḥaṭaʾ) against God?" (Genesis 39:9).[12] Joseph's brothers, upon the death of their father, beg Joseph to tolerate (or "forgive") them for their trespass (peshaʿ) and sin (ḥaṭaʾ), and for the evil (rāʿāh) that they have done him (Genesis 50:17). Joseph denies that he occupies the place of God, and it may be intimated that forgiveness for sin is God's province. Sin (ḥaṭaʾ), then, seems to be associated with consciousness of guilt and the need for atonement, specifically in relation to God, in and around the lineage of Abraham. So, too, the pharaoh's hardness of heart is tested by ten plagues, and by the seventh he confesses that he has sinned (Exodus 9:27) and that God is righteous whereas his own people are wicked, although he chooses to sin again (9:34; cf. 10:16–17).

In delivering the commandments, God affirms that he will punish evil (Exodus 20:5) for generations afterward (contrast Deuteronomy 24:16, Ezekiel 18:4), and Moses explains that God has established these rules so that the people will not sin (20:20). It is perhaps possible to understand that the commandments transform simple wrongdoing into the sin of violating divine injunction (cf. the Greek Wisdom 2:12, a late text not included in the Tanakh, for the phrase, "sins against the law"). But among the detailed instructions of God that follow, the only offense specifically described as a sin (Exodus 23:33) is worshipping neighboring gods: "You shall make no covenant with them, nor with their gods. They shall not dwell in your land, lest they make you sin against me. For if you serve their gods, it will surely be a snare to you." So too, among God's instructions for carrying out warfare we read: "You shall annihilate them—the Hittites and the Amorites, the Canaanites and the Perizzites, the Hivites and the Jebusites—just as the Lord your God has commanded, so that they may not teach you to do all the abhorrent things that they do for their gods, and you thus sin [*ḥaṭaʾ*] against the Lord your God" (Deuteronomy 20:17–18). Moses characterizes the worship of the calf as sin (*ḥaṭaʾ*, Exodus 32:21; cf. 32:30–33; Deuteronomy 9:16–21), to which Aaron replies that the people are prone to evil. That these occurrences of *ḥaṭaʾ* are related in this way is overlooked in the commentaries. It is not the case, to be sure, that every reference to idolatry necessarily employs the term *ḥaṭaʾ*, for other terms for wickedness are used as well, as in the following passage:

> The Lord said to Moses, "Soon you will lie down with your ancestors. Then this people will begin to prostitute themselves to the foreign gods in their midst, the gods of the land into which they are going; they will forsake me, breaking my covenant that I have made with them. My anger will be kindled against them in that day. I will forsake them and hide my face from them; they will become easy prey, and many evils and troubles will come upon them. In that day they will say, 'Have not these evils come upon us because

our God is not in our midst?' On that day I will surely hide my face on account of all the evil they have done by turning to other gods.

> Deuteronomy 31:16–18; cf. Deuteronomy 5:9, where the word for sin does not occur; also Deuteronomy 32:15–27; Joshua 24:19; Judges 2:17; 1 Samuel 12:10.

But henceforward, as we shall see, when the word for sin (that is, *ḥaṭa'*) does occur, it refers predominantly (though not absolutely uniquely) to deserting God for the worship of foreign deities. It is just this specialized usage that justifies rendering *ḥaṭa'* as "sin," with the rich biblical overtones that "sin," like comparable words in other modern languages (German "*Sünde,*" French "*péché,*" Spanish "*pecado,*" Italian "*peccato,*" etc.), bears today.

There is one context in which the word for "sin" is used in a more latitudinarian way, and that is in connection with the ritual sacrifices called "sin offerings" (חֲטָאָה, from the same root as *ḥaṭa'*) and "guilt offerings." Although there is mention of sin offerings in Exodus (e.g., of a bull at Exodus 29:14, cf. 29:36, 30:10), it is in Leviticus that a detailed description of the nature of these offerings is laid out. Thus, Chapter 4 of Leviticus begins: "The Lord spoke to Moses, saying, Speak to the people of Israel, saying: When anyone sins unintentionally in any of the Lord's commandments about things not to be done, and does any one of them: If it is the anointed priest who sins, thus bringing guilt on the people, he shall offer for the sin that he has committed a bull of the herd without blemish as a sin offering to the Lord" (4:1–3). So too, the priest may make atonement for sins committed by rulers and ordinary people. Detailed instructions are given, followed by more general rules for burnt offerings and other forms of sacrifice. The emphasis is entirely on the performance of the rites. Thus we read: "The guilt offering is like the sin offering, there is the same ritual for them . . . The priest who offers anyone's burnt offering shall keep the skin of the burnt offering that he has offered. And every grain offering baked in the oven, and all that is prepared in a pan or on a griddle, shall belong to the priest who offers it. But every other grain offering, mixed with oil or dry, shall belong to all the sons of Aaron equally" (Leviticus 7:7–10). Interestingly, the passages mentioning sin and guilt offerings do not specify any particular sin, and the sin may be inadvertent.[13] Among the various kinds of sacrifice listed in Leviticus, for example, sin offerings atone for lapses committed in ignorance (4–5, etc.; cf. Numbers 7:16, 8:8, 15:22–29, etc.), and on this basis the offender may be forgiven or exonerated (*nasa'*, 4:20, 26, 31, 35; 5:10, 13; cf. 2 Chronicles 29:20–24, etc.; Ezekiel 40–46). The so-called "guilt-offering" or "trespass offering" (אָשָׁם, *'asham*, Leviticus 5:14–6:7) is made also for witting offenses (Leviticus 6:1–7), although it is unclear whether the two types are finally distinguishable on this or any other basis. In the Septuagint both terms are rendered as *peri tês plêmmeleias* or *eis plêmmeleian*, literally an offering "concerning or for a mistake, error," though verbs deriving both from *plêmmeleia* and *hamartia* (*eplêmmelêsen, hêmarten*), the usual word for "sin," occur in this connection (Leviticus 5:15–16). What is more, although the sacrifices are the means to atonement, there is no mention of confession or repentance in connection with these offerings. They bear rather the characteristics of purification rites, with the tripartite structure consisting in sin deriving from some (usually indefinite) form of transgression, a prescribed ritual, and consequent atonement.

Very different are God's direct threats of punishment, up to and including the extermination of the Israelites, for the sin of disobeying his laws: "If you continue hostile to me, and will not obey me, I will continue to plague you sevenfold for your sins (*hata'*). I will let loose wild animals against you, and they shall bereave you of your children and destroy your livestock; they shall make you few in number, and your roads shall be deserted. If in spite of these punishments you have not turned back to me, but continue hostile to me, then I too will continue hostile to you: I myself will strike you sevenfold for your sins" (Leviticus 26:21–24; cf. 26:18, 26, 39; Deuteronomy 28:15–68, 29:25–28). Here, the sin terminology occurs precisely in connection with the Jews abandoning their God and violating the covenant. God will nevertheless relent if the Israelites confess their sins: "But if they confess their iniquity and the iniquity of their ancestors, in that they committed treachery against me and, moreover, that they continued hostile to me—so that I, in turn, continued hostile to them and brought them into the land of their enemies; if then their uncircumcised heart is humbled and they make amends for their iniquity, then will I remember my covenant with Jacob; I will remember also my covenant with Isaac and also my covenant with Abraham, and I will remember the land" (Leviticus 26:40–42; cf. Numbers 7:5, 14:18–19, 21:7, 22:34).

To be sure, confession is not always sufficient to escape punishment; confession and remorse may dispose God favorably, but they do not compel his mercy. After conquering Jericho, the Israelites destroyed all living things, "both men and women, young and old, oxen, sheep, and donkeys" (Joshua 6:21); Joshua decreed, however, that "all silver and gold, and vessels of bronze and iron, are sacred to the Lord; they shall go into the treasury of the Lord" (6:19). But Achan, of the tribe of Judah, kept some of the devoted spoils. God expressed his displeasure by allowing the defeat of a contingent of Joshua's troops as they attacked the people of Ai. Responding to Joshua's despair, God explains: "Israel has sinned; they have transgressed my covenant that I imposed on them. They have taken some of the devoted things; they have stolen, they have acted deceitfully, and they have put them among their own belongings" (Joshua 7:11). Achan confesses to the theft, saying, "It is true; I am the one who sinned against the Lord God of Israel" (7:20), and the Israelites stone him to death for his perfidy (7:25–26). Here again, the offense that is characterized as "sin" is a form of sacrilege, tantamount to idolatry, perhaps, in that it consists in valuing precious objects above duty or fidelity to God. The Israelites themselves, who are innocent of the sin, are redeemed once they have punished the offender.

Consciousness of sin causes anxiety, and one can at best hope that acknowledgment of one's disobedience and infidelity toward God may, by way of confession and repentance, induce his forgiveness. Similarly, the Israelites who have sexual relations with the women of Moab are punished, since such intercourse is regarded as tantamount to worshipping their god Baal. Hence, "Moses said to the judges of Israel, 'Each of you shall kill any of your people who have yoked themselves to the Baal of Peor'" (Numbers 25:5). When the Zimri son of Salu was seen leading a Midianite woman into his house, Phinehas, the grandson of Aaron, grabbed a spear and "went after the Israelite man into the tent, and pierced the two of them, the Israelite and the woman, through the belly. So the plague was stopped among the people of Israel" (25:8). Although the word for sin does not occur in this passage, the motive for divine wrath is clear and Phinehas' action reconciles God with the Israelites. The Israelites are in constant danger of deserting their God. As Moses affirms to the people as they are on the point crossing the Jordan river: "It is not because of your righteousness or the uprightness of your heart that you are going in to occupy their land; but because of the wickedness of these nations the Lord your God is dispossessing them before you, in order to fulfill the promise that the Lord made on oath to your ancestors, to Abraham, to Isaac, and to Jacob" (Deuteronomy 9:5; cf. Judges 3:7, 4:1, 6:6, etc.). The story of the

Israelites is one of continual lapsing into sin, consequent suffering and remorse, and the hope, but never the certainty, of ultimate redemption.

In the historical books, it is characteristically Israel and Judah that commit sins, whereas their enemies are accused rather of wickedness or iniquity. To take some illustrative examples: the sons of Eli were priests but "they had no regard for the Lord or for the duties of the priests to the people. When anyone offered sacrifice, the priest's servant would come, while the meat was boiling, with a three-pronged fork in his hand, and he would thrust it into the pan, or kettle, or caldron, or pot; all that the fork brought up the priest would take for himself … Thus the sin of the young men was very great in the sight of the Lord; for they treated the offerings of the Lord with contempt" (1 Samuel 2:13–14, 17). Besides such abuse of ritual offerings, they slept with women shamelessly (2:22). Word of their evil behavior (*rā'āh*, in the plural) comes to old Eli, and he warns his sons: "If a man sins against a man, God will mediate for him; but if a man sins against the Lord, who can intercede for him?" (2:25). The verb "sins" here, from the root *ḥaṭa'*, is applied to offenses against one's fellows as well as to those against God himself. This is not so much evidence, I think, that the word for sin applies equally to human interactions and the relationship with God. Rather, the parallelism serves to underline the contrast between transgressions among human beings—here called "sinning" for rhetorical effect—and those that specifically violate the covenanted relationship to the deity, which is the proper sphere of sin. In the end, Eli's wicked and unrepentant sons will die prematurely on the same day (2:34). The people as a whole sin by worshipping foreign gods, but at the direction and intercession of Samuel, who succeeded Eli as priest, they confess their error:

> Then Samuel said to all the house of Israel, "If you are returning to the Lord with all your heart, then put away the foreign gods and the Ashtaroth from among you, and direct your heart to the Lord, and serve him only, and he will deliver you out of the hand of the Philistines." So Israel put away the Baals and the Ashtaroth, and they served the Lord only. Then Samuel said, "Gather all Israel at Mizpah, and I will pray to the Lord for you." So they gathered at Mizpah, and drew water and poured it out before the Lord, and fasted on that day, and said there, "We have sinned against the Lord." And Samuel judged the people of Israel at Mizpah.
>
> 1 Samuel 7:6; cf. 12:10–11

As a result, they rout the Philistines. We see here the paradigmatic structure of the sin script, as we may call it. There is the primal offense of chasing after foreign gods, the confession (as often, at the behest of a priest or prophet) of the error, and God's forgiveness, manifested here and often elsewhere as his favor in battle.

Samuel denounces the decision of the Israelites to subject themselves to a king as wickedness or evil (*rāʿāh*, 1 Samuel 12:17), and they fear having added this evil to their sins (12:19). Samuel in turn prays for the people, for not to do so would be a sin (12:23), the implication being, it would appear, that to desert his role as prophet and intercessor is tantamount to turning away from God. On the day that they defeated the Philistines, Saul's soldiers sinned by eating the blood along with meat of the animals they had captured (1 Samuel 14:33–34); this is directly to violate a ritual prescription (Genesis 9:4) and so a sign of infidelity to God rather than an ordinary crime. So too, Saul, after conquering the Amalekites, sins by sparing the king Agag and keeping the best cattle as spoils (which were then sacrificed), even though God had commanded him to destroy them root and branch. So Samuel intones:

> Behold, to obey is better than sacrifice,
>   and to hearken than the fat of rams.
> For rebellion is as the sin of divination,
>   and stubbornness is as iniquity and idolatry.
>
> 1 Samuel 15:22–23

A clear analogy is drawn between disobedience and the worship of idols. Saul confesses to having sinned and begs Samuel to pardon him (15:25), with the excuse that he had bowed to the will of the people. But Saul's sin against God cannot be forgiven by a human being, even a prophet like Samuel, and he falls from grace with God. Samuel, however, sees to the fulfillment of God's instructions by personally cutting Agag into pieces.

David asks Jonathan, "What have I done? What is my iniquity and what is my sin (*haṭaʾ*) before your father, that he seeks my life?" (1 Samuel 20:1). Sin here may be simply a poetic doublet of iniquity, but I venture to suggest that the original audience may have perceived a distinction between merely personal injuries to which Saul may have taken offense and sinful violations of divinely prescribed prohibitions. Jonathan had already interceded with his father on David's behalf:

> And Jonathan spoke well of David to Saul his father, and said to him, "Let not the king sin against his servant David; because he has not sinned against you, and because his deeds have been of good service to you; for he took his life in his hand and he slew the Philistine, and the Lord wrought a great victory for all Israel. You saw it, and rejoiced; why then will you sin against innocent blood by killing David without cause?" And Saul hearkened to the voice of Jonathan; Saul swore, "As the Lord lives, he shall not be put to death".
>
> 1 Samuel 19:4–6

In the covenant with Noah, after the flood, God had specified two sorts of offenses that must be avoided: "Only you shall not eat flesh with its life, that is, its blood. For your lifeblood I will surely require a reckoning; of every beast I will require it and of man; of every man's brother I will require the life of man. Whoever sheds the blood of man, by man shall his blood be shed; for God made man in his own image" (Genesis 9:4–6). Saul's troops, as we saw, violated the first of these commandments; here Saul himself is about to contravene the second. It is this kind of offense, I suggest, that David is denying in his plea to Jonathan. So too, David avers that he spared Saul's life when he had the opportunity to kill him, and so did not sin (1 Samuel 24:11). In a similar vein, Saul later admits to having sinned in seeking to kill David (1 Samuel 26:21). There seems to be a something of a self-contained mini-narrative of Saul's sinfulness in his various states of derangement, as he jealously plots to slay an innocent man.

David himself confesses to having sinned in regard to Uriah, and here the offense is specifically indicated as being against God. Nathan quotes the words of God himself:

> "Why have you despised the word of the Lord, to do what is evil in his sight? You have smitten Uriah the Hittite with the sword, and have taken his wife to be your wife, and have slain him with the sword of the Ammonites. Now therefore the sword shall never depart from your house, because you have despised me, and have taken the wife of Uriah the Hittite to be your wife." Thus says the Lord, "Behold, I will raise up evil against you out of your own house; and I will take your wives before your eyes, and give them to your neighbor, and he shall lie with your wives in the sight of this sun. For you did it secretly; but I will do this thing before all Israel, and before the sun." David said to Nathan, "I have sinned against the Lord".
>
> 2 Samuel 12:9–13

Nathan reassures David that God has put away his sin, and he will not die, but the child born to him by Bathsheba will not live (12:13–14). David in turn spares Shimei, who was of the clan of Saul, when he confesses to having sinned against him (2 Samuel 19:20) at the time when he cursed him and declared his support for the rebellious Absalom (16:5–13). At the end of his life, David admits that he sinned (2 Samuel 24:10; cf. 1 Chronicles 21:8), and of the three forms of atonement offered him, chooses a plague. He then affirms that the sin is his, not that of his people (2 Samuel 24:17; cf. 1 Chronicles 21:17), who ought not to suffer; he offers proper sacrifice, and the plague is lifted. Here again, David's kingship is framed by his sin, confession, atonement, and the ultimate, albeit partial, forgiveness on the part of God. In his dedicatory prayer for the temple, which serves as something of a coda to the story of David, Solomon asks for forgiveness for the people's sins if they repent and confess in their prayers (1 Kings 8:33–36, 39, 46–51; cf. 2 Chronicles 6:24–31, 36–39). The word for "forgiveness" here is *salakh*, סָלַח, a verb that throughout the Hebrew Bible always takes God as subject (cf. Leviticus 6.6 = 5.16 in the Hebrew Bible; Leviticus 19:20–22; Numbers 14:19–20; Deuteronomy 29:20 = 29:19 in the Hebrew Bible; 1 Kings 8:30; Isaiah 55:7, etc.). As Jože Krašovec observes: "The subject of words denoting mercy is usually God, more rarely humans; while that of words meaning forgiveness is always God … The terminology of forgiveness is more closely related to guilt and repentance than is that of mercy or compassion."[14] The association of *ḥaṭa'*, confession, and forgiveness in these episodes, always in reference to the Israelites, is evident.

For all their faults, the first kings, Saul, David, and Solomon do not lapse into worshipping foreign gods, although Saul's failure to slay the king Agag and destroy all the livestock of the defeated Amalekites, as God had ordered, is compared to idolatry (1 Samuel 15:22–23). After these founding figures, however, backsliding into idolatry becomes endemic among the kings of Judah and Israel. Jeroboam, the first ruler of the northern kingdom of Israel after the division of the united realm inherited from Solomon into Israel and Judah (where Solomon's immediate successor Rehoboam continued to reign), sins in making two golden calves. In what was probably a strategy to offer his people an alternative to the worship in Jerusalem, the capital of Judah, he proclaimed: "'It is too much for you to go up to Jerusalem. Here are your gods, O Israel, which brought you up from the land of Egypt!' And he set up one in Bethel, and the other he put in Dan. Now this thing became a sin, for the people went to worship before the one as far as Dan. He made shrines on the high places, and made priests from every class of people, who were not of the sons of Levi" (1 Kings 12:28–31; cf. Sirach 47:23). Nor did Jeroboam return to the fold: "Jeroboam did not turn from his evil way, but again he made priests from every class of people for the high places; whoever wished, he consecrated him, and he became one of the priests of the high places. And this thing was the sin of the house of Jeroboam, so as to exterminate and destroy it from the face of the earth" (1 Kings 13:33–34).

Judah, the southern kingdom, was no more true to God. "Judah did what was evil in the sight of the Lord, and they provoked him to jealousy with their sins which they committed, more than all that their fathers had done. For they also built for themselves high places, and pillars, and Asherim on every high hill and under every green tree; and there were also male cult prostitutes in the land. They did according to all the abominations of the nations which the Lord drove out before the people of Israel" (1 Kings 14:22–24). Abijam (or Abijah) succeeded Rehoboam "and he walked in all the sins which his father did before him; and his heart was not wholly true to the Lord his God, as the heart of David his father" (1 Kings 15:3). Abijam's son Asa, however, brought the realm back to the proper worship of God:

> Asa did what was right in the eyes of the Lord, as David his father had done. He put away the male cult prostitutes out of the land, and removed all the idols that his fathers had made. He also removed Maacah his mother from being queen mother because she had an abominable image made for Asherah; and Asa cut down her image and burned it at the brook Kidron. But the high places were not taken away. Nevertheless the heart of Asa was wholly true to the Lord all his days.
>
> 1 Kings 15:11–14

Back in Israel, Jeroboam's son Nadab was no better than his father; he reigned for two years and "did what was evil in the sight of the Lord, and walked in the way of his father, and in his sin which he made Israel to sin" (1 Kings 15:26). Baasha, son of the prophet Ahijah, assassinated Nadab and exterminated the house of Jeroboam, because of Jeroboam's sins (15:30). But alas, even if he was the instrument of God's vengeance against Jeroboam and his line, he turned out to be no better: "He did what was evil in the sight of the Lord, and walked in the way of Jeroboam and in his sin which he made Israel to sin" (15:34). Baasha's son Elah reigned briefly before he was slain by one of his commanders, Zimri, who seized the throne and exterminated Baasha's line, "for all the sins of Baasha and the sins of Elah his son which they sinned, and which they made Israel to sin, provoking the Lord God of Israel to anger with their idols" (1 Kings 16:13). Zimri lasted only a few days before Omri overthrew him in turn, "because of his sins which he committed, doing evil in the sight of the Lord, walking in the way of Jeroboam, and for his sin which he committed, making Israel to sin" (16:19). But—as the reader will have guessed (or remembered)—"Omri did what was evil in the sight of the Lord, and did more evil than all who were before him. For he walked in all the way of Jeroboam the son of Nebat, and in the sins which he made Israel to sin, provoking the Lord, the God of Israel, to anger by their idols" (16:25–26). He was succeeded by his son Ahab, who "did evil in the sight of the Lord more than all that were before him" (16:30). Ahab married Jezebel (this can't be good), worshipped Baal, and "erected an altar for Baal in the house of Baal, which he built in Samaria. And Ahab made an Asherah [that is, a grove or sanctuary dedicated to the mother goddess by that name]. Ahab did more to provoke the Lord, the God of Israel, to anger than all the kings of Israel who were before him" (16:32–33). Thus Elijah communicates to Ahab the judgment of God: "Behold, I will bring evil upon you; I will utterly sweep you away, and will cut off from Ahab every male, bond or free, in Israel; and I will make your house like the house of Jeroboam the son of Nebat, and like the house of Baasha the son of Ahijah, for the anger to which you have provoked me, and because you have made Israel to sin" (1 Kings 21:21–22). Ahab's sons Ahaziah and Jehoram (also known as Joram) follow their father's ways. Ahaziah "served Baal and worshiped him, and provoked the Lord, the God of Israel, to anger in every way that his father had done" (1 Kings 22:52). Jehoram was not quite so bad: "He did what was evil in the sight of the Lord, though not like his father and mother, for he put away the pillar of Baal which his father had made. Nevertheless he clung to the sin of Jeroboam the son of Nebat, which he made Israel to sin; he did not depart from it" (2 Kings 3:2–3). Another Jehoram, son of Jehoshaphat, reigned in Judah at much the same time that his namesake ruled in Israel (to add to the confusion, this Jehoram too is sometimes referred to as Joram).

Jehu, whose genealogy is somewhat confused but is described as the son of Jehoshaphat, pretended that he would reinstall the worship of Baal, gathered all of Baal's worshippers in one place, and gave orders that they be exterminated (2 Kings 10:18–25); at his orders, his men "demolished the pillar of Baal, and demolished the house of Baal, and made it a latrine to this day" (10:27). But the reform was incomplete: "Jehu did not turn aside from the sins of Jeroboam the son of Nebat, which he made Israel to sin, the golden calves that were in Bethel, and in Dan . . . Jehu was not careful to walk in the law of the Lord the God of Israel with all his heart; he did not turn from the sins of Jeroboam, which he made Israel to sin" (10:29, 31). Jehu's son Joash, who succeeded him, "did what was right in the eyes of the Lord all his days, because Jehoiada the priest instructed him. Nevertheless the high places were not taken away; the people continued to sacrifice and burn incense on the high places" (2 Kings 12:2–13). Jehu's other son, Jehoash, however, "did what was evil in the sight of the Lord, and followed the sins of Jeroboam the son of Nebat, which he made Israel to sin; he did not depart from them" (2 Kings 13:2–3; cf. 13:6). Jeroboam the Second followed in the path of his namesake, the founder of the kingship in Israel, and "he did what was evil in the sight of the Lord; he did not depart from all the sins of Jeroboam the son of Nebat, which he made Israel to sin" (2 Kings 14:24). The very same thing is recorded concerning Jeroboam II's son Zechariah (2 Kings 15:9). He was slain by Shallum, who reigned for just one month, when Gadi's son Menahem slew him and occupied the throne, and sure enough, Menahem behaved just like Zechariah and the rest of the sinners (15:18). Menahem's son Pekahiah, in turn, "did what was evil in the sight of the Lord; he did not turn away from the sins of Jeroboam the son of Nebat, which he made Israel to sin" (15:24). Pekah son of Remaliah overthrew Pekahiah, and he too sinned in the same way as his slaughtered predecessor (15:28).

The reader's patience may be wearing thin, given the repetitiveness of these abominations, but it is just this accumulation that reveals how the writers and editors of these texts understood the nature of sin. Thus, back in Judah, Jehoshaphat succeeded his father, the faithful Asa, as king and he too was loyal to God: "He walked in all the way of Asa his father; he did not turn aside from it, doing what was right in the sight of the Lord; yet the high places were not taken away, and the people still sacrificed and burned incense on the high places" (1 Kings 22:43; at 2 Chronicles 19:10 he is said to have advised the priests not to trespass, אָשָׁם, *'asham*). Ahaziah took the throne upon the death of Jehoram (who had succeeded Jehoshaphat), and he was followed by Joash, who in turn yielded the throne to his son Amaziah. Amaziah's son Uzziah was next in line, who was followed by his son Jotham. Jotham "did what was right in the eyes of the Lord, according to all that his father Uzziah had done. Nevertheless the high places were not removed; the people still sacrificed and burned incense on the high places" (2 Kings 15:34). Jotham's son Ahaz, however, reinstated idolatry: "he did not do what was right in the eyes of the Lord his God, as his father David had done, but he walked in the way of the kings of Israel. He even burned his son as an offering, according to the abominable practices of the nations whom the Lord drove out before the people of Israel. And he sacrificed and burned incense on the high places, and on the hills, and under every green tree" (2 Kings 16:2–4). The end finally came when Hoshea reigned as king in Israel:

> Then the king of Assyria invaded all the land and came to Samaria, and for three years he besieged it. In the ninth year of Hoshea the king of Assyria captured Samaria, and he carried the Israelites away to Assyria, and placed them in Halah, and on the Habor, the river of Gozan, and in the cities of the Medes. And this was so, because the people of Israel had sinned against the Lord their God, who had brought them up out of the land of Egypt from under the hand of Pharaoh king of Egypt, and had feared other gods and walked in the customs of the nations whom the Lord drove out before the people of Israel, and in the customs which the kings of Israel had introduced. And the people of Israel did secretly against the Lord their God things that were not right. They built for themselves high places at all their towns, from watchtower to fortified city; they set up for themselves pillars and Asherim on every high hill and under every green tree; and there they burned incense on all the high places, as the nations did whom the Lord carried away before them. And they did wicked things, provoking the Lord to anger, and they served idols, of which the Lord had said to them, "You shall not do this".
>
> 2 Kings 17:5–12

It is the sin of worshipping foreign gods that leads to the exile of the Israelites: they "had sinned against the Lord their God" (17:7). The Assyrian king resettled the cities of abandoned Samaria, bringing people from "Babylon, Cuthah, Avva, Hamath, and Sepharvaim." They were ignorant of the God of that land, and for failing to worship him God sent lions to plague them. The Assyrian king thus instructed a priest of the Israelites to go to Samaria and teach the new inhabitants how to do proper reverence to God. And yet, every nation still made gods of its own, and put them in the shrines of the high places which the Samaritans had made, every nation in the cities in which they dwelt; the men of Babylon made Succoth-benoth, the men of Cuth made Nergal, the men of Hamath made Ashima, and the Avvites made Nibhaz and Tartak; and the Sepharvites burned their children in the fire to Adrammelech and Anammelech, the gods of Sepharvaim. They also feared the Lord, and appointed from among themselves all sorts of people as priests of the high places, who sacrificed for them in the shrines of the high places. So they feared the Lord but also served their own gods, after the manner of the nations from among whom they had been carried away. To this day they do according to the former manner.

2 Kings 17:29–34

Here is the crucial point: in worshipping their own deities, these peoples were not chasing after foreign gods; idolatry it may be, but it does not represent a turning away from God. Thus, there is no mention of sin here, nor would it be in place. The case is entirely different with the Israelites. The other peoples "do not follow the statutes or the ordinances or the law or the commandment which the Lord commanded the children of Jacob, whom he named Israel" (17:34). Nor have they reason to do so. As for the children of Jacob,

> The Lord made a covenant with them, and commanded them, "You shall not fear other gods or bow yourselves to them or serve them or sacrifice to them; but you shall fear the Lord, who brought you out of the land of Egypt with great power and with an outstretched arm; you shall bow yourselves to him, and to him you shall sacrifice. And the statutes and the ordinances and the law and the commandment which he wrote for you, you shall always be careful to do. You shall not fear other gods, and you shall not forget the covenant that I have made with you. You shall not fear other gods, but you shall fear the Lord your God, and he will deliver you out of the hand of all your enemies." However they would not listen, but they did according to their former manner.
>
> 2 Kings 17:35–40[15]

These are the laws laid down for the Israelites, and their failure to observe them and their worship of the gods of their neighbors is the sin for which they are punished by exile. As for the new inhabitants of the land, "these nations feared the Lord, and also served their graven images; their children likewise, and their children's children—as their fathers did, so they do to this day" (17:41). They have not sinned, and so they are not chastised.

The story continues—with more of the same. Back in Judah, the king Hezekiah, son of Ahaz, was faithful:

> he did what was right in the eyes of the Lord, according to all that David his father had done. He removed the high places, and broke the pillars, and cut down the Asherah. And he broke in pieces the bronze serpent that Moses had made, for until those days the people of Israel had burned incense to it; it was called Nehushtan. He trusted in the Lord the God of Israel; so that there was none like him among all the kings of Judah after him, nor among those who were before him.
>
> 2 Kings 18:3–5

Hezekiah's son Manasseh, however, restored idolatry: "he did what was evil in the sight of the Lord, according to the abominable practices of the nations whom the Lord drove out before the people of Israel. For he rebuilt the high places which Hezekiah his father had destroyed; and he erected altars for Baal, and made an Asherah, as Ahab king of Israel had done, and worshiped all the host of heaven, and served them" (2 Kings 21:2–3; cf. 21:4–6, 11). What is more, "Manasseh shed very much innocent blood, till he had filled Jerusalem from one end to another, besides the sin which he made Judah to sin so that they did what was evil in the sight of the Lord" (21:16). There is, I think, an implicit contrast between Manasseh's sin in the strict sense of the term, which consists in the worship of foreign gods, and the shedding of innocent blood. The latter too was prohibited, as we have seen; as Jonathan said to his father Saul, "will you sin against innocent blood by killing David without cause?" (1 Samuel 19:4–6). In the present context, however, the author or editor is keen to focus on the fundamental offense of turning away from God and worshipping idols, which is what overwhelmingly earns the name of sin.[16] We see it again in Manasseh's son Amon, who "did what was evil in the sight of the Lord, as Manasseh his father had done. He walked in all the way in which his father walked, and served the idols that his father served, and worshiped them; he forsook the Lord, the God of his fathers, and did not walk in the way of the Lord" (2 Kings 21:20–22). Amon's son Josiah was righteous—"he did what was right in the eyes of the Lord, and walked in all the way of David his father" (2 Kings 22:2; cf. 23:1–20 for a list of his activities)—but his son Jehoahaz "did what was evil in the sight of the Lord" (2 Kings 23:32), and the pharaoh Neco deposed him and placed Amon's next son Eliakim (also called Jehoiakim) on the throne, who did what was evil as well (23:37). Under Jehoiakim, Judah came under attack: "Surely this came upon Judah at the command of the Lord, to remove them out of his sight, for the sins of Manasseh, according to all that he had done, and also for the innocent blood that he had shed; for he filled Jerusalem with innocent blood, and the Lord would not pardon" (2 Kings 24:3–4). There seems again to be a distinction drawn between sin proper, which consists in worshipping foreign gods, and the evil deed of shedding innocent blood, although both are causes of God's wrath. Jehoiakim's son Jehoiachin succeeded his father to the throne, and it was during his reign that Nebuchadnezzar king of Babylon captured Jerusalem. Nebuchadnezzar installed Jehoiachin's uncle Mattaniah on the throne, changing his name to Zedekiah, and when Zedekiah rebelled, the Babylonian king finally conquered Judah, sacked the temple, and carried off the people.[17]

The dismal and repetitive histories of the kings of Israel and Judah make for tedious reading, and it seems to have been difficult even for the early chroniclers to keep the various stories straight. It is natural to wonder why the kings, one after another, persisted in worshipping idols or practicing other forbidden rites (such as offering incense in high places), despite the punishments that God kept inflicting upon them for their perfidy. So few seem to have chosen to remain faithful to the covenant, and their reforms were so quickly overturned. Some scholars have supposed that obeisance to other deities was not in fact deemed inconsistent with fidelity to the Hebrew God in this period, and that it is only after the exile that a more rigorous monotheism evolved; it is only from this later perspective that the backsliding of the earlier kings was regarded as apostasy. For the purposes of the investigation of sin in the Hebrew Bible, however, I have chosen to leave aside the reconstruction of the actual events and outlooks of the period of the divided kingdom, and also, perhaps more controversially, the identification of different strands in the composition of the biblical texts. I have already noted differences in the treatment of these figures in the books called First and Second Kings and First and Second Chronicles (in Christian Bibles), and other inconsistencies can be identified with the individual books. What matters most in the present context is that in these books sin, which is to say, the root *ḥaṭaʾ*, in its various verbal and nominal forms, designates the violation of the covenant with God, specifically by way of idolatry and the adoption of the devotional practices of the surrounding populations. There are other kinds of wickedness of which the kings of Judah and Israel are guilty, but they are not typically designated as sins but by other terms signifying evil or iniquity.

A further consequence of this conception of sin is that it is only the Israelites (understood broadly to include both parts of the divided kingdom) who sin. For it is only they who are bound by or are heirs to the covenant, and so they alone, by worshipping Baal and the rest, are chasing after foreign gods. Those peoples who persist in their antique religions may be enemies of the Israelites, when they occupy land that is destined for the newcomers or when their practices threaten to contaminate the heirs of the covenant; in such cases, God may go so far as to instruct his people to exterminate the cities and populations that pose such a danger. But their worship is not sinful in and of itself. When, after the Israelites are deported from their land, new groups are settled in what were the kingdoms of Judah and Israel, these peoples were expected to acknowledge the local God, who is Jehovah. It was not incumbent on them, however, to abandon their own deities and rituals; for them, the two practices could coexist in a way that was denied to the Israelites. From the earliest books of the Bible, that is to say, the Torah itself, with its narratives of creation, the fall, the time of the patriarchs, the servitude in and exodus from Egypt, and the covenant delivered by Moses, the conception of sin tended to coalesce around the relationship between God and his chosen people. It is violations of this bond or commitment that constitute the primary locus of sin. In the narratives of the kingdom under Saul, David, and Solomon and then, after it was divided, under the successive monarchs of Israel and Judah, the term ḥaṭa' is ever more narrowly focused on the institution of idolatrous practices, but the roots of this conception were already laid in the earlier books. What differs is that remorse and confession are relatively rare among the kings of Israel and Judah, and so, therefore, is forgiveness, although God persists in supporting his people, for all his wrath. From the captivity onward, the conception of sin will be refined and developed, and a greater emphasis will be placed on repentance and confession; but sin always maintains its primary significance as the abandonment of God and the worship of strange deities.

Explicitly post-exilic texts (in contrast to those that were undoubtedly composed or redacted after the capture of Jerusalem but narrate earlier events) introduce a new emphasis on sin and forgiveness in relation to the collective fault of the people. Ezra was a descendant of high priests, who was living in exile in Babylon when Artaxerxes, then king of Persia, decided to send him to Jerusalem in order to instruct the people in the laws of God (circa 457 BC). Ezra brought a great number of exiles with him, where he found a troubling situation. As he records it, officials approached him and reported: "The people of Israel and the priests and the Levites have not separated themselves from the peoples of the lands with their abominations, from the Canaanites, the Hittites, the Perizzites, the Jebusites, the Ammonites, the Moabites, the Egyptians, and the Amorites. For they have taken some of their daughters to be wives for themselves and for their sons; so that the holy race has mixed itself with the peoples of the lands" (Ezra 9.1–2). At this news, Ezra tore his garments and pulled out his hair. He observed that "for a brief moment favor has been shown by the Lord our God, to leave us a remnant, and to give us a secure hold within his holy place" (9:8), but the people have continued to commit abominations by intermarrying with the other peoples who inhabited Jerusalem. The situation was saved, however, when the people confessed their wrongdoing and encouraged the despairing Ezra to take heart:

> Ezra prayed and made confession, weeping and casting himself down before the house of God, a very great assembly of men, women, and children, gathered to him out of Israel; for the people wept bitterly. And Shecaniah the son of Jehiel, of the sons of Elam, addressed Ezra: "We have broken faith with our God and have married foreign women from the peoples of the land, but even now there is hope for Israel in spite of this. Therefore let us make a covenant with our God to put away all these wives and their children, according to the counsel of my lord and of those who tremble at the commandment of our God; and let it be done according to the law. Arise, for it is your task, and we are with you; be strong and do it.
>
> Ezra 10:1–4

With this, they put away their foreign wives and children, and returned to the path of God. To be sure, already in Deuteronomy there is the warning, "You shall not make marriages with them, giving your daughters to their sons or taking their daughters for your sons. For they would turn away your sons from following me, to serve other gods; then the anger of the Lord would be kindled against you, and he would destroy you quickly" (7:3–4). The Deuteronomy injunction, however, focuses on the danger that intermarriage would lead the people into idolatry; that seems to be the primary concern, rather than impurity deriving from mixing with foreign brides as such. This same anxiety is expressed in 1 Kings 11:1–2. Ezra, however, seems worried about the contamination resulting from such intercourse, since "the holy race has mixed itself with the peoples of the lands".[18] But it may be relevant that Ezra does not employ the language of sin in this connection, but speaks rather of uncleanliness (נִדָּה, *niddāh*) and impurity (root טָמֵא, *tame*, 9:11). The word for "holy," as applied to the Israelites, is קֹדֶשׁ (*qōdeš*), which means "apartness" and hence "sacredness"; the latter term derives from the Latin *sacer*, which again has a root sense of setting apart or dedication. This is why putting away the wives and children seems to suffice to appease God and avert punishment. The book known as 1 Esdras, which survives in Greek, was probably composed in the second or first century BC (Esdras is the Greek form of Ezra); it is not part of the Hebrew Bible, though it is recognized in the Eastern Orthodox tradition. It partly overlaps with the canonical Ezra, but there are considerable differences in the order and nature of the episodes recounted. In this version, Ezra says to the people, "You have broken the law and married foreign women, and so have increased the sin of Israel" (1 Esdras 9:7). Here the key word is *hamartia*, the standard Greek term for "sin." So too, the people confess: "this is not a work we can do in one day or two, for we have sinned [verbal form of *hamartia*] too much in these things" (9:11). But this late text may reflect an evolution in the conception of sin, and in any case it is difficult to be certain what Hebrew term, if any, lay behind the Greek word.

A few years later, Artaxerxes sent Nehemiah in turn to Jerusalem, with the commission to rebuild the walls of the city. Nehemiah confesses the sins of the people, including his own: "O Lord God of heaven, the great and terrible God who keeps covenant and steadfast love with those who love him and keep his commandments; let thy ear be attentive, and thy eyes open, to hear the prayer of thy servant which I now pray before thee day and night for the people of Israel thy servants, confessing the sins of the people of Israel, which we have sinned against thee. Yea, I and my father's house have sinned. We have acted very corruptly against thee, and have not kept the commandments, the statutes, and the ordinances which thou didst command thy servant Moses" (1:5–7). The surrounding peoples, and in particular Sanballat, a leader of the Samaritans, were opposed to the reconstruction of the walls, greeting the project with a mixture of contempt and hostility. Nehemiah prays, "Hear, O our God, for we are despised; turn back their taunt upon their own heads, and give them up to be plundered in a land where they are captives. Do not cover their iniquity, and let not their sin be blotted out from thy sight; for they have provoked thee to anger before the builders" (4:4–5). The ascription of sin to non-Jews is unusual, and vague; in the present context it may refer simply to their opposition to Nehemiah's project of rebuilding the wall and so, in his view, impeding the will of God. But there may also be an element of symmetry: the Jews were punished for their sins, which resulted in the destruction of the walls of Jerusalem; may God now turn the tables and reduce their enemies, indeed send them into exile, the way he did his covenanted people—likewise for their sins. The term may not be strictly appropriate from a theological perspective but it is a neat rhetorical inversion. It should also be noted that Sanballat was in league with Jews opposed to Nehemiah's scheme. Thus Shemaiah the son of Delaiah, of a priestly family but acting in the service of Sanballat, tries to lure Nehemiah into locking himself in the temple, so that, as he says, "I should be afraid and act in this way and sin, and so they could give me an evil name, in order to taunt me" (6:13). But it is only the Israelites who confess their sins and seek God's forgiveness: "And the Israelites separated themselves from all foreigners, and stood and confessed their sins and the iniquities of their fathers" (Nehemiah 9:2; cf. 9:29, 37). What is more, they acknowledge God's forgiveness, graciousness, and mercy; for all their evil ways, "when they turned and cried to thee thou didst hear from heaven, and many times thou didst deliver them according to thy mercies" (9:28).[19] The sins of the people are only vaguely indicated; they are principally invoked as the cause of their sufferings, whether in ancient times or, above all, in connection with the destruction of Jerusalem and the temple and the exile in Babylon. By acknowledging them and humbly begging God's forgiveness, the Israelites may hope for better things in the future. God remains merciful, and confession serves to renew the covenant that had been betrayed.

This close association between sin, confession, and God's pardon and reconciliation with his wayward people is the dominant motif in this period. It is a tripartite script, in which sin is defined by its place in this paradigmatic scenario. The pattern is not new in the Bible: it has been present, implicitly or explicitly, since the beginning, although one or another element may be emphasized, as when the idolatrous kings of Judah and Israel fail to repent and do not earn forgiveness. The remission of sins may never be taken for granted. But it is always potentially there for God's people, if they sincerely and remorsefully return to his fold and beg for his pity. Instances of wrongdoing are legion, and roundly condemned in the Bible. But such offenses, which needless to say the Israelites share with all other peoples, do not constitute the essence of *ḥaṭa'*, the specialized term that, I have been arguing, distinguishes biblical sin from the mere violation of divine law as such.

The Greeks and Roman recognized infractions of divine laws, as we saw in Chapter 1, even if this specific kind of transgression never crystallized into a fundamental religious concept. What was missing, however, was the element of remorse and confession, and without this, there was no proper forgiveness on the part of the gods. Forgiveness implies that the offender recognizes that she or he has done wrong; what is more, it entails sincere remorse and the determination not to commit the same offense in the future. In many descriptions, the repentant sinner seems to undergo a profound change of self, to the extent of becoming a new person. To be sure, "forgiveness" has several connotations in modern English, as do the comparable terms in other languages. It is sometimes used in the judicial sense of "pardon," that is, excusing an offense or commuting the penalty, as when the president pardons someone convicted of a crime. It may also be employed in an economic context, where it means the remission of a debt; thus, Jesus advises that we beseech the Lord: "Forgive us our debts as we also have forgiven our debtors" (Matthew 6:12). Sometimes too, "forgive" is used in the relatively inconsequential sense of overlooking discourteous behavior, roughly equivalent to the expression, "Excuse me!" But these usages do not capture the rich meaning of forgiving, which consists in the restoration of a moral relationship between the offender and the person who has been mistreated. It is not enough simply to confess one's error: one must repudiate the action and the values that enabled it. One must, in short, repent. Such a change of heart, in the words of Charles Griswold, "is a step toward showing that one is not simply the 'same person' who did the wrong."[20] Without such a transformation in the offender, giving up one's resentment at the injury would be tantamount to condoning it.

To win the favor of the gods, the pagan Greeks and Romans did not acknowledge wrongdoing; this would have gained them nothing but punishment.²¹ Rather, they sought to justify themselves, and by this earn, not forgiveness, but at least the pity of the offended deity. To be sure, as Kenneth Dover has observed, the Greeks in classical antiquity "did not expect gods to be merciful."²² But to have even a chance of being pitied (in Greek and Latin, there is no distinct term for "mercy": it is *eleos* or *misericordia*, the same word that designates "pity"), one had to prove one's innocence, not admit to guilt. In his youthful treatise on rhetoric called *De inventione*, or *On Devising Arguments*, Cicero explains that, in desperate straits, where the facts are clear, a defendant may be obliged to admit to a deed but will deny any guilt. When things are still worse, the accused may concede that he did wrong deliberately (*consulto peccasse*) but will nevertheless beg to be pardoned. Cicero says that this happens, and should happen, very rarely. The proper strategy in such a pass is to mention past services, and insist that one acted either foolishly, or at the instigation of another, or else for some decent and upright reason (*sed aut stultitia aut inpulsu alicuius aut aliqua honesta aut probabili causa*, 2, 106). The point is that the defendant must seek to extenuate the crime rather than give any sign of repentance.

There survive five long prose novels, in Greek, dating roughly from the first to the third or possibly fourth centuries AD, centering on the love between a young man and woman—hardly more than adolescents. In each of them, the protagonists fall in love at first sight, are separated, and go through various misadventures and tribulations, but they retain their passion for one another and are happily reunited in the end. Naturally, when they are most hopeless, they may beg the gods to deliver them from their misfortunes. The way they do so is profoundly illuminating.

At the beginning of the *Ephesiaca* or *Ephesian Tale*, Xenophon (writing in the first or perhaps second century AD) explains that the great physical beauty and other virtues of the protagonist, Habrocomes, induced him to despise the attractiveness of anyone else so far as to deny that Eros himself was a god (1.1.5). Such arrogant contempt for a deity was bound to lead to no good. Eros is predictably furious (1.2.1) and, by way of revenge and to teach the boy a lesson, causes him to fall in love with the beautiful Anthia. One might have expected Habrocomes to confess his error and plead with Eros for forgiveness. But nothing of the sort occurs. The first time either of the two protagonists offers supplication to a deity, it is Anthia, and she appeals to Isis rather than to

Eros. She declares that she has remained chaste and kept her marriage to Habrocomes pure, and prays that she either be restored to her husband, if he is still alive, or else that she remain faithful to his corpse (4.3.3–4; cf. the similar plea at 5.4.6). Habrocomes, for his part, finds himself on the point of being crucified because Kyno, a married woman, having fallen in love with him, murdered her husband and then, when he rejected her, accused him of having committed the crime. Habrocomes proclaims his innocence as he prays to the god of the Nile: if he has done any wrong, he declares, let him die a miserable death (4.2.4), but let the gracious Nile not look on indifferently at the death of a man who has committed no injustice. The god at once takes pity on him (οἰκτείρει, 4.2.6), since his suffering is in fact unmerited. In the end, when the pair are reunited, they give thanks to Isis for their salvation (5.13.4). There is no mention of Habrocomes' pride, or any suggestion that he or she might be guilty of some offense against the gods; there is thus no question of repentance or forgiveness.

In the novel by Chariton, conventionally titled *Callirhoe* for the heroine, the reason why the gods are hostile to her and her husband, Chaereas, is unclear. Callirhoe herself blames her plight upon malicious fortune (*Tukhê baskanê*, 1.14.7; cf. 2.8.3–6, 3.3.8, 4.1.12, 4.4.2, 4.7.4, 5.1.4, 6.8.1, 8.1.2). Once she is reunited with Chaereas, Callirhoe offers thanks to Aphrodite for being reconciled with her (8.4.10), although there is no indication of why the goddess was wroth with her—if indeed, she was angry. In the end, back home in Syracuse, Callirhoe visits the temple of Aphrodite to give thanks once again, and adds: "I do not blame you, mistress, for what I have suffered: it was my fate" (8.8.16). Clearly, there is no place for forgiveness here. In Achilles Tatius' novel, *Leucippe and Clitophon*, the hero, Clitophon, once begs Aphrodite not to take it as an insult to her dignity (she is, after all, the goddess of erotic passion) that he and Leucippe preserved their virginity until they might be properly married (8.5.8). This is hardly an expression of contrition. Daphnis and Chloe, for their part, in the novel named for them and ascribed to a certain Longus, are under the protection of Pan and the Nymphs. When Chloe is carried off in a raid, Daphnis reproaches the Nymphs for betraying them (2.21.3), upon which the Nymphs appear to him in a dream and reply that they are not to blame (2.23.2), and they reassure Daphnis that all will be well and that Pan is already coming to Chloe's defense.

Toward the beginning of Heliodorus' *Aethiopica*, the latest of the Greek novels (third or fourth century AD), Chariclea and Theagenes are taken prisoner by the bandit Thyamis and his gang. In her grief, Chariclea berates Apollo for her sufferings (1.8.2–3): "You are retaliating too much and too harshly for our sins [*hamartêmata*], and all that we have gone through does not suffice for your vengeance—Where will you put an end to these things?" Like other novelistic heroines, she asserts that rather than suffer shame she will slay herself, and so remain chaste until death. "But," she adds, "there is no judge harsher than you." Theagenes, however, advises her to leave off such reproaches, since lamentations merely irritate the god further: "for one must not censure but rather beseech, for the powerful are rendered propitious by prayers, not by reproofs" (1.8.4). Chariclea seems to acknowledge faults, but is certain that they do not merit such extreme chastisement; Theagenes, for his part, suggests entreaty as opposed to blame, thus finessing the question of guilt. Neither gives any hint of apology or remorse. Much later, when, thanks to the plots of the queen Arsace, Chariclea is condemned to be burnt at the stake, she, like Habrocomes in Xenophon's novel, cries out to the Sun and Earth and the spirits above and below the earth who watch over human injustice (8.9.12): "You are witnesses that I am innocent of the charges brought against me." This in a novel that a certain Socrates, in his *History of the Church* (fifth century AD), ascribed to Heliodorus, the bishop of Trikka, and there are indeed some indications that the author was at least familiar with some episodes in the Bible.[23]

There are, of course, many other passages in classical Greek and Roman literature where people beseech the mercy of the gods. I have selected these narratives because, as novels, they bear comparison with the so-called *Life of Adam and Eve*, which was discussed earlier in this chapter. There, as we saw, the entire emphasis was on Eve's confession of her sin and hope for God's forgiveness, despite her disobedience, which she highlights rather than conceals. Pity is a different matter: according to a dominant view in antiquity, pity was a response to undeserved suffering, not to misfortune *per se*.[24] In the novels and other texts, accordingly, the threefold complex of offense against a deity, remorseful confession, and forgiveness, which we have identified as constitutive of the biblical conception of sin, is absent.

Let us return, after this excursus on classical appeals to divine pity, to sin in the Hebrew Bible, and more particularly, to the Book of Job, where we may detect a superficial analogy to the Greek novels. Before his affliction, Job worried each morning that his children might have sinned; "for Job said, 'It may be that my sons have sinned, and cursed God in their hearts.' Thus Job did continually" (Job 1:5). And indeed, Bildad, one of the so-called comforters who tries to convince Job that he has deserved his suffering and must therefore repent, remarks: "Does God pervert justice? Or does the Almighty pervert the right? If your children have sinned against him, he has delivered them into the power of their transgression" (Job 8:3–4). Nevertheless, despite his torments, which the reader knows from the prologue have been inflicted not because he has erred but simply as a test of his faith, proposed by Satan, Job does not blame God: "In all this Job did not sin or charge God with wrong" (Job 1:22). His wife came to him and said, "Do you still hold fast your integrity? Curse God, and die," but Job replied, "You speak as one of the foolish women would speak. Shall we receive good at the hand of God, and shall we not receive evil?" The author of the text comments: "In all this Job did not sin with his lips" (Job 2:9–10). The sin that is at stake in the narrative, then, is rejecting God— precisely the idea most closely associated with the term *ḥaṭa'*.

Job's visitors, however, maintain that his affliction must be due to some offense he or his family committed. As Zophar affirms, "Know then that God exacts of you less than your iniquity [*'awon*] deserves" (Job 11:6), and "If iniquity is in your hand, put it far away, and let not wickedness [*'awlāh*] dwell in your tents" (11:14). Job himself asks God defensively: "If I sin, what do I do to thee, thou watcher of men? Why hast thou made me thy mark? Why have I become a burden to thee?" (Job 7:20). But when it comes to answering his comforters, Job resolutely denies their accusations; appealing directly to God, he cries out: "Then call, and I will answer; or let me speak, and do thou reply to me. How many are my iniquities and my sins? Make me know my transgression and my sin" (Job 13:22–23). Job is confident of his innocence: "thou knowest that I am not guilty" (Job 10:7; cf. 14:16). Insisting on his innocence, Job asks, "Does not calamity befall the unrighteous, and disaster the workers of iniquity?" (Job 31:3). Had he committed adultery, that, he admits, would have been a crime and an injustice (31:11); had he mistreated an orphan, or withheld alms from the poor, or any of a multitude of forms of unrighteousness, he would have deserved his misery (31:1–40). Elihu, the last of the comforters to speak, insists that those who confess to having sinned may receive God's favor

(Job 33:26–28), and he further suggests that, besides his obstinate refusal to acknowledge his iniquity, wickedness, and wrongdoing, Job has now added rebellion to his sins (Job 34:37). But Job has nothing to confess. He is the counterexample to the many instances of sin, repentance, and forgiveness in the Bible. He maintained his faith despite his tribulations, and so he is not in need of forgiveness. But neither does he ask for pity, like the characters in the novels. Job's trial is a test of faith. This is the focus of the narrative, and he does not waver. The standard paradigm, invoked repeatedly by the comforters, is not negated; indeed, it is reinforced by the demonstration that, although the innocent may suffer, it is only sin that demands confession and remorse.

It will have been noticed that the word for sin, which occurs relatively infrequently in the book of Job, is often paired with terms for transgression, iniquity, wickedness, error, evil, and the like (e.g., Job 15:5, 19:4, 20:12, 21:30, 22:5, 23; 24:19–20, 35:6, 8). This association is facilitated by the parallelism characteristic of Hebrew verse, which is not based on stress (like modern English), quantity (like Greek, Latin, and Arabic), or number of syllables (as in French poetry), but rather on sequences of two or (more rarely) three verses that repeat in slightly different language the same idea. Since all of Job, apart from the frame narrative in Heaven, is in verse, an abundance of synonyms is inevitable. Nevertheless, the word *ḥaṭaʾ* is especially associated with criticism of God, inscrutable as his will may be.

The personal nature of the Psalms invites confession and the plea for God's forgiveness. The first Psalm begins with a contrast between the righteous and the wicked, and recommends avoiding the path of sinners: "Blessed is the man who walks not in the counsel of the wicked, nor stands in the way of sinners, nor sits in the seat of scoffers; but his delight is in the law of the Lord, and on his law he meditates day and night" (1:1–2; cf. 1:5). The advice is clearly addressed to worshippers of God, who respect the covenant and God's injunctions. So too, in the fourth Psalm, the singer enjoins: "But know that the Lord has set apart the godly for himself; the Lord hears when I call to him. Be angry, but sin not; commune with your own hearts on your beds, and be silent. Offer right sacrifices, and put your trust in the Lord" (4:3–5). Enemies, on the contrary, are castigated for transgressions: "Lead me, O Lord, in thy righteousness because of my enemies; make thy way straight before me. For there is no truth in their mouth; their heart is destruction; their throat is an open sepulchre, they flatter with their tongue. Make them bear their guilt, O God; let them fall by their own counsels; because of their many transgressions cast them out, for they have rebelled against thee" (Psalm 5:8–10; cf. 10:2, 11:2). So too, the singer exclaims: "The Lord tests the righteous and the wicked, and his soul hates him that loves violence. On the wicked he will rain coals of fire and brimstone; a scorching wind shall be the portion of their cup. For the Lord is righteous, he loves righteous deeds; the upright shall behold his face."[25] The singer's enemies are not foreign nations but rather, it appears, evildoers and slanderers within his own community. But he regards them as beyond the pale, and hopes not for their acknowledgement of their wrongdoing and return to the path of God, but for their utter destruction.

The case is different when the singer confesses his own sins and begs God for forgiveness, as in Psalm 25:

> [16] Turn thou to me, and be gracious to me;
>   for I am lonely and afflicted.
> [17] Relieve the troubles of my heart,
>   and bring me out of my distresses.
> [18] Consider my affliction and my trouble,
>   and forgive all my sins.
> [19] Consider how many are my foes,
>   and with what violent hatred they hate me.
> [20] Oh guard my life, and deliver me;
>   let me not be put to shame, for I take refuge in thee.
> [21] May integrity and uprightness preserve me,
>   for I wait for thee.
> [22] Redeem Israel, O God,
>   out of all his troubles.

The word sin is closely associated with the appeal for pardon. What is more, the appeal to God's mercy is conceived of as a more universal plea for Israel as a whole, suggesting that the enemies in question are not merely personal antagonists but foes of God's chosen people. Again, in Psalm 32:

> [1] Blessed is he whose transgression is forgiven,
>   whose sin is covered.
> [2] Blessed is the man to whom the Lord imputes no iniquity,
>   and in whose spirit there is no deceit.

> ³When I declared not my sin, my body wasted away
>   through my groaning all day long.
> ⁴For day and night thy hand was heavy upon me;
>   my strength was dried up as by the heat of summer.
> ⁵I acknowledged my sin to thee,
>   and I did not hide my iniquity;
>   I said, "I will confess my transgressions to the Lord";
>   then thou didst forgive the guilt of my sin.

So too, the singer cries out in Psalm 38: "I confess my iniquity, I am sorry for my sin. Those who are my foes without cause are mighty, and many are those who hate me wrongfully. Those who render me evil for good are my adversaries because I follow after good" (38:18–20; cf. 41:4–7). Psalm 51 brings together various themes in a complex combination. The singer begins by pleading: "Have mercy on me, O God, according to thy steadfast love; according to thy abundant mercy blot out my transgressions. Wash me thoroughly from my iniquity, and cleanse me from my sin!" (51:1–2; cf. 9). The sinner acknowledges having offended God and God alone: "Against thee, thee only, have I sinned, and done that which is evil in thy sight" (51:4). The metaphor of washing, however, summons up ideas of purity, and rather than indicate any specific offenses, the singer avows: "Behold, I was brought forth in iniquity, and in sin did my mother conceive me" (51:5). It is tempting to compare Isaiah, where the prophet cites the words of God:

> ²⁵"I, I am He
>   who blots out your transgressions for my own sake,
>   and I will not remember your sins.
> ²⁶Put me in remembrance, let us argue together;
>   set forth your case, that you may be proved right.
> ²⁷Your first father sinned,
>   and your mediators transgressed against me.
> ²⁸Therefore I profaned the princes of the sanctuary,
>   I delivered Jacob to utter destruction
>   and Israel to reviling".
>
> Isaiah 43:25–28

The fundamental sin remains that of abandoning the way of God, as inscribed in the covenant; this is not original or inherited sin but the repeated tendency among the Israelites to desert their God.[26] The singer himself struggles not to sin (Psalm 119:11).

Repentance and confession are the means of overcoming sin; as the singer continues in Psalm 51: "Restore to me the joy of thy salvation, and uphold me with a willing spirit. Then I will teach transgressors thy ways, and sinners will return to thee" (51:12–13). Repeatedly, the sin of abandoning God's ways (e.g., Psalm 78:17, 32) is followed by a petition for forgiveness: "Help us, O God of our salvation, for the glory of thy name; deliver us, and forgive our sins, for thy name's sake!" (Psalm 79:9; cf. 85:2, 103:3, 106:6). Occasionally, iniquity rather than sin may be paired with forgiveness (Psalm 130:3–4), but here too, no specific offenses are indicated. By contrast, others are condemned for their evil-doing:

> [1] The fool says in his heart,
>   "There is no God."
> They are corrupt, doing abominable iniquity;
>   there is none that does good.
> [2] God looks down from heaven
>   upon the sons of men
>   to see if there are any that are wise,
>   that seek after God.
>
> Psalm 53:1–2[27]

On occasion, the singer ascribes sin to enemies (e.g., Psalm 104:35; 109:7, 14), and he may contrast the utter destruction that awaits them with his own confession and hope of absolution. Thus, he prays: "Deliver me from my enemies, O my God, protect me from those who rise up against me, deliver me from those who work evil, and save me from bloodthirsty men. For lo, they lie in wait for my life; fierce men band themselves against me. For no transgression or sin of mine, O Lord, for no fault of mine, they run and make ready" (Psalm 59:1–4). Later in the same Psalm, however, he curses his enemies: "For the sin of their mouths, the words of their lips, let them be trapped in their pride. For the cursing and lies which they utter, consume them in wrath, consume them till they are no more" (59:12–13). The core scenario remains that of sin as the betrayal of God's will, contrition, and the hope of forgiveness.

The book of Proverbs has relatively little to say about sin. There is advice against heeding sinners ("My son, if sinners entice you, do not consent,"

Proverbs 1:10), and warnings about the fate of sinners ("The iniquities of the wicked ensnare him, and he is caught in the toils of his sin," Proverbs 5:22). Typically, the punishment of sinners is contrasted with the rewards expected by the righteous: "The wage of the righteous leads to life, the gain of the wicked to sin" (Proverbs 10:16; cf. 11:31; 13:6, 21, 22; 14:21, 34). More generally, no one can claim to be free of sin: "Who can say, 'I have made my heart clean; I am pure from my sin'?" (Proverbs 20:9; cf. Ecclesiastes 7:20: "Surely there is not a righteous man on earth who does good and never sins").[28] Pride (Proverbs 21:4) and foolishness (Proverbs 24:9) are identified with sin, both of these causes of neglecting God and turning from his tutelage.

The prophets add some new wrinkles to the tradition concerning sin, and no wonder: castigating the backsliding Israelites is their stock in trade. Isaiah intones against the sins of Judah, which he regards as a sinful people: "Ah, sinful nation, a people laden with iniquity, offspring of evildoers, sons who deal corruptly! They have forsaken the Lord, they have despised the Holy One of Israel, they are utterly estranged" (Isaiah 1:4). Ezekiel is especially hard on Judah, whose sins are more than twice those of neighboring Samaria: "Samaria has not committed half your sins; you have committed more abominations than they, and have made your sisters appear righteous by all the abominations which you have committed. Bear your disgrace, you also, for you have made judgment favorable to your sisters; because of your sins in which you acted more abominably than they, they are more in the right than you" (Ezekiel 16:51–52).[29] In general, the righteous will live and those who sin will die (Ezekiel 3:20–21; cf. 18:21, 33:10–16), above all those who do not abandon sinful ways (Ezekiel 18:24; cf. Isaiah 1:28, 13:9, 30:1 on adding sin to sin by seeking shelter in Egypt).[30]

Nevertheless, the sins of the people will be atoned if they are obedient to the Lord: "I will restore their fortunes, both the fortunes of Sodom and her daughters, and the fortunes of Samaria and her daughters, and I will restore your own fortunes in the midst of them, that you may bear your disgrace and be ashamed of all" (Ezekiel 16:53–54). So too in Isaiah, God appeals to his people: "Come now, let us reason together, says the Lord: though your sins are like scarlet, they shall be as white as snow; though they are red like crimson, they shall become like wool. If you are willing and obedient, you shall eat the good of the land; but if you refuse and rebel, you shall be devoured by the sword; for the mouth of the Lord has spoken" (Isaiah 1:18–20; cf. 3:9, 6:7, 27:9, 38:17). God orders Jeremiah to proclaim:

> 'Return, faithless Israel,
>   says the Lord.
> I will not look on you in anger,
> for I am merciful,
>   says the Lord;
> I will not be angry for ever.
> ¹³Only acknowledge your guilt,
>   that you rebelled against the Lord your God
> and scattered your favors among strangers under every green tree,
>   and that you have not obeyed my voice,
>   says the Lord.
> ¹⁴Return, O faithless children,
>   says the Lord;
> for I am your master.
>
> Jeremiah 3:12–14

Jeremiah records the plea of the people: "We acknowledge our wickedness, O Lord, and the iniquity of our fathers, for we have sinned against thee" (Jeremiah 14:20).[31] To Ezekiel God declares: "Because you have made your guilt to be remembered, in that your transgressions are uncovered, so that in all your doings your sins appear—because you have come to remembrance, you shall be taken in them" (Ezekiel 21:24). Daniel prays: "O Lord, the great and terrible God, who keeps covenant and steadfast love with those who love him and keep his commandments, we have sinned and done wrong and acted wickedly and rebelled, turning aside from thy commandments and ordinances" (Daniel 9:4–5; cf. 9:8–9, 11, 15–20, 24). In Second Isaiah, composed at the time when Cyrus was king of Persia, it is affirmed that Jerusalem has paid doubly for her sins: "Speak tenderly to Jerusalem, and cry to her that her warfare is ended, that her iniquity is pardoned, that she has received from the Lord's hand double for all her sins" (Isaiah 40:2). Although sinners offend God (Isaiah 42:24; cf. 58:1, 59:2, 64:5), sins may be blotted out. Thus God declares: "I, I am He who blots out your transgressions for my own sake, and I will not remember your sins. Put me in remembrance, let us argue together; set forth your case, that you may be proved right. Your first father sinned, and your mediators transgressed against me" (Isaiah 43:25–27; cf. 44:22).³² For those who deny having sinned, however, there is no forgiveness: "you say, 'I am innocent; surely his anger has turned from me.' Behold, I will bring you to judgment for saying, 'I have not sinned'" (Jeremiah 2:35).³³

As often, the particular sins are not identified, save in general terms as disobedience to God's commandments.³⁴ But idolatry remains the prime manifestation or locus of sin; thus Jeremiah, in continuation of the passage quoted above:

> ²¹A voice on the bare heights is heard,
>   the weeping and pleading of Israel's sons
> because they have perverted their way,
>   they have forgotten the Lord their God.
> ²²"Return, O faithless sons,
>   I will heal your faithlessness."
> "Behold, we come to thee;
>   for thou art the Lord our God.
> ²³Truly the hills are a delusion,
>   the orgies on the mountains.
> Truly in the Lord our God
>   is the salvation of Israel.
>
> Jeremiah 3:21–23

Later, Jeremiah warns (in the voice of God): "They have turned to me their back and not their face; and though I have taught them persistently they have not listened to receive instruction. They set up their abominations in the house which is called by my name, to defile it. They built the high places of Baal in the valley of the son of Hinnom, to offer up their sons and daughters to Molech, though I did not command them, nor did it enter into my mind, that they should do this abomination, to cause Judah to sin" (Jeremiah 32:33–35). Isaiah repeats the words of God: "Turn to him from whom you have deeply revolted, O people of Israel. For in that day every one shall cast away his idols of silver and his idols of gold, which your hands have sinfully made for you" (Isaiah 31:6–7). Ezekiel quotes the Lord: "Son of man, these men have taken their idols into their hearts, and set the stumbling block of their iniquity before their faces" (Ezekiel 14:3; cf. 23:49: "And your lewdness shall be requited upon you, and you shall bear the penalty for your sinful idolatry; and you shall know that

I am the Lord God"). Hosea reports: "And now they sin more and more, and make for themselves molten images, idols skilfully made of their silver, all of them the work of craftsmen. Sacrifice to these, they say. Men kiss calves!" (Hosea 13:2).[35] Micah transmits the reproach of God: "You shall sow, but not reap; you shall tread olives, but not anoint yourselves with oil; you shall tread grapes, but not drink wine. For you have kept the statutes of Omri, and all the works of the house of Ahab; and you have walked in their counsels" (Micah 6:15–16).

Since sin, as we have seen, consists primarily in the violation of the covenant, it is ascribed chiefly to God's people and only rarely to foreigners. In Hosea, God says of Israel, "The more they increased, the more they sinned against me" (Hosea 4:7), and he goes on to accuse the Israelites of idolatry (cf. 8:11, 13; 9:9; 10:8–9, where again the sin is idolatry; Hosea's prophecy ends with a hope of forgiveness, 14:4–7).[36] However, Daniel urges Nebuchadnezzar, "break off your sins by practicing righteousness, and your iniquities by showing mercy to the oppressed, that there may perhaps be a lengthening of your tranquillity" (Daniel 4:27), and in Ezekiel, God accuses the King of Tyre of sinning (Ezekiel 28:16).[37] But the proclamations recorded in Ezekiel against the many foreign nations, from Edom to Egypt, mention evil and iniquity but not sin, in conformity with the general conception of sin as a violation of God's injunctions to his own people, with a primary emphasis on idolatry.[38]

We cannot conclude the discussion of sin in the prophets without noting the remarkable passage in Isaiah, in which there is mention, for the first time, of the idea that a righteous person may bear the sins of others. This is the so-called "suffering servant," of whom it is written:

> [10]Yet it was the will of the Lord to bruise him;
>   he has put him to grief;
> when he makes himself an offering for sin,
>   he shall see his offspring, he shall prolong his days;
> the will of the Lord shall prosper in his hand;
> [11]he shall see the fruit of the travail of his soul and be satisfied;
> by his knowledge shall the righteous one, my servant,
>   make many to be accounted righteous;
>   and he shall bear their iniquities.
> [12]Therefore I will divide him a portion with the great,

> and he shall divide the spoil with the strong;
> because he poured out his soul to death,
> > and was numbered with the transgressors;
> yet he bore the sin of many,
> > and made intercession for the transgressors.
>
> Isaiah 53:10–12

We need not enter here into Christian exegeses of this passage as an anticipation of the Messiah's arrival on earth in the form of Jesus Christ (Jewish tradition identifies him with Israel itself). There are, of course, antecedents to the idea of an intercessor who pleads with God for the remission of the people's sins (cf., for example, 1 Samuel 7:6, discussed above), and it may even be argued that this is the chief, and most thankless, responsibility of prophets in the Hebrew Bible. Yet the image of the scapegoat whose suffering gathers to himself and expurgates the sins of others is new in the Tanakh, though it may have parallels in contemporary cultures.[39]

We have come to the conclusion of our survey of sin, represented by the key term *ḥaṭaʾ*, in the Hebrew Bible, and it is time to summarize the results. What has emerged, in the first instance, is a confirmation, I believe, of the decision to focus on this one word, as opposed to the variety of terms signifying evil, wickedness, iniquity, and the like. These latter terms are, needless to say, immensely significant for the ethical vision inscribed in the Hebrew Bible. But they refer to a wider range of offenses than those characteristically designated by *ḥaṭaʾ*, and do not identify a concept that is uniquely biblical, in comparison with the various terms for vice, injustice, or wrongdoing in contemporary classical cultures. The notion implied by *ḥaṭaʾ*, by contrast, turns out in fact to be novel, and inaugurates a religious conception that is specific to the biblical tradition. Very broadly, sin in the Tanakh, as conveyed by the term *ḥaṭaʾ*, consists principally in unfaithfulness to God and his covenant (earlier instances of the term, for example in connection with Cain's murder of Abel, necessarily have a looser application). This is the reason why sin is largely restricted to the chosen people, for they, and they alone, can be charged with violating the covenant with God (exceptions have been noted above, in the course of presenting the evidence). The Hebrew God is of course concerned with ethics in the wider sense, and his commandments cover a range of infractions, including murder, adultery, and more. Further instances of misconduct include the mistreatment of the poor, of widows, of orphans, theft, violations of temple rules, and much more. After all, there is a staggering number of prohibitions listed in the Torah. But these are not what the concept of sin is primarily about. When it comes to sin proper, the particular nature of the offense is often left vague, and is expressed by such general formulas as abandoning the way of God, committing treachery against God, "despising the Holy One of Israel," reviling God, and such like. When it is specified more closely, sin is crucially identified with the worship of foreign gods, which proves to be an extraordinary temptation. The emphasis here is on "foreign"—for the Israelites, the worship of idols or the deities of neighboring populations constitutes precisely a breach of the covenant: these idols or gods are not their gods but those of their neighbors. The neighboring peoples themselves may be the very incarnation of evil, and no doubt this has to do at some level with the nature of their worship, as perceived by the authors of the Tanakh. But the gods they revere and to whom they sacrifice are their own, and not foreign; and thus, however false their cults may be, they cannot be charged with abandoning the God of the Hebrews—and so, in this fundamental respect, they cannot be charged with sinning.

To be sure, some sins are accidental and atoned for by ritual acts; these do indeed have analogies in rituals and cultic practices in the ambient world, as we saw in Chapter 1 for the case of classical Greece. But infringements on these codes is not primarily what sin is about, and they may be atoned for by prescribed sacrifices and other acts. Straying from God is another matter entirely, and is punished severely, by the threat of the wholesale destruction of his people. In spite of the evidence of such chastisements in the course of their history, culminating in the fall of the kingdoms of Judah and Israel and the exile of the Jewish people, the sin of falling away from God proves to be a constant temptation. There is, however, a remedy, in the form of repentance and the humble confession of guilt. Such acknowledgement of error can earn God's forgiveness, although there is no guarantee that it will be effective: all depends on God's will and mercy. Still, the pattern of sin, confession, and the hope of pardon and redemption is a fundamental leitmotiv of the Hebrew Bible. It is a script involving three moments, and taken together, as a narrative paradigm or archetype, they define the very nature of sin in the Tanakh. It is this pattern of offending an exclusive and possessive national deity, which leads to punishment and the possibility of reconciliation through the acknowledgement of error, that distinguishes biblical sin from anything in the classical Greek and Roman tradition.

One final point deserves mention. The punishments that God inflicts in response to sin—that is, turning away from his covenant—are not typically regarded as miracles. They are historical defeats, scourges, afflictions, that can perfectly well be explained in naturalistic terms. The primary fact is that of the suffering of the Israelites; it is this that is interpreted as an affliction delivered by God for the faithlessness of his people. It is true that, on occasion, prophets may perform wonders of the kind that anticipate those of Jesus. Elijah, for example, provides an endless supply of flour and oil (1 Kings 17:14), resurrects a widow's son (17:22), and seems able to bring about rain (1 Kings 18:45). So too Elisha resurrects a child (2 Kings 4:34), increases small amounts of olive oil or flour (4:4, 43), heals leprosy (2 Kings 5:14), and blinds the enemy (2 Kings 6:18), though he subsequently restores their sight (6:20). But these marvels do not occur in the context of sin and confession, and they are not represented as motives for faith or respect for the covenant. The connection between miracles and faith, and the role of both in the paradigmatic conception of sin and forgiveness, is a feature specific to the New Testament, especially the Gospels, where it is precisely faith or trust, rather than repentance and confession, that is the key operator or middle term in the dynamic, tripartite structure that constitutes the sin paradigm. It is to this subtle but profound transformation of the role of sin that we turn in the following chapter.

3

The New Testament: Jesus' Sense of Sin

Let us begin by taking a close look at what appears to be a paradigmatic instance of sin in the Gospels, namely, the healing of the paralytic or palsied man (translations of the Greek word vary), who was brought to Jesus by his friends. In the version recorded by Mark (2:1–12), the passage begins:

> And when he [that is, Jesus] returned to Capernaum after some days, it was reported that he was at home. And many were gathered together, so that there was no longer room for them, not even about the door; and he was preaching the word to them. And they came, bringing to him a paralytic carried by four men. And when they could not get near him because of the crowd, they removed the roof above him; and when they had made an opening, they let down the pallet on which the paralytic lay.

We may omit discussion of any insurance claims that may have arisen in connection with the damaged roof, but it is important to note that already at this point, in the second chapter of Mark's Gospel, Jesus is so widely known as a healer that people flock to wherever he chances to be. The passage continues:

> And when Jesus saw their faith, he said to the paralytic, "My son, your sins are forgiven." Now some of the scribes were sitting there, questioning in their hearts, "Why does this man speak thus? It is blasphemy! Who can forgive sins but God alone?" And immediately Jesus, perceiving in his spirit that they thus questioned within themselves, said to them, "Why do you question thus in your hearts? Which is easier, to say to the paralytic, 'Your sins are forgiven,' or to say, 'Rise, take up your pallet and walk'"?

We may observe that Jesus seems to mention the faith of those who brought the paralytic to him, though we may be justified in supposing that he was including the faith of the ill man himself. We may also call attention to what may appear to be an element of frivolity in Jesus' response to the scribes. They look to his declaration concerning the forgiveness of sins, which is indeed a blasphemous claim, in light of the ample evidence in the Hebrew Bible that the only one who may pardon sin is God himself. Indeed, so much is this the case that, as we noted in the previous chapter, God alone is the subject of the verb *salakh* (סָלַח), which is the term par excellence for the remission of sins. As John Chrysostom, writing toward the end of the fourth century, expressed it in his *Homily* 40, in which he expounded on Corinthians 1–2: "But rulers and kings, whether it is adulterers whom they forgive or homicides, release them indeed from the present punishment; but their sin they do not purge out . . ., it being God alone who does this." Jesus will reply directly to this charge in a moment, as we shall see, but his first answer seems to be that mere words are easy—anyone can declare, "Your sins are forgiven!" Deeds, however, are another matter, and the proof of Jesus' exceptional abilities lies not in the words he pronounces, bidding the paralytic to get up and walk, but in the fact that the lame man actually does so. Whether or not the man's sins are forgiven is not immediately apparent to onlookers, and so can seem like mere blustering. But that the crippled man in fact stands up, lifts his makeshift bed and starts walking away is irrefutable evidence of the power of Jesus' pronouncements.[1] There is no law that prohibits the scribes from uttering these words; if they do not, it is because they know that, on their lips, the words will be ineffectual. Having said this much, however, Jesus proceeds to make a further claim:

> "But that you may know that the Son of man has authority on earth to forgive sins"—he said to the paralytic—"I say to you, rise, take up your pallet and go home." And he rose, and immediately took up the pallet and went out before them all; so that they were all amazed and glorified God, saying, "We never saw anything like this!".
>
> New Revised Standard Version, NRSV

Jesus here ups the ante and affirms that he can indeed forgive sins because his status is special—as the Son of Man, a somewhat opaque formula that seems equivalent in force to Son of God, he is unlike any other human being, the scribes included, and this is what authorizes him to remit the sins of the paralytic. In saying this he is truly blaspheming in the eyes of the scribes, and he proceeds to back up his claim with the visible proof of his extraordinary, that is to say, divine powers: he instructs the crippled man to get up, gather his pallet, and walk—and behold, he does just that, in the presence of all (and we know that there is quite a crowd on hand). The bystanders testify openly to their astonishment: "they were all amazed and glorified God, saying, 'We never saw anything like this!'" Jesus invokes the miracle of the healing of the paralytic precisely as proof of his ability to occupy the place of God and forgive sins. Since he can do that, which, as he suggests, is the harder task, no doubt because a false pretense can be immediately exposed, Jesus can expect others to believe his claim to forgive sins as well, since this is easier to assert, though not to do, in that the truth or falsity of the pardon is not so readily visible.

So far, I have been treating Jesus' two actions—healing the crippled man and forgiving his sins—as distinct and in principle unrelated, save insofar as the miraculous cure lends a certain plausibility to Jesus' claim that he can remit the disabled man's sins as well. Now, one might suppose that there is a deeper connection between the forgiving of sins and the healing of the paralytic, namely that the man's handicap is in fact the result of his prior sins. Understood this way, it is because his sins have been pardoned that the paralytic is now cured and able to walk again. This view naturally leads one to speculate on the kinds of offenses the man might have committed and so were the cause of his affliction.[2] Thus one nineteenth-century authority, Albert Barnes, writes: "The man might have brought on this disease of the palsy by a long course of vicious indulgence," accompanied by vices such as "gluttony, intemperate drinking, lewdness, debauchery."[3] Of course, Mark says nothing at all about such sins as Barnes imagines, and this is simply guesswork on Mr. Barnes' part—guesswork, or still worse, an inference concerning the nature of sin that may not have been on Jesus' mind at all.

Barnes and others may, however, have found some support for their interpretation in the version of the story of the paralytic that is narrated in the Gospel of John, which exhibits some significant differences from the way it is related in Mark, Matthew (9:1–8), and Luke (5:17–26), and so it is worth quoting at length:

> Now there is in Jerusalem by the Sheep Gate a pool, in Hebrew called Bethzatha, which has five porticoes. In these lay a multitude of invalids, blind, lame, paralysed. One man was there, who had been ill for thirty-eight years. When Jesus saw him and knew that he had been lying there a long time, he said to him, "Do you want to be healed?" The sick man answered him, "Sir, I have no man to put me into the pool when the water is troubled, and while I

am going another steps down before me." Jesus said to him, "Rise, take up your pallet, and walk." And at once the man was healed, and he took up his pallet and walked. Now that day was the Sabbath. So the Jews said to the man who was cured, "It is the sabbath, it is not lawful for you to carry your pallet." But he answered them, "The man who healed me said to me, 'Take up your pallet, and walk.'" They asked him, "Who is the man who said to you, 'Take up your pallet, and walk'?" Now the man who had been healed did not know who it was, for Jesus had withdrawn, as there was a crowd in the place. Afterward, Jesus found him in the temple, and said to him, "See, you are well! Sin no more, that nothing worse befall you." The man went away and told the Jews that it was Jesus who had healed him. And this was why the Jews persecuted Jesus, because he did this on the Sabbath. But Jesus answered them, "My Father is working still, and I am working." This was why the Jews sought all the more to kill him, because he not only broke the Sabbath but also called God his own Father, making himself equal with God.

John 5:2–18

Jesus' words, "See! You have become well. Sin no longer, so that nothing worse may happen to you" (Ἴδε ὑγιὴς γέγονας μηκέτι ἁμάρτανε ἵνα μὴ χεῖρόν σοί τι γένηται, 5:14, my translation), would seem to indicate that the sick man had sinned before; this is the force of the Greek μηκέτι (*mêketi*), "no longer," "no further." If he continues to sin, then he may suffer something even worse than that which has already befallen him. May we infer, then, from Jesus' admonition that the man's prior sins were the cause of his present disorder?

Let us examine the case more closely. The man has been ill, we are informed, for thirty-eight years. There is no indication of his current age, but it is likely that he was not very old when he was beset by his infirmity. Had he already committed sins so great as to be deserving of such an affliction? Since, as we shall see, Jesus often heals people whose infirmities are clearly not the result of any offenses on their part, it is wise to exercise caution in assuming that Jesus is ascribing the lame man's condition to specific sins.

In fact, the bare term *eti*, which commonly means "yet, still, longer," may also signify "hereafter," with no implication of continuity with the past. Prometheus, in the Aeschylean tragedy, *Prometheus Bound*, declares that "Zeus, although he thinks arrogant thoughts, will be humble in the future [*eti*]" (vv. 906–7); Zeus has certainly been anything but humble so far. Jesus may, then, be admonishing the paralytic not to sin henceforward, now that he has recovered. But even if we take

Jesus to imply that the man had indeed sinned in the past—and this is surely the more likely interpretation of the word *mêketi*—it does not follow that these prior sins were the cause of his infirmity. It is equally possible to understand Jesus' statement as implying that, however grim the man's suffering has been so far, and John's description makes it clear that the illness was severely distressing, if he should sin in the future, then something far worse will happen to him. This will be not just physical illness, such as he and many others (the "multitude of invalids" round the washing pool) have suffered, but rather the wages of sin, that is to say, spiritual death and lasting damnation. For that is what sin entails, not physical disability as such. Whatever the cause of his paralysis, then, and we may well imagine that there is a perfectly natural explanation for it, the crucial thing is to avoid sinning henceforward, for that will entail truly disastrous consequences.

There is another consideration in respect to whether the man's paralysis is due to sin, the full implication of which we shall see further on. John mentions that the onset of the disease occurred a full thirty-eight years earlier than the encounter with Jesus. This apparently incidental detail informs us that, if indeed the cause of the paralytic's disability was some kind of sin, it must have been committed prior to the birth of Christ, since Christ, at the time when he began to teach, was "around thirty years of age" (Luke 3:23). Jesus' encounter with the paralytic occurred fairly early in his preaching (we recall that it is recounted in the second chapter of Mark's Gospel), and at the time of his crucifixion Jesus is commonly supposed to be thirty-three (on no reckoning was he older than thirty-six). However, as we shall see, the coming of Jesus marks a crucial watershed in the very nature of sin. For, in a passage that has given rise to profound controversy, John quotes Jesus as saying: "If I had not come and spoken to them, they would not have sin; but now they have no excuse for their sin . . . If I had not done among them the works that no one else did, they would not have sin" (John 15:22, 24). We will return to this affirmation of Jesus further on; for the moment, we may simply observe that, by John's own reckoning, the paralytic could not have sinned, strictly speaking, or at least not in the eyes of Jesus, at the time when he fell ill, since that occurred before Jesus was born. Indeed, I venture to suggest that this may be the reason why John specifies how long the man had suffered from the malady. There is other evidence in the Gospels, as we shall soon see, that shows that mortal afflictions of the common kind are not in principle due to sinning—any more that Job's trials were the result of any sins of which he may have been guilty. For the moment, however, we may examine one aspect of the episode that we have so far neglected, and which will prove to be of critical importance.

Mark records that "when Jesus saw their faith, he said to the paralytic, 'My son, your sins are forgiven.'" Whatever the cause of the paralysis, the reason why the man's sins are pardoned lies in his faith—or perhaps, more particularly, the faith of the men who brought him to Jesus. But what is the nature of their faith? The Greek word that is rendered in English as "faith" is *pistis*, and, as we shall see, it is intimately connected with the forgiveness of sin. It thus deserves more particular attention.

What is the basis of the *pistis* of the four men who lift the paralytic to the roof of the house and then lower him inside so that Jesus may heal him? Presumably the men acquired this *pistis*, which is the motive for Jesus' remission of the paralytic's sin, thanks to what they have seen or heard of Jesus previously. Since, as we have seen, the story of the paralytic is recounted in the second chapter of Mark, the events that inspired their conviction must have been those described in the opening chapter of the Gospel. This begins with John the Baptist's proclamation of Jesus' coming, his baptism of Jesus, Jesus' temptation in the desert, and the summoning of the first disciples. What follows deserves quotation in full:

> [21] And they went into Capernaum; and immediately on the Sabbath he entered the synagogue and taught. [22] And they were astonished at his teaching, for he taught them as one who had authority, and not as the scribes. [23] And immediately there was in their synagogue a man with an unclean spirit; [24] and he cried out, "What have you to do with us, Jesus of Nazareth? Have you come to destroy us? I know who you are, the Holy One of God." [25] But Jesus rebuked him, saying, "Be silent, and come out of him!" [26] And the unclean spirit, convulsing him and crying with a loud voice, came out of him. [27] And they were all amazed, so that they questioned among themselves, saying, "What is this? A new teaching! With authority he commands even the unclean spirits, and they obey him." [28] And at once his fame spread everywhere throughout all the surrounding region of Galilee.
>
> Mark 1:21–28

Jesus is clearly impressive as a preacher, surpassing the lessons of the scribes. There is no indication, however, of the content of his teaching. Very likely he expounded some passage or passages in the Hebrew Bible more profoundly than the scribes had done, but nothing is said of his exegesis. Rather, the narrative shifts to the exorcism of the possessed man, and the demon that bears witness both to Jesus' divinity and to his ability, should he so wish, to destroy the evil spirits. This is the teaching that astonishes the onlookers, and the source of his sudden fame in the region. Jesus proceeds directly to a second, somewhat different act of healing, this time witnessed only by his immediate circle:

> [29] And immediately he left the synagogue, and entered the house of Simon and Andrew, with James and John. [30] Now Simon's mother-in-law lay sick with a fever, and immediately they told him of her. [31] And he came and took her by the hand and lifted her up, and the fever left her; and she served them.
>
> Mark 1:29–31

But thanks to Jesus' growing reputation, a great many people seek him out, both to cure diseases and to drive out evil spirits:

> [32] That evening, at sundown, they brought to him all who were sick or possessed with demons. [33] And the whole city was gathered together about the door. [34] And he healed many who were sick with various diseases, and cast out many demons; and he would not permit the demons to speak, because they knew him.
>
> Mark 1: 32–34

Jesus retires to pray in solitude, but is discovered by his disciples who report that everyone is looking for him, presumably to be cured by his now evident powers:

> [35] And in the morning, a great while before day, he rose and went out to a lonely place, and there he prayed. [36] And Simon and those who were with him pursued him, [37] and they found him and said to him, "Every one is searching for you".
>
> Mark 1:35–37

Jesus, in turn, bids them to follow him to nearby towns, so that he may preach more widely—always accompanied, however, by the performance of exorcisms:

> [38] And he said to them, "Let us go on to the next towns, that I may preach there also; for that is why I came out." [39] And he went throughout all Galilee, preaching in their synagogues and casting out demons.
>
> Mark 1:38–39

Finally, Jesus is approached by a leper, who declares his confidence in his ability to cleanse or purify (*katharisai*) him. Jesus is moved by compassion (*splankhnistheis*) and heals him, but bids him not to reveal the miracle to anyone:

> [40] And a leper came to him beseeching him, and kneeling said to him, "If you will, you can make me clean." [41] Moved with pity, he stretched out his hand and touched him, and said to him, "I will; be clean." [42] And immediately the leprosy left him, and he was made clean. [43] And he sternly charged him, and sent him away at once, [44] and said to him, "See that you say nothing to any one; but go, show yourself to the priest, and offer for your cleansing what Moses commanded, for a proof to the people." [45] But he went out and began to talk freely about it, and to spread the news, so that Jesus could no longer openly enter a town, but was out in the country; and people came to him from every quarter.
>
> Mark 1:40–45

As we see, despite Jesus' injunction the leper reports the miraculous cure far and wide, with the result that Jesus must now avoid cities where the Jewish authorities might hold him to account. But his efforts to shun notoriety are unsuccessful and multitudes come to him in the countryside, presumably, though it is not said so explicitly, to benefit from his healing powers. This is the entire run-up to the episode of the paralytic, and it is what his friends will have known of Jesus prior to delivering him into his care. It is this, then, that is the source of their faith or *pistis*.[4]

Today, we think of faith as being largely synonymous with "belief," at least in religious contexts. Faith has several senses. It often signifies a firm conviction, one so deeply rooted that it resists or is impervious to contrary arguments. One defense of such inalterable belief is that it is not based simply on rational argument or demonstration, but rather is thought of as transcending reason or that it begins where reason leaves off. This is in part due to the nature of its object: faith relates to higher truths that cannot be verified by ordinary experience or scientific demonstration. Another sense of faith today is credence in a specified set of doctrines, that is, a set of propositions that constitute what we may call the content of belief. Rather than referring to what is not seen or beyond the senses, faith in this latter sense consists in the belief that something is the case, for example that there is a God, or that Christ died for our sins.[5] We may call these two ways of believing the "how" of faith, as when we say, "I believe in my heart," and the "what" of faith, as when we say, "I believe that this is the case."

Now, as it happens, neither of these two meanings or aspects of faith corresponds to the normal semantic range of the classical Latin word *fides*, from which the English "faith" derives, or the corresponding Greek word *pistis* (which is ultimately cognate with *fides* and with the English "bide"). At a later date, to be sure, the words *pistis* and *fides* began to assume something like the modern sense of "faith." As Teresa Morgan observes in her splendid and thoroughly documented study of the Greek and Latin terms in early Christian texts and in the Septuagint, the semantic shift is evident in Augustine's distinction between *fides quae creditur* ("that which is believed") and *fides qua creditur* ("that by which it is believed"). As Morgan explains, the latter is "that which takes place in the heart and mind of the believer."[6] For the first sense—that is, faith as surpassing reason—we may compare Pope Gregory the Great, who preached in his 26th *Homily* in the year 591-92: "Neither does our faith have any value, if human reason furnishes it with experimental proof."[7] Gregory's phrase is quoted by Thomas Aquinas in his *Summa Theologica* (III, Question 55, Article 5, Objection 2), in the course of his discussion of whether Christ's resurrection was demonstrated by proofs. In the Bible, however, this later sense of faith is marginal. In Hebrews 11:1, to be sure, faith is defined as "conviction of things not seen." But this is an exceptional affirmation in an exceptional book.[8]

Teresa Morgan identifies an incipient instance of the other, propositional sense of "faith" in James, when he writes:

> What does it profit, my brethren, if a man says he has faith but has not works? Can his faith save him? [15]If a brother or sister is ill-clad and in lack of daily food, [16]and one of you says to them, "Go in peace, be warmed and filled," without giving them the things needed for the body, what does it profit? [17]So faith by itself, if it has no works, is dead. [18]But some one will say, "You have faith and I have works." Show me your faith apart from your works, and I by my works will show you my faith. [19]You believe that God is one; you do well. Even the demons believe—and shudder.
>
> James 2:14-19

There seems to be a suggestion here of faith in a particular doctrine, namely that God is one. This sense is indicated by the relatively rare use in the New

Testament of the verb for "believe" (*pisteuein*, obviously related to *pistis*) with the conjunction "that" (in Greek, *hoti*); to "believe that" something is the case is not quite the same as simply believing in someone. John too favors the expression *pisteuein hoti* ("believe that"), but, as Morgan remarks, his usage does not indicate "the deliberate, counter-rational acceptance of something which cannot be known for certain"[9]—that is, the first or semi-mystical use of "believe." With these possible exceptions to the rule, by and large faith in the metaphysical or the propositional sense of the word is not emphasized in the New Testament, and still less so in the Gospels and the epistles of Paul. Nor for that matter, is it evident in the Septuagint, where the Greek terminology is sometimes influenced by the Hebrew words that are being translated.

What, then, does *pistis* primarily mean in the New Testament, and what is its relation to sin and forgiveness? The answer, as Morgan shows, is that *pistis*, like Latin *fides*, almost always bears its classical meaning of "trust" or "confidence" (or sometimes "trustworthiness" or "reliability"). It is faith in this sense that salvation and the remission of sin depend upon. We have already seen this kind of faith at work in the story of the paralytic, who is restored to health thanks to the belief of his friends (and possibly his own) in Jesus' capacity to perform miraculous cures. To see that this sense prevails in the New Testament as a whole, we must look briefly at the passages in which the noun *pistis* and the related adjective and verb occur, before returning to the relationship between faith and sin.

A woman who has been suffering from hemorrhages for a dozen years and succeeds in touching Jesus' garment despite the press of the crowd is healed (Mark 5:25–31); she "had heard about Jesus" (5:27) and thought to herself, "If I but touch his clothes, I will be made well" (5:28). When the woman reveals herself to Jesus, he says to her, "Daughter, your *pistis* has made you well; go in peace, and be healed of your disease" (5:31). What is it that she believes? She is confident that Jesus can heal her. There is no question of faith in the sense of commitment to a credo or belief in some ineffable truth beyond reason and the senses. Nor, we may note, is there the least indication that the woman has sinned. This absence is not to be explained by stylistic compression, and still less by assuming that the evangelist took it for granted that his readers would understand that her disease must be a result of sin, and so thought it otiose to mention this explicitly. If Mark had wished us to suppose that the woman's hemorrhage was due to prior sin, he could easily have said so. But the emphasis is elsewhere, on the woman's confidence that Jesus can cure her condition. It is this that Jesus remarks upon, and it tells us all we need to know.

The account of the healing of the paralytic is related in the ninth chapter of the Gospel of Matthew, and again follows a series of miraculous cures narrated in the preceding chapter. These include the healing of the leper, similar to the story as it is recounted in Mark; it is followed by the episode of the servant of the centurion. The story is worth quoting in full for what it demonstrates about the nature of *pistis* and salvation:

> [5] As he entered Capernaum, a centurion came forward to him, beseeching him [6] and saying, "Lord, my servant is lying paralyzed at home, in terrible distress." [7] And he said to him, "I will come and heal him." [8] But the centurion answered him, "Lord, I am not worthy to have you come under my roof; but only say the word, and my servant will be healed. [9] For I am a man under authority, with soldiers under me; and I say to one, 'Go,' and he goes, and to another, 'Come,' and he comes, and to my slave, 'Do this,' and he does it." [10] When Jesus heard him, he marveled, and said to those who followed him, "Truly, I say to you, not even in Israel have I found such faith. [11] I tell you, many will come from east and west and sit at table with Abraham, Isaac, and Jacob in the kingdom of heaven, [12] while the sons of the kingdom will be thrown into the outer darkness; there men will weep and gnash their teeth." [13] And to the centurion Jesus said, "Go; be it done for you as you have believed." And the servant was healed at that very moment.
>
> Matthew 8:5–13

The faith of the centurion consists in his confidence that Jesus can heal his servant—and this from a man with considerable authority, a captain in the army in charge of a hundred men, a Roman and not a Jew. And yet, unlike the Jews who persecute Jesus and from whom he seeks to conceal his wonder-working, this officer trusts the mere word of Jesus to effect the cure. The others, the "sons of the kingdom," will be banished to the outer darkness because they did not believe in Jesus' powers, whereas the pagan officer will be saved. Thus, Jesus says, "be it done for you as you have believed" (the verbal form of *pistis* is used here), and the servant is indeed healed, confirming the centurion's faith that Jesus could cure him.

Next, Jesus performs a different sort of miracle, the calming of the winds at sea:

> [23] And when he got into the boat, his disciples followed him. [24] And behold, there arose a great storm on the sea, so that the boat was being swamped by the waves; but he was asleep. [25] And they went and woke him, saying, "Save, Lord; we are perishing." [26] And he said to them, "Why are you afraid, O men of little faith?" Then he rose and rebuked the winds and the sea; and there was a great calm. [27] And the men marveled, saying, "What sort of man is this, that even winds and sea obey him?".
>
> Matthew 8:23–27

Again, what is the nature of the faith that the disciples fell short of in this instance? It is the faith that they will be safe with Jesus in the boat, since the winds respect him. It is not clear whether the disciples would have been entirely safe had they allowed Jesus to continue sleeping; presumably the mere knowledge that he was among them ought to have sufficed to calm their fears. But even if they were justified in disturbing his sleep, they ought to have trusted him to master the winds when he awoke and not have feared that they were about to die. The faith they ought to have exhibited is not just an abstract belief in Jesus' divinity but a confidence in his abilities to perform actions that are beyond the capacity of ordinary mortals. Of course, these miracles testify to Jesus' more than human powers, and indirectly the disciples and all the others who seek Jesus' ministrations manifest their faith in his godhood. This is why they are disposed to accept as well his ability to forgive sins. But the immediate object of their confidence is Jesus' ability to perform wonders, and this is the faith to which Jesus responds and justifies by his acts. After the calming of the winds, Jesus drives the demons out of men who have been possessed and casts them into swine, which immediately rush to sea and drown.

Further miracles follow the healing of the paralytic, and reveal all the more clearly the nature of the faith to which Jesus responds. We read next:

> [18] behold, a ruler came in and knelt before him, saying, "My daughter has just died; but come and lay your hand on her, and she will live." [19] And Jesus rose and followed him, with his disciples.
>
> Matthew 9:18–19

This tale is clearly a doublet of the episode with the centurion. It is interrupted by the story of the hemorrhaging woman, and then continues:

> ²³And when Jesus came to the ruler's house, and saw the flute players, and the crowd making a tumult, ²⁴he said, "Depart; for the girl is not dead but sleeping." And they laughed at him. ²⁵But when the crowd had been put outside, he went in and took her by the hand, and the girl arose. ²⁶And the report of this went through all that district.
>
> Matthew 9:23–26

Although the word "faith" is not used here, it is clear, just as in the interposed story of the hemorrhaging woman, that it is the ruler's confidence in Jesus' curative powers that leads him to seek out Jesus; it is this, in turn, that induces Jesus to oblige by resurrecting his daughter. The episode that immediately follows this one leaves no doubt as to the sense of *pistis* and the verb *pisteuein*:

> ²⁷And as Jesus passed on from there, two blind men followed him, crying aloud, "Have mercy on us, Son of David." ²⁸When he entered the house, the blind men came to him; and Jesus said to them, "Do you believe [verb, *pisteuein*] that I am able to do this?" They said to him, "Yes, Lord." ²⁹Then he touched their eyes, saying, "According to your faith [*pistis*] be it done to you." ³⁰And their eyes were opened. And Jesus sternly charged them, "See that no one knows it." ³¹But they went away and spread his fame through all that district.
>
> Matthew 9:27–31[10]

In the Catholic edition of the *Revised Standard Version of the Bible*,[11] a note is appended to the healing of the leper, as related at the beginning of chapter 8 of the Gospel of Matthew. Exceptionally, the comment is not on alternative readings in the Greek manuscript tradition, but touches on the interpretation of the episode: "The miracles of Jesus were never performed to amaze people and shock them into belief. They were worked with a view to a real strengthening of faith in the recipient or beholder, from whom the proper dispositions were required." It is not a question, however, of shocking anyone into believing; the evidence of Jesus' powers is clear, and those who trust in them do so on the basis of what they have seen or heard. This is what *pistis* means in the Gospels. Jesus tests human beings and discovers whether they are prepared to recognize him as the Messiah and the Son of God. The only clue they have lies in his prior acts of healing and driving out demons. If, like the blind men, people believe that Jesus can cure their affliction, then he does it, which then serves as still further proof of his abilities. Those who are opposed to what they see as blasphemous pretentions are naturally concerned at the likelihood that the more wonders he performs, the more people will trust in his powers, and so they will naturally attempt to stop him. This is why Jesus discourages people from spreading the word of his miracles. But the word gets out all the same, setting the conditions for his persecution and final crucifixion. The final miracle recorded in the ninth chapter of Matthew makes the danger clear:

> [32] As they were going away, behold, a dumb demoniac was brought to him. [33] And when the demon had been cast out, the dumb man spoke; and the crowds marveled, saying, "Never was anything like this seen in Israel." [34] But the Pharisees said, "He casts out demons by the prince of demons".
>
> Matthew 9:32–34

The Pharisees recognize Jesus' extraordinary power—how could they not?—but interpret it as a gift of the devil rather than inherent in Jesus himself as the Son of God. They thus fail to have proper trust in his words and deeds, which alone is the condition for salvation.

The Pharisees' anxiety is not without reason, as Jesus' acts immediately thereafter demonstrate:

> [35] Then Jesus went about all the cities and villages, teaching in their synagogues, and proclaiming the good news of the kingdom, and curing every disease and every sickness. [36] When he saw the crowds, he had compassion for them, because they were harassed and helpless, like sheep without a shepherd. [37] Then he said to his disciples, "The harvest is plentiful, but the laborers are few; [38] therefore ask the Lord of the harvest to send out laborers into his harvest".
>
> Matthew 9:35–38

The new laborers are the twelve disciples themselves, on whom Jesus now bestowed "authority over unclean spirits, to cast them out, and to cure every disease and every sickness" (Matthew 10:1). His method is clear. He instructs them: "As you go, proclaim the good news, 'The kingdom of heaven has come near.' Cure the sick, raise the dead, cleanse the lepers, cast out demons. You received without payment; give without payment" (10:7–8). They are to canvas house by house, and those who fail to accept them are in dire trouble. "If anyone will not welcome you or listen to your words, shake off the dust from your feet as you leave that house or town. Truly I tell you, it will be more tolerable for the land of Sodom and Gomorrah on the day of judgment than for that town" (10:14–15). No doubt, the disciples are to proclaim Jesus' divinity; but the basis for conviction in their words, apart from Jesus' own reputation, is the miracles they have just been empowered to perform. In turn, they, like Jesus, will suffer persecution: "Beware of them," he counsels (that is, the Pharisees and their supporters), "for they will hand you over to councils and flog you in their synagogues; and you will be dragged before governors and kings because of me, as a testimony to them and the Gentiles" (10:17–18). But they must endure the hatred of all, since the stakes are high: "Everyone therefore who acknowledges me before others, I also will acknowledge before my Father in heaven; but whoever denies me before others, I also will deny before my Father in heaven" (10:32–33).

The reader may suspect by this point that I am belaboring the obvious: passage after passage confirms the importance of Jesus' wonder-working. But it is necessary to present the evidence abundantly, because the vast weight of modern opinion has placed the emphasis on Jesus' teachings, rather than on his miracles.[12] His teachings are indeed radical and deeply humane, and they are innovative in the context of ancient ethics generally, whether popular or propounded by philosophers. But they are not in the first instance the basis for faith, nor for the absolution from sin, and this requires patient demonstration. Let us proceed a bit further, then, case by case. Following Jesus' instructions to the disciples, there is an interlude concerning John the Baptist, who is now in prison:

> [2]When John heard in prison what the Messiah was doing, he sent word by his disciples [3]and said to him, "Are you the one who is to come, or are we to wait for another?" [4]Jesus answered them, "Go and tell John what you hear and see: [5]the blind receive their sight, the lame walk, the lepers are cleansed, the deaf hear, the dead are raised, and the poor have good news brought to them. [6]And blessed is anyone who takes no offense at me".
>
> Matthew 11:2–6

If this is how Jesus chooses to reassure John the Baptist that he is the Messiah, why suppose that these are not the principal means by which he persuades the people at large?

Immediately thereafter, Jesus turns his attention to the cities in which he has performed his miracles:

> [20]Then he began to reproach the cities in which most of his deeds of power had been done, because they did not repent. [21]"Woe to you, Chorazin! Woe to you, Bethsaida! For if the deeds of power done in you had been done in Tyre and Sidon, they would have repented long ago in sackcloth and ashes. [22]But I tell you, on the day of judgment it will be more tolerable for Tyre and Sidon than for you. [23]And you, Capernaum, will you be exalted to heaven? No, you will be brought down to Hades. For if the deeds of power done in you had been done in Sodom, it would have remained until this day. [24]But I tell you that on the day of judgment it will be more tolerable for the land of Sodom than for you".
>
> Matthew 11:20–24

Jesus proceeds to enter a synagogue on the Sabbath and cure the withered hand of a man he finds there. The Pharisees fasten on the legalistic detail of violating the injunction not to work on the Sabbath, to which Jesus answers with a trenchant analogy. But their real concern is with his manifest powers, and this is why they begin to conspire and seek to destroy him (Matthew 12:9–14).

There is more in this vein—much more. When Jesus casts out a demon that has rendered a man blind and mute, thereby restoring his sight and ability to speak, the Pharisees accuse him of deriving his power from Beelzebub rather than from God. Jesus cleverly replies that, if that were so, the ruler of demons would be warring with his own (Matthew 12:22–28). Back in Nazareth, however, Jesus did not perform many "works of power" (*dunameis*), because the people of his own town (*patris*) did not honor him (Matthew 13:53–58). Upon hearing of the death of John the Baptist, Jesus withdrew to an isolated place. "But when the crowds heard it, they followed him on foot from the towns. When he went ashore, he saw a great crowd; and he had compassion for them and cured their sick" (Matthew 14:13–14). By dinner time, the disciples wished to send the crowd away, but Jesus proposed to feast them then and there. Although they had only five loaves of bread and two fish on hand, thanks to Jesus, these were sufficient so that "those who ate were about five thousand men, besides women and children" (14:21), and food was left over besides. After this, Jesus walks on water to the boat where the disciples have spent the night, causing them some consternation. Peter, apparently to test whether it is really Jesus approaching, asks that he may be granted the ability to do likewise, and so meet Jesus halfway. But he takes fright in midcourse and begins to sink.

Jesus grasps his hand, and says: "You of little faith, why did you doubt?" (14:31). The message is clear: Jesus' miracles work for those who trust him. Then, "those in the boat worshiped him, saying, 'Truly you are the Son of God'" (14:33). Having crossed over by boat, they landed in Gennesaret, where the people recognized Jesus "and brought all who were sick to him, and begged him that they might touch even the fringe of his cloak; and all who touched it were healed" (14:35–36). Jesus' treatment of the Canaanite woman, which follows, is exemplary. The woman begs Jesus to cure her daughter, who is possessed by a demon. At first, Jesus refuses, on the grounds that he was sent to tend only to the Israelites, and he will not throw their food to the dogs. But when the woman affirms that even dogs get to eat the crumbs from their master's table, Jesus replies: "'Woman, great is your faith! Let it be done for you as you wish.' And her daughter was healed instantly" (Matthew 15:28). Faith or *pistis* here means the confidence that Jesus can heal the girl; nothing else is at stake. Jesus goes on to cure "the lame, the maimed, the blind, the mute, and many others" (15:30), and when the crowd perceived this, "they praised the God of Israel" (15:31). To feed the multitude, Jesus again performs the miracle of the loaves and the fish (this time, seven loaves and "a few fish"), and this proves enough to satisfy four thousand men, plus women and children, not to mention the leftovers.

The miracles are not yet done. Jesus appears transfigured to his disciples, who hear a voice emerge from a cloud, saying, "This is my Son, the Beloved" (Matthew 17:5). Though the vision appears only to the chosen, the record of it, originally no doubt circulated orally, serves to inform others of the marvel. Jesus then cures an epileptic child, whom his disciples were unable to treat. When the disciples ask, "Why could we not cast out?," Jesus replied, "Because of your little faith" (17:19–20). Those who believe in Jesus can be healed; but to heal others also requires faith. The faith here, as in the case of Peter sinking in the sea as he attempts to walk across its surface at Jesus' bidding, is again trust in Jesus' ability to perform wonders, as a precondition to mending others in the case of his disciples, to whom he granted the power. Of course, this implies belief in his divinity, but there is nothing either transcendental or credal about this kind of faith. It is belief in Jesus, nothing more. Upon his arrival in Jerusalem, as his final hour draws near, Jesus heals the blind and the lame in the temple (Matthew 21:14), a bold provocation. So too, Jesus tells the priests in the temple, "John came to you in the way of righteousness and you did not believe him, but the tax collectors and the prostitutes believed him; and even after you saw it, you did not change your minds and believe him" (21:32). "Believe" here (the verb is *pisteuein*) means "have credence in," "hold what he says to be true"; this is the condition for salvation. Jesus continues to baffle the Pharisees and Sadducees with clever ripostes and parables, another sign of his election, since this too amazes his opponents and wins him trust among the people. In his last moments, he prophesies concerning the future and the end of days, and when he is crucified, there is darkness at noon and upon his death the earth quaked and tombs were opened (Matthew 27:45, 51–52), which causes the guards to exclaim, "Truly this man was God's Son!" (27:54). The final miracle, of course, is the resurrection, and Jesus' apparition before the two Marys and the disciples (Matthew 28:9–10, 16–17), although even then, we are told, most worshipped him but "some doubted" (*hoi de edistasan*, 28:17). It is the ultimate test of faith, and it depends, once again, on trusting that the vision is true and that "all authority in heaven and on earth" (28:18) has indeed been granted to Jesus.

Although I have followed the order of the narrative in the Gospel of Matthew, the wonders are recounted in much the same form in Mark and, with some elaboration and variation, in Luke and in John. For example, in John's version of the blind man whose sight was restored, we are told that the Pharisees denied that Jesus could have performed such a wonder, since he is himself a sinner (*hamartôlos*), having violated the Sabbath (John 9:16; cf. 24). The blind man replies that "God does not listen to sinners" (9:31), but he did heed Jesus, who must therefore be from God. The Pharisees counter: "You were born entirely in sins, and are you trying to teach us?" (9:34). It may be that the Pharisees infer the man's sinfulness from the very fact that he was born sightless. But this is not Jesus' view, nor that of John. As John explains:

> [35] Jesus heard that they had driven him out, and when he found him, he said, "Do you believe in the Son of Man?" [36] He answered, "And who is he, sir? Tell me, so that I may believe in him [*hina pisteusô eis auton*]." [37] Jesus said to him, "You have seen him, and the one speaking with you is he." [38] He said, "Lord, I believe [*pisteuô*]." And he worshiped him. [39] Jesus said, "I came into this world for judgment so that those who do not see may see, and those who do see may become blind." [40] Some of the Pharisees near him heard this and said to him, "Surely we are not blind, are we?" [41] Jesus said to them, "If you were

blind, you would not have sin [*ouk an eikhete hamartian*]. But now that you say, 'We see,' your sin remains [*hê hamartia humôn menei*]".

John 9:35–41

As with every passage and even word in the Bible, there have been reams of commentary and interpretation concerning this episode. I do not propose to investigate all the theological implications of Jesus' words, but rather to call attention once again to the sense of *pistis* (and the corresponding verb *pisteuein*) here, which, as in the other uses we have surveyed so far, continues to signify "trust" rather than some doctrinal or supernatural faith. What is more, we see here a clear connection between *pistis* and sin, and it is now time (if not high time) to return from this excursus on faith and miracles to a consideration of sin itself.

To begin with, it is clear that the blind man's infirmity is not due to a prior offense, as the Pharisees suppose: "His disciples asked him, 'Rabbi, who sinned, this man or his parents, that he was born blind?' Jesus answered, 'Neither this man nor his parents sinned; he was born blind so that God's works might be revealed in him'" (John 9:2–3). This may bear on our interpretation of the innocence of the paralytic as well, with which we began this chapter. What is more, sin is associated closely with the absence of confidence in Jesus; indeed, this is its sole significance. Those whose eyes are truly open and so trust in Jesus as the Son of God will be free of sin; those who believe that they perceive the truth but deny Jesus' divinity will abide in sin, and so are damned. The implied structure is an initial state of sin or *hamartia*, which is annulled by trust in Jesus; this, in turn, is the condition for salvation. We see here a version of the tripartite pattern of sin leading to deliverance that is paradigmatic in the Hebrew Bible, such as we examined in Chapter 2. But the differences are also apparent. There is no falling away, no backsliding, no betrayal of God's covenant here. One turns, not returns, to Jesus. Jesus is new in the world, and confidence in his godhood, rendered visible by his miracles, is a fresh beginning, not a restoration. Faith in Jesus is not contrasted with the worship of idols; there is no chasing after foreign gods, here or elsewhere in the accounts of Jesus' mission. Jesus was primarily addressing fellow Jews, whose God was, he claimed, his father. Nor is there confession: there is nothing to reveal, no fault to admit. The only fault or error is not believing in Jesus, and this is remedied by a change of heart, a conversion, a turning to Jesus. God was now, for the first time, manifesting himself in this world in a human form, and believing this, rather than restoring the relationship defined by the covenant, was the path to eternal life. Sin, in turn, was the rejection of Jesus, the failure to recognize him despite his many wonders. Sin was *apistia*, the lack of belief that he was who he said he was. The formal configuration is the same as in the Tanakh, but the content has been radically transformed.

To see the new status and nature of sin in the Gospels, we must, once again, track the term—in this case, *hamartia* and the corresponding verb—through the texts. So let us look. The intimate connection between sin and forgiveness or absolution in the Gospels is abundantly clear. In the first chapter of the Gospel of Matthew, an angel tells Joseph that Mary "will bear a son, and you are to name him Jesus, for he will save his people from their sins" (Matthew 1:21). Mark introduces the matter of sin in connection with John the Baptist: "John the baptizer appeared in the wilderness, proclaiming a baptism of repentance for the forgiveness of sins. And people from the whole Judean countryside and all the people of Jerusalem were going out to him, and were baptized by him in the river Jordan, confessing their sins" (Mark 1:4–5). Luke cites the prophecy of Zecharia in regard to Jesus: "You, child, will go before the Lord to prepare his ways . . ., to give knowledge of salvation to his people by the forgiveness of their sins" (Luke 1:76–77). But shortly afterwards he says of John the Baptist: "He went into all the region around the Jordan, proclaiming a baptism of repentance for the forgiveness of sins" (Luke 3:3). Matthew too introduces John: "In those days John the Baptist appeared in the wilderness of Judea, proclaiming, 'Repent, for the kingdom of heaven has come near'" (Matthew 3:1–2). And he continues: "Then the people of Jerusalem and all Judea were going out to him, and all the region along the Jordan, and they were baptized by him in the river Jordan, confessing their sins [*exomologoumenoi tas hamartias autôn*]" (3:5–6).[13] But wait! I have just asserted that confession marks one of the differences between the way sin and salvation are represented in the Hebrew Bible and in the New Testament: in the Tanakh, repentance and confession are essential to receiving God's pardon, whereas in the New Testament, faith or trust in Jesus replaces the role of confession. Yet here we find, in two of the four Gospels, people confessing their sins in the hope that they will be forgiven. The distinction that I have drawn would seem to fail at the very first mentions of sin in the New Testament.

We may note, to begin with, that confession is very rare in the New Testament. The verb in question is *exomologeisthai*, or in the simple form (without the prefix *ex-*), *homologein*. These words, and the corresponding nouns, are not in themselves infrequent. The compound verb occurs ten times in the New Testament—twice in Matthew, once in Mark, and twice in Luke, along with once in Acts, twice in Romans, once in Philippians, and once in James—and the simple form, *homologein*, twenty-three times (the abstract noun *homologia* occurs six times).[14] But in most instances, the meaning of the word is not "confess," but rather "acknowledge," "reveal," or "profess"—the older sense of "confess" that survives in the use of the word "confession" to mean "religion" or "faith." To take a couple of examples, at Matthew 11:25 we read: "At that time Jesus said, 'I praise You, Father'"; the word for "praise" is *exomologeisthai*.[15] So too at Luke 10:21, the same verb is rendered, "I thank you, Father" (both in the NRSV translation). At Romans 15:9, we have "glorify." The same word is translated as "confess" at Philippians 2:11, but in the sense of "affirm": "every tongue will confess that Jesus Christ is Lord, to the glory of God the Father." At Luke 22:6 it is rendered as "consented." In Acts 19, however, *homologeisthai* does seem to mean "confess" in the usual modern sense of "admit":

> [11]God did extraordinary miracles through Paul, [12]so that when the handkerchiefs or aprons that had touched his skin were brought to the sick, their diseases left them, and the evil spirits came out of them. [13]Then some itinerant Jewish exorcists tried to use the name of the Lord Jesus over those who had evil spirits, saying, "I adjure you by the Jesus whom Paul proclaims." [14]Seven sons of a Jewish high priest named Sceva were doing this. [15]But the evil spirit said to them in reply, "Jesus I know, and Paul I know; but who are you?" [16]Then the man with the evil spirit leaped on them, mastered them all, and so overpowered them that they fled out of the house naked and wounded. [17]When this became known to all residents of Ephesus, both Jews and Greeks, everyone was awestruck; and the name of the Lord Jesus was praised. [18]Also many of those who became believers confessed and disclosed their practices [*polloi te tôn pepisteukotôn êrkhonto exomologoumenoi kai anangellontes tas praxeis autôn*]. [19]A number of those who practiced magic collected their books and burned them publicly; when the value of these books was calculated, it was found to come to fifty thousand silver coins. [20]So the word of the Lord grew mightily and prevailed.

What is being disclosed or confessed to in this passage is not sin as such but, it would appear, magical practices that are either pure fraud or at worst the work of the devil, as opposed to the miracles performed by Paul.[16]

There are only two places outside the Gospels where there is mention of the confession of sin in the New Testament; one of them, using the word *exomologeisthai*, is in the Epistle of James:

> The prayer of faith [*hê eukhê tês pisteôs*] will save the sick, and the Lord will raise them up; and anyone who has committed sins will be forgiven [*k'an hamartias êi pepoiêkôs aphethêsetai autôi*]. Therefore, confess your sins to one another [*exomologeisthe oun allêlois tas hamartias*], and pray for one another so that you may be healed. The effective prayer of a righteous man can accomplish much.
>
> James 5:15–16

We may note that the faithful are enjoined to confess to one another (*allêlois*) rather than to God, as is generally the case in the Hebrew Bible. The passage suggests a group meeting or congregation of the faithful, where self-revelation can lead to healing (some commentators speak of a "messianic community"). The forgiving of sins, however, is God's work. There is thus a certain gap between the confession of sins, which leads to healing (presumably of physical ailments), and the forgiveness of sins, which depends on the "prayer," or *eukhê*, of faith. *Eukhê* occurs only three times in the New Testament, here and in Acts 18:18 (at Cenchreae Paul had his hair cut, "for he was under [literally, had] a *eukhê*") and 21:23, where it is rendered rather as a "vow" or "oath." In the present passage, "an avowal of faith" is a perfectly legitimate translation, consistent with the use of the term in Acts.[17] Read this way, we have another confirmation that, in the New Testament, it is *pistis* above all that brings about the forgiveness of sins.

At 1 John 1:9, there is again mention of forgiveness of sins, where it is associated more directly with confession: "If we confess our sins [*ean homologômen tas hamartias hêmôn*], he is faithful [*pistos*] and just to forgive us our sins, and to cleanse us from all unrighteousness." Here the crucial word is the simple *homologein*; it recurs at 1 John 2:23, 4:2–3, and 4:15, and again at 2 John 1:7, where, however, it means "acknowledge" or "declare," the usual sense of the verb.[18] Commentators have pointed to a potential inconsistency between what John says here and his remarks a page later, in which he appears to affirm that those who believe in Jesus cannot sin:

> ⁴Everyone who commits sin is guilty of lawlessness; sin is lawlessness [*hê hamartia estin hê anomia*]. ⁵You know that he was revealed to take away sins, and in him there is no sin. ⁶No one who abides in him sins; no one who sins has either seen him or known him. ⁷Little children, let no one deceive you. Everyone who does what is right is righteous, just as he is righteous. ⁸Everyone who commits sin is a child of the devil; for the devil has been sinning from the beginning. The Son of God was revealed for this purpose, to destroy the works of the devil. ⁹Those who have been born of God do not sin, because God's seed abides in them; they cannot sin, because they have been born of God.
>
> 1 John 3:4–9

Thus, Colin Kruse comments on this latter passage: "Still another theme which receives considerable emphasis in 1 John is that those who are born of God do not sin … Such teaching, however, stands in apparent contradiction to what the author says in 1:8–9." Kruse suggests as a way of eliminating the paradox: "The tension between these two parts of the letter is best resolved by recognizing that sin in Chapter 3 is defined as *anomia*, which in context is to be understood as rebellion, and is related to the devil's opposition to God. It is impossible for those born of God to have any part in *anomia*."[19] This seems rather a forced solution. John is not restricting the meaning of sin, he is explaining that sin is as bad as violating the law. That said, John goes on to affirm that those who have seen and known Jesus do not sin: these are the ones whom John describes as "born of God." Those who have not acknowledged Jesus are children of the devil. The message is clear: trust in Jesus is the condition—the only condition—for the remission of sin. As we shall see, this is precisely the lesson of the Gospels as well. What, then, has forgiveness to do with confession, as opposed to faith? In the earlier passage, God is said to be *pistos*—that is, "worthy of trust" (rendered as "faithful" in the NRSV); but still, there is the prior condition of confession. The reason, I suspect, is that John, who may well have been the author of the fourth Gospel, had in mind the tradition of the Hebrew Bible, and in this one instance imported it into his account of salvation through belief in Jesus.[20] Which brings us back to John the Baptist.

The reason why John the Baptist, in contradistinction to Jesus, insists on repentance and the confession of sins as a condition for forgiveness is that he is essentially a prophet in the style of the Tanakh. John wears ashes and sackcloth, in the manner of Hebrew mourners (cf. Nehemiah 9:1; Daniel 9:3), not that of Jesus and his disciples. He cannot appeal to trust in Jesus as the basis for salvation, because Jesus has not yet made himself manifest or provided the proof of his divinity in the form of multiple miracles. Once he has been known and seen, in the words of John's epistle, then the entire story changes. From now on, it is *pistis* or faith in Jesus that constitutes the path to pardon.

We may begin with Luke's account of Jesus and the "sinful woman" (*gunê hamartôlos*, 7:37), who washes his feet and dries them with her hair. "Therefore," Jesus declares: "her sins, which were many, have been forgiven" (7:47). The narrative continues:

> [48] Then he said to her, "Your sins [*hamartiai*] are forgiven." [49] But those who were at the table with him began to say among themselves, "Who is this who even forgives sins [*hamartias*]?" [50] And he said to the woman, "Your faith [*pistis*] has saved you; go in peace".
>
> Luke 7:48–50

What were the woman's sins? There is no indication. Commentators sometimes make guesses. Alternatively, as John Carroll suggests, "the account leaves that gap to be filled by the reader," although he adds: "readers acquainted with the stereotypical depiction in Greco-Roman culture of women slaves and prostitutes as available for music ('flute girls'), conversation, and sexual activity at banquets would likely sympathize with the scandalized dinner host."[21] But Jesus, or the author of the Gospel, shows no interest in identifying the woman's sins, any more than the Gospel writers do in the case of the paralyzed man. She does not confess them, nor does she express repentance. We may infer, if we like, that her gesture toward Jesus intimates a desire to abandon her former ways. Carroll writes: "Willingness to leave behind a disordered life brings one to Jesus, and his acceptance, embodying divine mercy, then invites deepened commitment, perhaps even the radical step of discipleship." And he adds: "All that remains is for the woman to live as one forgiven, as one made whole (healed, saved) because, in her openness to divine mercy, she dared, vulnerable and without shame, to approach Jesus."[22] Perhaps, but Jesus says nothing of this, nor does the woman give any sign of remorse for her previous way of life—if indeed, she will henceforth abandon it. The issue here, again as in the narrative of the crippled man, concerns Jesus' claim to forgive sins, which alarms the Pharisees among whom he is dining. What is Jesus' response? The bare statement that the woman has earned the remission of her sins through her faith or trust in him: "Your *pistis* has saved you." Sin, trust, and forgiveness or salvation: that is the pattern of the remission of sin in the Gospel. It is otiose and misleading to assimilate it to the paradigm of the Hebrew Bible, or to later conceptions of sin.

Contrary to the great majority of cases in the Gospels, in the story of the adulterous woman who is condemned by the Pharisees to be stoned to death, the sin in question is clearly identified. The episode is related only in John, and it is to be noted that it does not appear in the earliest manuscripts. Jesus saves the woman by enjoining anyone who is without sin (ἀναμάρτητος, John 8:7) to cast the first stone. When no one does, Jesus tells the adulterous woman that neither will he condemn her, and he sends her on her way, bidding her not to sin again (8:11). Jesus may be cautioning the woman not to commit adultery any more, but again, there may be the latent implication that now that she has known Jesus and perceived how he saved her life against all expectations, to sin again would be to deny him. We may note that Jesus, or the writer of the Gospel, betrays no interest in what the bystanders' sins may have been. They have seen how he stayed their hands; perhaps this demonstration of his powers, achieved by insight rather than wonder-working in this instance, was enough to spark their faith in him.

John the Baptist says of Jesus: "Here is the Lamb of God who takes away the sin of the world!" (John 1:29). He is the one whom one must know. When Jesus foretells his death to the Jews, he warns them: "I told you that you would die in your sins, for you will die in your sins unless you believe [*pisteusête*, verbal form of *pistis*] that I am he [*hoti egô eimi*]" (John 8:24). Jesus' words are unambiguous: it is belief or trust in him that wipes away sins and brings redemption.[23] The author of Acts (probably Luke of the Gospel) affirms: "Of him all the prophets bear witness that through his name everyone who believes in him receives forgiveness of sins" (Acts 10:43; cf. Luke 19:7–10). Again, "let it be known to you, brethren, that through Him forgiveness of sins is proclaimed to you; by this Jesus everyone who believes is set free from all those sins from which you could not be freed by the law of Moses" (Acts 13:38–39); both times the verb is *pisteuein*. So too, the apostle urges: "Now why do you delay? Get up and be baptized, and wash away your sins, calling on his name" (Acts 22:16). Paul tells King Agrippa how Jesus opened his eyes and sent him among the people, "that they may receive forgiveness of sins and an inheritance among those who have been sanctified by faith in me" (Acts 26:18). Paul continues: "After that, King Agrippa, I was not disobedient to the heavenly vision, but declared first to those in Damascus, then in Jerusalem and throughout the countryside of Judea, and also to the Gentiles, that they should repent and turn to God and do deeds consistent with repentance" (26:19–20). Paul would seem to be reverting to John the Baptist in his emphasis on repentance, but as we shall see shortly, the Greek word in question in fact has quite another significance.

Paul's epistle to the Romans contains more references to sin than any other book in the New Testament: thirty with the noun *hamartia* (the runner up is the Epistle to the Hebrews, with twenty-four), six with the verb (surpassed only by 1 John with seven), and one with *hamartêma* (synonymous with *hamartia*, but occurring only four times in the New Testament). Only with the adjective *hamartôlos* does it fall behind (three occurrences; Luke wins hands down with seventeen). Paul, unlike Jesus, tends to associate *hamartia* with the weakness of the flesh; as he says, "with the mind I myself serve the law of God; but with the flesh the law of sin" (Romans 7:25). Or again: "For what the law could not do, in that it was weak through the flesh, God sending his own Son in the likeness of sinful flesh, and for sin, condemned sin in the flesh" (Romans 8:3). Paul's sense of a division in the self, an inability to control the promptings of the body, may well be indebted to Platonism, as Emma Wasserman has argued. As she puts it, "a Platonic discourse about the soul provides for a more coherent interpretation of Paul's diverse statements about sin"; the "new life in Christ" that Paul promises is best understood, she explains, as "a new state of self-control."[24] The body, in turn, stands for the irrational part of the soul. As Wasserman states, "the self of Romans 7 is not whole but rather split between its rational and irrational parts"; thus, Paul's notion of sin must be understood in relation to a tension internal to the spirit.[25] But the way to overcome sin is not through Socratic reasoning or dialectic but through faith. Of the various prohibitions concerning food in the Hebrew Bible, Paul says: "I know and am persuaded in the Lord Jesus that nothing is unclean in itself." Still, he reasons, one must not offend the sensibilities of others; thus, "it is unclean for anyone who thinks it unclean" (Romans 14:14–15). In the end, what counts is *pistis*: "But he who doubts is condemned if he eats, because his eating is not from faith; and whatever is not from faith is sin" (14:23).[26]

As in the Hebrew Bible and in English, there are various words in Greek that indicate evil or iniquity, for example, *ponêron, kakon, rhadiourgia, adikia, anomia, skandalon, planê, alisgêma,* and *paraptôma*. These terms, which are variously rendered in English, refer to vices or transgressions, but usually do not bear the same relation to forgiveness as *hamartia*. In the Gospel of Mark, when the Pharisees criticize the disciples for not washing before eating, as ritual demands (Mark 7:1–8), Jesus counters that all foods are clean (7:19), and he explains: "For it is from within, from the human heart, that evil intentions [*hoi dialogismoi hoi kakoi*] come: fornication, theft, murder, adultery, avarice, wickedness, deceit, licentiousness, envy, slander, pride, folly. All these evil things [*panta tauta ta ponêra*] come from within, and they defile a person" (7:21–23). The behavior that Jesus condemns is unequivocally bad, but he does not employ the word *hamartia* in this connection. So too, in listing the commandments that one must observe, Jesus says: "You shall not murder; You shall not commit adultery; You shall not steal; You shall not bear false witness; Honor your father and mother; also, You shall love your neighbor as yourself" (Matthew 19:18–19). But Jesus does not apply here the word *hamartia*. At Acts 15:20, Paul recommends that gentiles should abstain from things that are polluted (*alisgêmata*), such as idols, fornication, and blood.[27] In his epistle to the Romans, Paul declares: "For the wrath of God is revealed from heaven against all ungodliness and wickedness of those who by their wickedness suppress the truth" (Romans 1:18). Shortly afterwards, Paul goes into greater detail:

> And since they did not see fit to acknowledge God, God gave them up to a debased mind and to things that should not be done. They were filled with every kind of wickedness, evil, covetousness, malice. Full of envy, murder, strife, deceit, craftiness, they are gossips, slanderers, God-haters, insolent, haughty, boastful, inventors of evil, rebellious toward parents, foolish, faithless, heartless, ruthless.
>
> Romans 1:28–31

When Paul accused the magician Elymas of doing works of the devil, as he attempted to turn the proconsul, Sergius Paulus, away from *pistis* (Acts 13:8), he berated him: "You son of the devil, you enemy of all righteousness, full of all deceit and villainy" (Acts 13:10). Paul did not accuse Elymas of sinning, since that would have elicited the possibility of forgiveness. Rather, Paul blinded him, by way of teaching a lesson to Sergius.

It is true that forgiveness is sometimes associated with one or another of these words for iniquity, as opposed to sin proper. Thus, in the Sermon on the Mount, Jesus says that God will forgive trespasses (*paraptômata*) if humans do so among themselves (Matthew 6:14–15). This locution is motivated, I believe, by the context, in which divine and human forgiveness are contrasted. Since humans cannot pardon sins, Jesus avoids the term *hamartia* here.[28] Matthew uses the language of debts, which of course human beings may cancel, along with trespasses: "And forgive us our debts [*opheilêmata*], as we also have forgiven our debtors... For if you forgive others their trespasses [*paraptômata*], your heavenly Father will also forgive you, but if you do not forgive others, neither will your Father forgive your trespasses" (Matthew 6:12, 14–15). In Luke's version of the Lord's Prayer, God's forgiveness of sins is compared to, and at the same time contrasted with, human beings' remission of debts: "And forgive us our sins, for we ourselves forgive everyone indebted to us." (11:4). Human beings cannot remit sins; cancelling a debt—a perfectly human gesture of kindness or liberality—is analogous to God's forgiveness. So too, in exhorting people not to judge or condemn others, Jesus affirms, "Acquit [*apoluete*] and you will be acquitted" (Luke 6:37), avoiding the usual term for forgiving (*aphienai*), more properly used of God; we may compare the Hebrew *salakh* [סָלַח], which takes only God as subject (see Chapter 2, p. 48). An apparent exception to the rule is Acts 8:22, where Peter says: "Turn away [*metanoêson*] from this *kakia* [evil] and beg God that this thought in your heart may be forgiven [*aphethêsetai*]." Perhaps we are to understand that the thought is sinful, although the behavior that one is enjoined to abandon is, in itself, iniquitous but not a sin proper. As Paul says, "whatever is not from faith is sin" (Romans 14:23).

Contrariwise, where forgiveness is not mentioned, another term often substitutes for *hamartia*, e.g. *skandalizein* or "cause to stumble"; an example is Matthew 5:29–30: "If your right eye offend you [*skandalizei*], etc." At Matthew 13:41–42, the NRSV reads: "The Son of Man will send his angels, and they will collect out of his kingdom all causes of sin and all evildoers." But the Greek for "sin" here is *skandala* and that for "evildoers" is, more literally, those who do things contrary to the law" (*tous poiountas tên anomian*; cf. *skandalisêi* [verbal form] and *skandala* at Matthew 18:6–9, Mark 9:42–48). It makes a difference that the Gospel writer here avoided the word *hamartia*. In the parable of the prodigal son (Luke 18–21), the son affirms that he sinned against Heaven and the father feels pity (*esplankhnisthê*); he of course cannot forgive sins. So too, God may be gracious (*khrêstos*) toward the wicked and ungrateful (*tous akharistous kai ponêrous*), and pitying (*oiktirôn*) to those who show pity (Luke 6:35–36); again, the analogy between God and human beings invites vocabulary other than that of sin and forgiveness. There is an anomalous case in which Peter is told to forgive his brother (*aphêsô autôi*) even if he sins against him (*hamartêsei eis eme*) multiple times (Matthew 18:21–22; but see below, p. 108, on the possible meaning of "brother" here; cf. *hamartêsêi eis se* at 18:15, where Jesus offers instructions for resolving conflict). In the following parable of the unforgiving servant, however, Jesus speaks of the remission of a debt (*daneion*), not of sin. Human reconciliation may be signified also by the term *kharizesthai*, "be gracious." An example is Ephesians 4:32, where Paul exhorts his readers to "be kind [*khrêstoi*] to one another, tenderhearted [*eusplankhnoi*], forgiving [*kharizomenoi*] one another, as God in Christ has forgiven [*ekharisato*] you" (NRSV). To be sure, sin is not mentioned here, but neither, in fact, is forgiveness. As so often, when comparing human and divine clemency, the authors of the New Testament eschew the technical language of forgiveness (*aphesis*, or the verbal form, *aphiêmi*), and resort to other terms more appropriate to interpersonal relations (cf. Colossians 3:12–13, where much the same vocabulary is in play).[29]

The negative affirmation that only sins against the Holy Spirit are not forgiven (Matthew 12:31–32, cf. Mark 3:28; Luke 12:10) reinforces the association between sin and forgiveness indirectly. For the forgiver par excellence, that is, God, nevertheless may withhold pardon for certain kinds of offenses (just which remains a matter of dispute among critics). There are various mentions of sins that are not necessarily pardoned. John speaks of the sin of the one who handed Jesus over to Pilate (19:11), and Mark affirms that forgiveness is denied to outsiders who fail to understand parables (4:12). Mark speaks too of a sinful [*hamartôlôi*] and adulterous generation (8:38), and, according to Luke, Peter says that he himself is sinful (5:8). Forgiveness is not mentioned, though of course it may be assumed, especially in the case of Peter. But it is not confession that will save him, but rather his faith.

When he perceives that Jesus has been sentenced to death, Judas experiences regret for having betrayed him—the verb is *metamelomai* rather than *metanoein*—and he declares that he sinned before the Jewish priests who had paid him:

> ³When Judas, his betrayer, saw that Jesus was condemned, he repented [μεταμεληθείς] and brought back the thirty pieces of silver to the chief priests and the elders. ⁴He said, "I have sinned [*hêmarton*] by betraying innocent blood." But they said, "What is that to us? See to it yourself." ⁵Throwing down the pieces of silver in the temple, he departed; and he went and hanged himself.
>
> Matthew 27:3–5; cf. Mark 14:41

In seeking absolution from the Jewish priests, Judas reveals yet again his failure to place his trust in Jesus, which is the only route to forgiveness. Even as he changes his mind, he misdirects his appeal and imagines that confessing to having sinned will earn redemption. The priests withhold even a gesture of compassion—it is not clear that they could forgive a sin—and with this, Judas despairs and takes his own life.

On rare occasions, forgiveness may be granted for behavior that is not strictly sinful, at least to the extent that there are extenuating circumstances. In a remarkable passage, which is not present in all manuscripts of the Bible, Jesus speaks from the cross and says, "Father, forgive [*aphes*] them; for they know not what they do" (Luke 23:34).[30] It is not clear to whom Jesus refers, but he might be taken to be exonerating all who conspired in his crucifixion. Peter Abelard, in his treatise, *Ethics or "Know Yourself"*, asks: "if such people's ignorance is hardly to be counted as a sin at all, then why does the Lord himself pray for those crucifying him, saying 'Father, forgive them, for they do not know what they are doing' …? For where no fault preceded, there doesn't appear to be anything to be excused."[31] Aristotle observed that pardon (his word is *sungnômê*, frequently rendered as "forgiveness") is granted when people act either under external compulsion or in excusable ignorance of the facts or circumstances (*Nicomachean Ethics*, 1109b18–1111a2). An example is Oedipus' slaying of his father: this is not culpable parricide, because Oedipus did not recognize Laius and because there was no reasonable way he could have known who he was. His action was, in this sense, not voluntary, and when he discovered the full truth of what he had done, Oedipus' response was to blind himself. As Aristotle observes, if someone commits an offence in ignorance, but later, upon learning the facts, feels no regret (*en metameleiâi*), then he or she is hardly worthy of pity or pardon (cf. 1110b33–1111a2). Those who condemned Jesus were in a condition similar to that of Oedipus: they did not know that he was the Son of God. Should they have known? Certainly, his miracles ought to have convinced them that he was no ordinary wonder-worker or charlatan; they ought to have believed and trusted him. The passage is unusual in the context of the Gospels because elsewhere a failure of faith counts precisely as sin. It appears to provide a loophole, by which those who have not had *pistis* in Jesus are not utterly condemned. If they acted in ignorance, then their deed, as Abelard noted, falls short of sin, and indeed the word *hamartia* does not appear in this episode.

There is no indication as to whether those ignorant people whom Jesus wished to forgive felt regret afterwards. Presumably they would have, once they were aware of his true nature. Would they have been expected to repent? We have seen that John the Baptist summoned the people repent and confess their sins: "John the baptizer appeared in the wilderness, proclaiming a baptism of repentance for the forgiveness of sins" (Mark 1:4). "Then he began to reproach the cities in which most of his deeds of power had been done, because they did not repent" (Matthew 11:20). But John, as we have remarked, preceded the appearance of Jesus, and his call may be seen as a vestige of the emphasis on remorse in the Hebrew Bible. Yet Jesus himself seems to demand penitence, as when he intones: "Woe to you, Chorazin! Woe to you, Bethsaida! For if the deeds of power done in you had been done in Tyre and Sidon, they would have repented long ago in sackcloth and ashes" (11:21). Luke records Jesus' rebuke to the Pharisees: "I have come to call not the righteous but sinners to repentance [*metanoian*]" (Luke 5:32). Jesus warns the Galileans: "unless you repent, you will all perish as they did" (Luke 13:3)—that is, those who were killed earlier by Pilate. He concludes the parable of the lost sheep with the words, "there will be more joy in heaven over one sinner who repents [*metanoounti*, verbal form of *metanoia*] than over ninety-nine righteous persons who need no repentance" (Luke 15:7). And the parable of the lost coin ends with the words: "Just so, I tell you, there is joy in the presence of the angels of God over one sinner who repents" (Luke 13:10). As Peter says in Acts, "Repent, and be baptized every one of you in the name of Jesus Christ so that your sins may be forgiven" (Acts 2:38); or again in Acts 3:19: "Therefore repent and return, so that your sins may be wiped away." Or this: "While God has overlooked the times of human ignorance, now he commands all people everywhere to repent, because he has fixed a day on which he will have the world judged in righteousness by a man whom he has appointed, and of this he has given assurance to all by raising him from the dead" (Acts 17:30–31). Or again, in Acts 5:31: "He is the one whom God exalted to His right hand as a Prince and a Savior, to grant repentance to Israel, and forgiveness of sins." In a somewhat more abstract vein, characteristic of the Epistle to the Hebrews, we read: "Therefore let us go on toward perfection, leaving behind the basic teaching about Christ, and not laying again the foundation: repentance [*metanoia*] from dead works and faith [πίστις] toward God" (Hebrews 6:1).[32]

Jesus is even more emphatic a few chapters later in the Gospel of Luke, as he admonishes the disciples: "If a brother sins [*hamartêi*], you must rebuke the offender, and if there is repentance, you must forgive. And if the same person sins against you seven times a day, and turns back to you seven times and says, 'I repent [*metanoô*]' you must forgive him [*aphêseis autôi*]" (Luke 17:3–4). This appears to be an exceptional case, in which human beings are appointed to forgive sins. But some translations, like the NRSV, render the Greek word for brother (*adelphos*) as "disciple." Indeed, Jesus not only endowed the disciples with the power to perform wonders (see Matthew 10:1; Mark 6:7), he also passed on to them the ability to forgive. As Jesus tells them: "If you forgive the sins of any, they are forgiven them; if you retain the sins of any, they are retained" (John 20: 23). This gift is the basis of the priest's capacity to absolve sins after confession in the Catholic Church. Cyprian, citing this very passage, affirms that "only they who are set over the Church and established in the Gospel law, and in the ordinance of the Lord, are allowed to baptize and to give remission of sins" (*Epistle* 72.7). The disciples are thus standing in for Jesus, as he stands in for his Father.

It would certainly appear, from the above passages, that repentance, and with it a focus on one's previous errors, is central to the remission of sins in the New Testament. But despite appearances, the case is not so clear. I have been citing throughout the New Revised Standard Version, which is often taken to be the authoritative and most accurate translation of the Bible into English. In every case, the word that is translated as "repentance" is *metanoia*, and the verb for "repent" is *metanoein*. But is this the proper rendering of the term? As it happens, a great many recent translations of the Bible in a wide variety of languages take *metanoia* rather to mean "conversion," or the like. This is a far cry from repentance, as we normally conceive of it. Before proceeding to argue the case, let me illustrate this new tendency by citing some examples of both the older translation of John the Baptist's mission and the newer (Mark 1:4; Luke 3:3).

The King James Bible gives "the baptism of repentance for the remission of sins." But the recent version by David Bentley Hart reads, "a baptism of the heart's transformation, for forgiveness of sins."[33] Clearly, this is no mere matter of stylistic variation: the heart's transformation is not at all the same idea as repentance, as we normally understand the word. The New Century Version, in turn, has: "John was baptizing people in the desert and preaching a baptism of changed hearts and lives for the forgiveness of sins." So too, recent translations of the Bible into languages other than English frequently render *metanoia* as "conversion." Thus, although the Spanish Nueva Versión Internacional (NVI) renders Luke 3:3 as "Juan recorría toda la región del Jordán predicando el bautismo de arrepentimiento para el perdón de pecados", and La Biblia de las Américas (LBLA), in turn, has "predicando un bautismo de arrepentimiento para el perdón de los pecados", the La Palabra version has "un bautismo como signo de conversión para recibir el perdón de los pecados"—"conversión" has replaced "arrepentimiento" or repentance here. So too, the Traducción en lenguaje actual (TLA) offers the locution, "Be baptized and turn to God": "'¡Bautícense y vuélvanse a Dios! Sólo así Dios los perdonará.'" A few more examples: The Italian Nuova Riveduta 2006 (NR2006) has "repentance": "un battesimo di ravvedimento per il perdono dei peccati"; but the Conferenza Episcopale Italiana (CEI) version gives "un battesimo di conversione per il perdono dei peccati". In what is still the standard Protestant Bible in German, Martin Luther rendered the verses as "die Taufe der Buße zur Vergebung Sünden", that is, "a baptism of penance." But the Gute Nachricht Bibel has "Kehrt um und lasst euch taufen, denn Gott will euch eure Schuld vergeben!"—literally, "turn round," that is, the basic sense of "convert" (cf. English "revert," etc.).[34] Dictionaries of the Bible and commentaries on particular books testify to the same uncertainty about how to understand the Greek term *metanoia*.[35]

Let me put my cards on the table: I firmly believe that "conversion" or "change of heart" is the proper rendering. Jesus is not asking his followers to look back to their sins and repent of them, but rather to look forward to their new faith in Jesus. It is time now to set forth the reasons for this judgment. To begin with, the meaning of *metanoia* in classical Greek is more like "second thoughts" or a change of mind, the recognition that a given action turned out wrong, or that it was wrong to do it. *Metanoia* is a compound, with the prefix, *meta-*, signifying "after," and the root *noein* meaning "think" (compare *nous* or "mind," "paranoia," etc.). It thus often was intellectual in nature, more like regret, in the non-moral sense, as in "I regret that I didn't bring an umbrella today, since it ended up raining." In Latin, the word *paenitentia*, which is obviously the source of the English "penitence," and its cognates have much the same range of meanings.

Let us look at some uses of the word. The great *Greek-English Lexicon of the New Testament and Other Early Christian Literature*, which is really much more than that since it also covers earlier, classical uses, offers as the first definition of *metanoia* "a change of mind."[36] Thus, Thucydides (3.36.4) reports that the Athenians changed their mind about the destruction of Mytilene, after the city revolted, and decided to execute only the ringleaders (who numbered, Thucydides affirms, more than a thousand, 3.50.1). There is no repentance here in the sense of a profound reckoning with one's former self. In the comical mock-epic, *The Battle of the Frogs and Mice*, a mouse regrets having accepted the offer to mount on the frog's back and set out upon the lake, once it finds itself amidst the waves (v. 79). A fragment of the comic poet Philemon, a contemporary of Menander, warns: "Whoever wishes to marry is heading for *metanoia*," that is, regret at the outcome, not remorse for former sins or crimes. The speaker in the first of Antiphon's tetralogies—that is, rhetorical exercises that offer condensed versions of speeches by and against the accused—declares that he is innocent of the charges and warns the jurors not to put him to death. "Do not recognize your error [*hamartian*] after having changed your minds [*metanoêsantes*]; *metanoia* for such things cannot be remedied," he says (2.4.12). The speaker's point is that a change of opinion after the fact is useless in capital cases. The next definition offered by the lexicon is "repentance, turning about, conversion," and it adds: "Mostly of the positive side of repentance, as the beginning of a new relationship with God," citing various passages in the New Testament.

In Acts 19:4, Paul states that "John baptized with the baptism of *metanoia*, telling the people to believe [*pisteusôsin*] in the one who was to come after him, that is, in Jesus." This affirmation is clearly an expansion of Mark and Luke's mention of John the Baptist's mission (Mark 1:4, Luke 3:3), but there is an important addition. The injunction to adopt the new faith can be interpreted not as a distinct and separate idea—repent *and* believe—but as a specification of the sense of *metanoia*: to be baptized in conversion is tantamount to belief or trust in Jesus. Paul says of Jesus: "All the prophets testify about him that everyone who believes in him receives forgiveness of sins through his name" (Acts 10:43). The phrasing is clearly parallel to a "baptism of repentance for the remission of sins," with *pistis* (or the corresponding verb) taking the place of *metanoia* as the condition of the remission (*aphesis*) of sins. So too, when Paul declares, "by this Jesus everyone who believes is set free from all those sins from which you could not be freed by the law of Moses" (Acts 13:39), it is *pistis*, rather than *metanoia*, that earns forgiveness of sin. We may see the equivalence still more clearly in Paul's phrasing, "as I testified to both Jews and Greeks about *metanoia* toward God and faith [*pistis*] toward our Lord Jesus" (Acts 20:21). Here, *metanoia* and *pistis* appear to be basically equivalent: conversion to God and faith in Jesus are parallel expressions ("repentance toward [Greek *eis*] God" sounds as odd in Greek as it is in English). We may compare Acts 13:38, where Paul avers that "through this man forgiveness of sins is proclaimed to you." We have seen that the standard translations of Acts 3:19 runs: "Repent [*metanoêsate*] therefore, and turn again [*epistrepsate*], that your sins may be blotted out" (Revised Standard Version. RSV); but the pairing of *metanoein*, literally "rethinking," with "turning toward" or conversion suggests that we understand *metanoia* in its normal classical meaning, that "positive side of repentance" of which the dictionary speaks. So too, Paul declared to all of Judaea and to the gentiles as well "that they should *metanoein* and turn to God [*epistrephein epi ton theon*] and do deeds worthy of *metanoia*" (Acts 26:20). It is perfectly possible to take the prepositional phrase "to God" with both *metanoein* and *epistrephein*: "convert to God and turn to God" (again, "repent to God" would be odd). And the deeds that believers are asked to perform are presumably worthy of their new faith, their change of heart (for *epistrephein* or turning to the Lord, cf. 2 Corinthians 3:16; 1 Thessalonians 1:9 on turning to [*pros*] God and away from [*apo*] idols). There is a similar conjunction of belief with the verb *metamelomai*, a synonym of *metanoein*, at Matthew 21:32: "For John came to you in the way of righteousness, and you did not believe him [*episteusate*], but the tax collectors and the harlots believed him; and even when you saw it, you did not afterward change your minds [*metemelêthête*] and believe [*pisteusai*] him" (RSV). Jesus' criticism follows directly upon the parable about the son who changed his mind [verb: *metamelomai*] about going to work in the vineyard (21:29); there is no suggestion of repentance here. The sense of a change of heart, as opposed to penance, is again evident at 2 Peter 3:9: "The Lord is not slow about his promise as some count slowness, but is forbearing toward you, not wishing that any should perish, but that all should reach *metanoia*" (RSV), or, more literally, "arrive to [*eis*] *metanoia*." At 2 Timothy 2:25, we read: "correcting his opponents with gentleness, God may perhaps grant them *metanoia* tending to a knowledge of the truth." God grants a new way of thinking that leads to knowledge, just as at 2 Corinthians 7:10 *metanoia* leads to salvation: true faith is the condition for being saved. A change of heart may be accompanied by outward signs of grief, exemplified paradigmatically by the image of sackcloth and ashes, associated above all with John the Baptist. It is true that Jesus employs the image, when he warns: "Woe to you, Chorazin! Woe to you, Bethsaida! For if the deeds of power done in you had been done in Tyre and Sidon, they would have repented long ago in sackcloth and ashes" (Matthew 11:21; cf. Luke 10:13). But it is worth noting that the reference here is to the kind of penitence that was practiced in by the Israelites before the coming of Jesus, so vividly evoked by Nehemiah (9:1–3):

> Now on the twenty-fourth day of this month the people of Israel were assembled with fasting and in sackcloth, and with earth on their heads. Then those of Israelite descent separated themselves from all foreigners, and stood and confessed their sins and the iniquities of their ancestors. They stood up in their place and read from the book of the law of the Lord their God for a fourth part of the day, and for another fourth they made confession and worshiped the Lord their God.

Metanoia and its cognates are concentrated above all in Luke and Acts and to a lesser degree in Revelation (together amounting to about two-thirds of the total occurrences). It is relatively infrequent in the Pauline epistles, but the instances are illuminating. A central passage is 2 Corinthians 7:8–10:

> For even if I distressed [*elupêsa*] you with my letter, I do not regret [*metamelomai*] it (although I did regret [*metemelomên*] it, [for] I see that

that letter distressed [*elupêsen*] you, if only briefly). Now I rejoice, not because you were distressed [*elupêthête*], but because you were distressed [*elupêthête*] toward *metanoia*; for you were distressed [*elupêthête*] in regard to God, so that you were not harmed in any way by us. For distress [*lupê*] in regard to God produces an unregretful [*ametamelêtos*] *metanoia* ... tending to salvation, but the distress [*lupê*] of the world produces death.

NRSV, much modified

This is the most salient passage in the Bible for a comparison between the values of *metanoia* and *metameleia*, and also for the relationship between distress and regret. It is perhaps natural to think of *lupê* as an aspect of repentance, understood as redemptive suffering,[37] but what Paul says is that a previous letter of his (probably not 1 Corinthians) produced dismay in its recipients; he does not say why, but it is reasonable to suppose that he was critical of their practices or beliefs. He professes to regret the pain he caused, but is nevertheless pleased because it moved them to *metanoia*. *Lupê* here is not a sign of remorse but a stimulus to a change of heart. They will not regret the change later, since it was, on Paul's view, a positive one: the paradoxical expression *metanoia ametamelêtos*, "a change of heart that will not be regretted," signifies the kind of alteration of opinion that is not subject to further afterthought. There is no evident contrast between *metanoia* and *metameleia*.[38]

The sense of *ametamelêtos* is confirmed by Romans 11:29, where Paul declares that "the gifts and the call of God are irrevocable [*ametamelêta*]" (RSV), that is, not subject to a change of heart on the part of God. For human beings, however, a refusal to change one's mind or heart can be blameworthy, if it means rejecting faith in the Lord. Thus, at Romans 2:4–5 Paul exclaims: "Do you not know that God's kindness [*to khrêston tou theou*] is meant to lead you to *metanoia*? But by your hardness and *ametanoêton* heart you are storing up wrath for yourself on the day of wrath when God's righteous judgment will be revealed" (RSV, slightly modified). The human heart must admit of change, or it will be damned on judgment day.

To sum up: the biblical terms typically rendered as "repent" and "repentance" are best understood as a change of mind leading toward true belief, that is, a conversion. *Metanoia* does not presuppose a painful reflection upon and rejection of one's past sins, like modern "remorse," nor is it an enduring state of mind, a permanent grief over one's sinful condition.[39] *Metanoia* is a punctual phenomenon, and when achieved it leads to joy and salvation, even if the association between *metanoia* and the remission of sin may insinuate a latent feeling of guilt. Jesus asks not for a reckoning of one's past faults as a condition for forgiveness, but for a change of heart directed toward God and belief or confidence in his own divinity. That is the route to the remission of sin, and sin itself, in this new dispensation, is precisely the failure to make the necessary turn, to convert to *pistis* in Jesus Christ.

The preceding discussion helps to clarify a passage in the Gospel of John that has been the cause of much discussion and perplexity. Jesus affirms: "If I had not come and spoken to them, they would not have sin; but now they have no excuse for their sin ... If I had not done among them the works that no one else did, they would not have sin" (John 15:22, 24). John Calvin, commenting on this passage, wrote: "It may be thought that Christ intended by these words to say, that there is no other sin but unbelief; and there are some who think so. Augustine speaks more soberly, but he approaches to that opinion; for, since faith forgives and blots out all sins, he says, that the only sin that damns a man is unbelief."[40] Calvin himself rejected this interpretation. He allows that it is true, to the extent that "unbelief not only hinders men from being delivered from the condemnation of death, but is the source and cause of all evils." However, he adds: "But the whole of that reasoning is inapplicable to the present passage; for the word *sin* is not taken in a general sense, but as related to the subject which is now under consideration." Calvin explains that it is "as if Christ had said, that their ignorance is utterly inexcusable, because in his person they maliciously rejected God; just as if we were to pronounce a person to be innocent, just, and pure, when we wished merely to acquit him of a single crime of which he had been accused. Christ's acquittal of them, therefore, is confined to one kind of *sin*, because it takes away from the Jews every pretense of ignorance in this *sin*, of despising and hating the Gospel."[41] This is ingenious, but unnecessary. As we have seen again and again, trust or faith in Jesus, or, what amounts to the same thing, a conversion or change of heart in their relation to him, wipes away sin. Jesus never demands confession, and no one confesses to him. The particularities of their prior offenses, iniquity, trespasses, or wickedness are of no concern to him. All are summed up in the condition of disbelief or *apistia*. As Jesus avers, the Paraclete will come and will convict the world of sin, "because they do not believe in me" (John 16:8–9). Had they believed, they would not have sin.

The author of Acts explains: "While God has overlooked the times of human ignorance, now he commands all people everywhere to repent [or rather, convert: μετανοεῖν], because he has fixed a day on which he will have the world judged in righteousness by a man whom he has appointed, and of this he has given assurance [or rather, confidence: *pistis*] to all by raising him from the dead" (17:30–31). The logic is clear: Jesus' resurrection is the sure indication of his divinity; this is the source of *pistis* for all people. God disregards ignorance of Jesus in the past, since he could not be known, save perhaps by the prophets who foresaw his arrival (as their words are interpreted in the New Testament). But now, when his miraculous deeds, culminating in the resurrection, are visible to all, those who experience a transformation or conversion will be among the saved, whereas those who do not trust in him are condemned. Paul writes to the Corinthians: "It is written: 'I believed; therefore I have spoken.' Since we have that same spirit of faith, we also believe and therefore speak, because we know that the one who raised the Lord Jesus from the dead will also raise us with Jesus and present us with you to himself" (2 Corinthians 4:13–14). Or again: "we walk by faith," (rendered in the NRSV as "we live by faith": 2 Corinthians 5:7). Paul writes to the Galatians (2:15–16): "We ourselves are Jews by birth and not Gentile sinners; yet we know that a person is justified not by the works of the law but through faith in Jesus Christ. And we have come to believe in Christ Jesus, so that we might be justified by faith in Christ, and not by doing the works of the law, because no one will be justified by the works of the law." And he adds: "And the life I now live in the flesh I live by faith in the Son of God, who loved me and gave himself for me" (2:20). Paul asks, "What does a believer have in common with an unbeliever?" (*tis meris pistôi meta apistou*, 2 Corinthians 6:15); the answer, of course, is nothing at all.

We might be inclined to suppose that belief in Jesus' resurrection is a kind of propositional faith: not trust that it happened so much as credence in the doctrine that Christ died for our sins. Paul seems to have subscribed to such a view, although the evidence is not decisive. At 1 Corinthians 15:3, Paul affirms: "For I delivered to you as of first importance what I also received, that Christ died for our sins according to the Scriptures." And he adds: "if Christ has not been raised, your faith is worthless; you are still in your sins" (1 Corinthians 15:17). Again, at Romans 4:25 Paul explains: "He was delivered over to death for our sins and was raised to life for our justification." Our old humanity (*palaios* ... *anthrôpos*) was crucified along with Christ (Romans 6:6), with the result that sin was annulled. At 1 Thessalonians 4:14, Paul affirms: "we believe that Jesus died and rose again, and so we believe that God will bring with Jesus those who have fallen asleep in him." The epistles ascribed to Peter make the point still more doctrinally: "He himself bore our sins in his body on the cross, so that we might die to sins and live for righteousness; by his wounds you have been healed" (1 Peter 2:24; cf. 1 Peter 3:18). These statements, it seems to me, constitute an interpretation of Jesus' crucifixion, but are not the motive that is given in the Gospels themselves. As Jesus explains to the disciples, when they try to discourage him from going to Jerusalem, where his life will be in danger: "Do you think that I cannot appeal to my Father, and he will at once send me more than twelve legions of angels? But how then would the scriptures be fulfilled, which say it must happen in this way?" (Matthew 26:53–54). Jesus died as he did because so was it prophesied.

Paul defends the unique importance of *pistis* by citing Abraham's faith, which in turn is reckoned as righteousness (*dikaiosunê*, Romans 4:5, 9–22; cf. Galatians 3:6); the claim is part of an argument to the effect that the uncircumcised too will be saved, if they believe. So too, the author of the Epistle to the Hebrews affirms that Moses was angry with those who sinned (*tois hamartêsasin*) during the crossing of the desert, because, he adds, of their unbelief (*apistia*, Hebrews 3:17–18; Moses himself was *pistos*, 3:2, 5). Abel, Enoch, Noah, Abraham, Isaac, and Jacob are all said to have lived and died by faith (*pistei*, dative of *pistis*, Hebrews 11:4–39). These ascriptions of *pistis* to revered figures in the Hebrew Bible are rhetorical strategies to project retroactively the kind of faith or trust in God that is the hallmark of belief in Jesus. More especially, Paul argues that sin (*hamartia*), and consequently death, came into the world as a result of one person—that is, Adam—and death spread to all mankind because all have sinned (Romans 5:12).[42] Adam's offense is not said to be the cause of all subsequent sin, although this passage has been invoked in support of the doctrine of original sin, a topic that will be discussed in the following chapter.

Paul notes, however, that although sin was in the world, it was not counted (or did not count) before there was law, and so it was death rather than sin that reigned from Adam to Moses (Romans 5:13–14). It is perhaps for this reason that Paul refers to Adam's transgression (*parabasis*),[43] trespass (*paraptôma*), or disobedience (*parakoê*), rather than to sin (5:14–20). The law itself (*nomos*) is not sin (*hamartia*), as Paul firmly asserts (Romans 7:7); and yet, as he says, "I would not have known sin, except through the law" (cf. 1 Corinthians 15:56 "the power of sin is the law"). As Paul explains, "I would not have known what it is to covet if the law had not said, 'You shall not covet'" (7:7). Before there is a prohibition, one cannot transgress or violate it. The thought is perhaps of a piece with the claim, in the first Epistle of John, that "sin [*hamartia*] is lawlessness [*anomia*], the violation of *nomos*" (1 John 3:4): there must be law if there is to be sin. But that kind of sin, which is a function of the law, belongs to Paul's past life, when he committed the sins that the law proscribed. As he says, "I died, and I found that the same commandment [*entolê*] that led to life led rather to death" (Romans 7:10). The sin that the commandment enabled deceived and killed him (7:11). But with the coming of Christ and Paul's own conversion, the sin that remains is rooted in the flesh and limbs of the body, and represents a law that wages war against the law of the mind (*antistrateuomenon tôi nomôi tou noos mou*, 7:23). This law Paul identifies with his authentic self (*autos egô*, 7:25, misleadingly translated in the NRSV as "with my mind"). Henceforth, if one dwells in the spirit (*en pneumati*, Romans 8:9) rather than in the flesh, then one may be counted among the elect of God. Although Paul in this passage speaks of hope (*elpis*, 8:24) and love (*agapê*, 8:35), these form part of the triad of "faith, hope, and charity," and for all that Paul assigns precedence to love (1 Corinthians 13:13), his point is that, without these, one is condemned to remain in the sin of the flesh (cf. the expression *sarx hamartias*, "the flesh of sin," Romans 8:3).[44]

Paul perceived clearly that sin in the Hebrew Bible was associated with violation of the law or commandments, although he failed to emphasize the intense focus on chasing after foreign gods. He also played down the possibility of the remission of sin, if the chosen people returned to God after their apostasy. Sin in the New Testament remains closely bound up with forgiveness, as it was in the Tanakh. What has changed is the means of obtaining pardon. In the Hebrew Bible, the principal offense, as we saw in the previous chapter, is the worship of idols, which violates the covenant with God; by its nature, sin is specific to the Israelites, and obtaining God's pardon requires confessing to having abandoned his ways and returning to his proper worship. In the Gospels and Acts of the Apostles, there is no question of a prior contract, no return to the proper path. Rather, all depends on one's confidence or belief, one's *pistis*, in Jesus, which consists in trusting that he is who he claims to be and can do what he promises. *Pistis* or faith replaces the function of confession. But the conviction that Jesus can heal the sick and forgive sin based not on blind faith, which is not the core sense of *pistis*, but on the abundant evidence of his divinity as manifested by his miraculous cures and other wonders. It is because confidence in Jesus is based on his works that miracles play a central role in the Gospels.

Sin, in turn, takes its contours from this paradigm or script. Whereas in the Tanakh, it lay in the act of disparaging God by deserting his worship, in the New Testament sin is redefined as the absence of that faith by which alone it can be redeemed. Where offenses against the law or the commandments are mentioned, they are typically characterized as evils, transgressions, or by other, broadly synonymous terms—but not, usually, as sins or *hamartiai*. *Hamartia*, in turn, appears in the Gospels primarily in connection with *pistis* in Jesus and consequent forgiveness (*aphesis*); rarely is it associated with specific faults or acts of wrongdoing. Sin is thus a negative state, the absence of faith or *apistia*, the lack of trust in Jesus and his works, despite the manifest evidence of his divinity. The entry of Jesus into the world is a unique event, and salvation and the remission of sin henceforward assume a new form. As a result, the meaning of sin is likewise transformed.

Although the Gospels and Acts in the form we have them were composed subsequently to the letters of Paul, very likely in the latter decades of the first century, they reflect Jesus' sense of sin in a consistent way. Jesus had supposed that some who were alive in his time would see the end of days. Salvation and the remission of sin depended on seeing his works firsthand, or hearing about them from those who had witnessed them. With the passing of time, it became necessary to record the traditions that had been passed on orally, first in Aramaic, the language of Jesus, and then in Greek. With a faithful record that drew on memory and no doubt written reminiscences, whether in Aramaic or in Greek, it was possible to know and trust in Jesus' miracles at second hand, and so the opportunity for forgiveness was given to future generations and to peoples scattered widely. This was the mission of the writers of the Gospels: to record the works of Christ so as to enable those who came afterward to trust in his powers and achieve remission of their sins.

Paul, who came earlier, had a different objective: he was concerned to preserve the faith among those who were already converted, and prevent them from lapses, misunderstandings, and deception on the part of false apostles. But his understanding of the role of faith was the same as that in the Gospels, for all that he developed and amplified its meaning. As he preached (Romans 3:21–26):

> now, apart from law, the righteousness of God has been disclosed, and is attested by the law and the prophets, the righteousness of God through faith in Jesus Christ for all who believe. For there is no distinction, since all have sinned and fall short of the glory of God; they are now justified by his grace as a gift, through the redemption that is in Christ Jesus, whom God put forward as a sacrifice of atonement by his blood, effective through faith. He did this to show his righteousness, because in his divine forbearance he had passed over the sins previously committed; it was to prove at the present time that he himself is righteous and that he justifies the one who has faith in Jesus.

To be sure, Paul sometimes uses *hamartia* in the more casual sense of "wrongdoing," as when he asks, rhetorically, "Did I commit a sin by humbling myself so that you might be exalted, because I proclaimed God's good news to you free of charge?" (2 Corinthians 11:7). So too, he counsels the Ephesians, "be angry but do not sin" (Ephesians 4:26), or again, in reference to those who prevented Paul from spreading the word to the gentiles, so that they too might be saved (1 Thessalonians 2:16). But all these uses are consistent with the emphasis on trust in Jesus as the single path to forgiveness, and the absence of such faith as the sure sign of sin.

There are some looser uses of the terminology for sin, especially in the books that are not securely attributed to Paul himself. Thus, we read in 1 Timothy that "the law is laid down not for the innocent but for the lawless and disobedient, for the godless and sinful, for the unholy and profane, for those who kill their father or mother, for murderers, fornicators, sodomites, slave traders, liars, perjurers" (1 Timothy 1:9–10). The inclusion of the adjective *hamartôlos* or "sinful" in this rather overwrought list may be chalked up to rhetorical effect. So too, the same writer intones: "Do not ordain anyone hastily, and do not participate in the sins of others; keep yourself pure. No longer drink only water, but take a little wine for the sake of your stomach and your frequent ailments.

The sins of some people are conspicuous and precede them to judgment, while the sins of others follow them there" (1 Timothy 5:22–24). Some novel offenses are characterized as sin, again especially in the non-Pauline books. For example, "if you show partiality, you commit sin and are convicted by the law as transgressors [*parabatai*]" (James 2:9). Or, more generally, "There is sin in anyone who knows what is good [*kalon*] and does not do it" (James 4:17). The apocryphal book called Sirach (also known as Ecclesiasticus) introduces some fresh indices of sin, in the somewhat indiscriminate manner of wisdom literature, for example, that "the onset of pride [*huperêphania*] is sin" (commonly translated, "the beginning of pride is sin," Sirach 10:13). So too, among the many maxims is the injunction not to receive or approach sinners (Sirach 12:4, 7, and 14). The same collection also informs us that the lot of women is most sinful, since no wickedness (*kakia*) compares with that of woman (Sirach 25:19; cf. 1 Esdras 4:27). Commerce too leads to sin (Sirach 27:1–2), and swearing oaths is sinful (Sirach 23:8–11; but cf. Sirach 19:16 for venial sins of the tongue). Crucially, in the first Epistle of John a distinction is drawn between mortal (*pros thanaton*) and non-mortal sin (1 John 5:16–17), a notion that was to have a long legacy. So too, the idea that those born of God cannot sin but those who sin are from the devil (1 John 3:8–9, discussed above), would later be invoked in arguments over whether post-baptismal sin could be forgiven (see Chapter 4).

The vocabulary for sin and absolution also becomes more varied, again particularly in the non-Pauline books, in comparison with the tripartite pattern of sin, faith (or conversion), and forgiveness characteristic of the Gospels. Honoring one's father may atone for sins (Sirach 3:3, 14). Christ's blood is associated with redemption (*apolutrôsis*), a word paired with the forgiveness of sins: "in whom we have redemption, the forgiveness of sins" (Colossians 1:14), whereas there is forgiveness (*aphesis*) for trespasses (*paraptômata*, Ephesians 1:7; cf. Ephesians 2:1 for the combination of sins and trespasses), and God may be gracious (*kharisamenos*) toward trespasses (Colossians 2:13). Perversion (*exestraptai*) too is associated with sin (Titus 3:11), as is lawlessness (*anomia*, 1 John 3:4; cf. Baruch 1:17, 2:12) and injustice (*adikia*, 1 John 5:17). "Reconciliation" (*katallagê*, 2 Corinthians 5:19–20) may stand in place of "forgiveness," and one may "cover" or "veil" sins by saving a sinner (James 5:20); so too love covers [*kaluptei*] sins (1 Peter 4:8). There is "purification" (*katharismos*) of sins (Hebrews 1:3), and atoning for or propitiating (*hilaskesthai*) sins (Hebrews

2:17; cf. 1 John 2:2). Thus, at 1 John 4:10 we read: "In this is love, not that we loved God, but that he loved us and sent his Son to be the propitiation for our sins." Further, a priest may offer sacrifices (*thusiai, prospherein*) for sins (Hebrews 5:1, 3), though it is Jesus' sacrifice that is crucial: "now once at the consummation of the ages he has been manifested to put away sin by the sacrifice of himself" (Hebrews 9:26). Or again: "He, having offered one sacrifice for sins for all time, sat down at the right hand of God" (Hebrews 10:12); and Hebrews 7:27: "Unlike the other high priests, he has no need to offer sacrifices day after day, first for his own sins, and then for those of the people; this he did once for all when he offered himself." By contrast, the blood of ordinary sacrifices cannot remove sin (Hebrews 10:4; cf. Revelation 1:5 on Christ "who loves us and freed us from our sins by his blood"). So too, the writer of Hebrews remarks on the futility of sacrifice (*thusia*) for those who sin voluntarily after they have acquired knowledge of the truth (Hebrews 10:26).

Sin, faith, and forgiveness: it is the place of sin or *hamartia* in this tripartite scenario that defines its role in Jesus' conception of sin, as it is transmitted in the Gospels and the Acts of the Apostles. Just as the relationship between sin, confession, and the return to God and renewal of the covenant characterized sin in the Hebrew Bible and distinguished it from the more elementary idea of violating a divine commandment, so too the role of trust in Jesus after his appearance on earth constitutes a further inflection of sin, that distinguishes it from the precedent in the Tanakh. Each term in the triad—sin or *hamartia*, faith in Jesus or *pistis*, and forgiveness or the remission (*aphesis*) of sin—was rich in associations and connotations, and so subject to interpretation and elaboration. We can already detect hints of this process in the later books of the New Testament, in which the authors engage with issues in the primitive Christian communities and seek to work out the implications of Jesus' mission. It would soon transpire that the original sense of sin as *apistia* or failure of belief would give way to a wider application of the term *hamartia* that encompassed offenses and trespasses of various kinds—a conception close to the modern notion of sin. Understood this way, sin in the Bible is not so very different from the transgression of divine laws adumbrated in a number of classical Greek texts, even if this idea never achieved the centrality in Greek religious thought that it did in the Bible. How that more contemporary but less distinctive notion of sin developed in the early centuries after Christ is the subject of the next and final chapter.

4

The Church Fathers and the Rabbis: The Transformation of Sin

Interpretations of sin on the part of early Christians, and of the Rabbis whose commentaries are recorded in the Mishnah and the Talmud, are varied and complex. In what follows I make no attempt to treat in detail the theological debates over the fall of mankind, redemption, or the relationship between sin and freewill, to take just a small sample of the issues that emerge as central in this period. The purpose of this chapter is more limited. I have argued in the previous chapters that sin in the Hebrew Bible consisted mainly in chasing after foreign gods and that for Jesus sin was equated with *apistia* or the lack of trust in his divinity. In the present chapter, I illustrate how the notion of sin expanded in the first few centuries after Christ to include the range of offenses that we today typically recognize as sinful, such as murder, fornication, and the rest. We will, accordingly, be examining those passages that most clearly reveal a wider or more latitudinarian sense of sin, and how the several thinkers found justification for their views in the Bible. We will necessarily touch on broader issues, but only insofar as they are relevant to showing how the biblical conception of sin was transformed in this period.

The close association between sin, faith, and forgiveness remains a constant among Christian commentators on the New Testament. Marius Victorinus, the first Latin commentator on the Pauline epistles and writing in the mid fourth century, cites Paul's affirmation in Galatians 2:15–16: "we know that people are not justified based on works of the Law, but through the faith in Christ Jesus," and comments: "faith itself alone grants justification and sanctification."[1] Stephen Cooper, the translator of Victorinus, compares Luther's doctrine: "As Luther would famously say in *The Freedom of a Christian*, 'whoever has faith will have everything, and whoever does not have faith will have nothing.'"[2] So too,

Ambrosiaster, as the anonymous author of several treatises formerly ascribed to Ambrose is called, writing sometime between the 460s and 480s, comments on Galatians 1:4: "Paul shows quite clearly that the law is of no use when he says that Christ offered himself up to suffer on our behalf, in order to justify us . . ., so that we should be delivered from the law by faith in Christ and be no longer sinners."[3]

But if faith alone, as these comments affirm, can save a person from sin, it does not follow that the only sin is the absence of faith, which, as I argued in Chapter 3, is how the evangelists represent Jesus' own view. Augustine, who was influenced by both Victorinus and Ambrosiaster, is more precise in his commentary on Galatians 3:1:

> Now from this point the apostle begins to show how the grace of faith [*gratia fidei*] is sufficient for justification apart from works of the law, in case anyone was saying that while he does not attribute a person's entire justification to works of the law alone, neither does he attribute it to the grace of faith alone, but rather claims that salvation is accomplished by both. (2) But in order to treat this question carefully and avoid being misled by ambiguity, one must first realize that the works of the law are in two divisions. Some come under sacraments [*in sacramentis*], others under morals [*in moribus*]. (3) Under sacraments are: circumcision of the flesh, the temporal Sabbath, new moons, sacrifices, and all the countless observances of this kind. Under morals are: You shall not kill, You shall not commit adultery, You shall not bear false witness [Exod. 20: 13–14, 16; Deut. 5: 17–18, 20], and the like. (4) Now surely, it is impossible that the Apostle does not care whether a Christian is a murderer and an adulterer or chaste and innocent, in the same way that he does not care whether a man is circumcised or uncircumcised in the flesh. (5) At present, therefore, he is dealing mainly with these latter, sacramental works (although he indicates that he sometimes includes the former as well).[4]

Paul, according to Augustine, was rightly dismissive of mere ritual, as enjoined by various prescriptions, such as circumcision, which Paul of course did not regard as indispensable to salvation after the coming of Christ. But he did not mean to suggest, Augustine insists, that moral offenses of the sort identified in the commandments were a matter of indifference, provided one had faith. These were sins.

In his comment on Galatians 5:22–23, Augustine quotes 1 Timothy 1:8–10: "For we know that the law is good, if one uses it lawfully, understanding this, that the law is not laid down for the righteous but for the unrighteous and disobedient, for the ungodly and sinners [*peccatoribus*], for the unholy and profane, for those who kill their father or mother, for murderers, fornicators, sodomites, kidnappers, liars, perjurers, and whatever else is contrary to sound teaching."[5] Even those who have not committed these terrible crimes are not free of sin. As Augustine writes, "It is one thing not to sin, another not to have sin. For one in whom sin does not rule, that is, one who does not obey his desires, does not sin. But one in whom those desires do not exist at all not only does not sin but does not have sin. But although in many respects this can be accomplished in this life, one cannot hope for this in every respect except in the resurrection and the transformation of the flesh" (my translation).[6]

The association of sin with various types of fault or misdeed contributed to blurring the terminological discrimination that was, as I have attempted to demonstrate, characteristic of the Bible. Justin Martyr, born around the year 100 and so one of the earliest interpreters of the New Testament, writes of Jesus:

> Concerning chastity, he uttered such sentiments as these: Whosoever looks upon a woman to lust after her, has committed adultery with her already in his heart before God. And, If your right eye offend you, cut it out; for it is better for you to enter into the kingdom of heaven with one eye, than, having two eyes, to be cast into everlasting fire. And, Whosoever shall marry her that is divorced from another husband, commits adultery. And, There are some who have been made eunuchs of men, and some who were born eunuchs, and some who have made themselves eunuchs for the kingdom of heaven's sake; but all cannot receive this saying [Matthew 19:12]. So that all who, by human law, are twice married, are in the eye of our master sinful [*hamartôloi*].
>
> *First Apology* 15

Later in the same essay, Justin observes:

> Since at our first birth we were born ignorant and by necessity from moist seed, by the union of our parents, and grew up in bad habits and wicked training, in order that we may not remain the children of necessity and of ignorance but become children of choice and knowledge and may obtain remission [*aphesis*] of sins [*hamartiai*] in which we sinned previously [*proêmartomen*], there is pronounced in the baptism over him who chooses

to be born again and has repented of his sins [*metanoêsanti epi tois hêmartêmenois*] the name of God the Father and Lord of the universe.

61.10

Clement of Alexandria, who lived from 150 to 215, offers a definition of sin as a voluntary act of wickedness: "a voluntary sin [*hamartia*] is an unjust act (*adikia*), and an unjust act is voluntary wickedness [*kakia*]. A sin, then, is a voluntary act of mine" (*Stromata* 2:15 = 8.1004A Migne). In the early third-century Acts of Thomas, one of the so-called apocryphal acts, a weeping crowd confesses to the apostle: "the works which we have done" are foreign to God. But if God would overlook their former deeds, and free them from "the evils which we committed, being in error [*en planêi ontes*], and forget their former sins [*tôn proterôn hamartêmatôn*]," then they will become his servants (38). Thomas reassures the people that God will not take account of the sins which they committed while they were in error (*tas hamartias has en planêi ontes diepraxasthe*), but will overlook the transgressions which they did in ignorance (*ta paraptômata ha kata agnôsian ête pepoiêkotes*). Note the interchangeability especially of the terms for sin (*hamartia*) and transgression (*paraptôma*).

Cyprian of Carthage, writing in Latin in the first half of the third century, affirms: "The crimes [*delicta*] of lying, of lust, of fraud, of cruelty, of impiety, of anger, God rebukes and finds fault with" (*An Address to Demetrianus* 9). But he goes on to say: "You are indignant that God is indignant, as if by living evilly you deserved something good, as if all things that happen to you were not much smaller and lighter than your sins [*peccatis vestris*]."[7] Tertullian is deeply concerned about relapsing into error after one has repented. In his essay, *De paenitentia*, he affirms that repentance, "when once learned and undertaken by us, ought never afterward to be cancelled by repetition of the offense [*delictum*]" (ch. 5). Later in the same chapter, Tertullian affirms: "one does not sin [*peccat*] lightly against the Lord—one who, having renounced his rival the devil by repentance ..., again raises him up by his relapse." The terms *delictum* and *peccatum* appear to be interchangeable. Augustine cites 1 Corinthians 5 and 10, Galatians 5, Ephesians 5, and other lists of prohibited conduct as examples of grave or mortal sins (*peccata*, e.g., *Expositio epistulae ad Galatas* 48, *De continentia* 9, etc.).[8] However, the term ἁμαρτία does not occur in these biblical passages—and this word, as I have been arguing, is key to Jesus' understanding of sin. For Augustine, on the contrary, sin is "any word, deed, or desire contrary to eternal law" (*peccatum est factum vel dictum vel concupitum aliquid contra aeternam legem*).⁹

The tract, *Against the Pelagians: Dialogue between Atticus, a Catholic, and Critobulus, a Heretic*, is one of Jerome's last works, composed in 417, just three years before his death. Critobulus, who represents Pelagius' views, cites the Epistle of James and asks: "Pray does not James the Apostle write that he who offends [*offenderit*] in one point is guilty of all?" Atticus, who is the mouthpiece for Jerome himself, replies:

> The passage is its own interpreter. James did not say, as a starting-point for the discussion, he who prefers a rich man to a poor man in honour is guilty of adultery or murder. That is a delusion of the Stoics who maintain that sins [*peccata*] are equal. But he proceeds thus: "He who said, Thou shalt not commit adultery, said also, Thou shalt not kill: but although thou dost not kill, yet, if thou commit adultery, thou art become a transgressor [*transgressor*, Greek *parabatês*] of the law" [2:11]. Light [sins] are compared with light ones, and heavy with heavy. A fault [*vitium*] that deserves the rod must not be avenged with the sword; nor must a crime [*scelus*] worthy of the sword, be checked with the rod.¹⁰

The confusion of terminology for sin in Latin was abetted by Jerome's translation of the Bible, the so-called Vulgate, in which he indiscriminately rendered as *peccatum* or *peccare* various terms in Greek. An example is Jerome's version of Matthew 6:14, where παραπτώματα or "transgressions" is translated as *peccata* (it is one of those passages in which human and divine forgiveness are paired, so it is particularly important to avoid the suggestion that human beings can remit sins; cf. Matthew 6:15; Mark 11:25–26; more generally, Ephesians 1:7, 2:5). So too, Jerome gives *peccare* where the Greek verb is *ptaiein*, "to stumble", in 2 Peter 1:10, and he translates the Greek adjective ἀπταίστους (literally, "not stumbling," "infallible") as *sine peccato*, "without sin" (Jude 1:24).

The wider application of the terms for sin and sinning, which now covered a variety of individual offenses and not merely a failure to trust in Jesus' miracles and divinity, coincided with new developments in Christianity itself and its relation to the ambient world. As the church evolved as a pastoral institution and Christ's words and those of the apostles became the basis for systematic theology and for vitriolic polemics among different sects, certain themes, implicit or latent in the Bible, received new emphasis and transformed the way sin figured in Christian thought. The paucity of references to specific kinds of sin—by sin I mean *ḥaṭa'* (חטא) in the Hebrew Bible and *hamartia* in the New Testament—as opposed to faithlessness as such, did not inhibit the Church Fathers from discovering such sins where they were not mentioned or even where they were specifically denied.

In this chapter, I focus on four such cases. First, I look at the episode of the healing of the paralyzed or palsied man, recounted in Matthew 9:1–8, Mark 2, and Luke 5:17–26, and in a different form, in John (some ancient commentators maintained that this episode referred to a different individual). Here, although Jesus pronounces that the man's sins have been forgiven, no specific offenses are mentioned. Next, I consider the restoration of sight to a blind man, who, Jesus affirms, had not sinned, and neither had his parents (John 9:1–3). Again, we will look at comments on this passage by early Christians, composed in Greek and in Latin, to see how they responded to this claim. After this, I turn to Jesus' denial that there was sin before he came (John 15:22); as we saw in Chapter 3, this assertion gave rise to a variety of interpretations, intended to salvage the ostensible fact that people generally, and Israelites in particular, were guilty of a great many sins prior to the manifestation of Jesus on earth. Finally, I return to the question of the fall, as recounted in Genesis, and whether Adam and Eve are guilty of having sinned. Here, I look also at the issue of original sin, which is traced to Adam's disobedience of God's injunction not to eat the fruit of the tree of the knowledge of good and evil, even though, as we saw in Chapter 2, the Hebrew word for sin does not occur in the narrative. Although the idea of original sin was to be the subject of a great deal of controversy in early Christianity, the crucial biblical source is a single passage in Paul's Epistle to the Romans (5:12), which is open to various interpretations. Jesus himself, at all events, does not so much as hint at this notion.

Squaring the sinfulness of all with Jesus' affirmation that the man who had been blind from birth had not sinned and that, before his own coming, people had no sin, did not prove to be an insurmountable hurdle to those who sought to identify specific sins, or original sin, as the object of absolution through faith in Jesus. With the attention to particular sins there arose as well a new emphasis on confession, which was, as we saw in the previous chapter, all but absent in the Gospels. In this connection, too, there emerged a deep anxiety over the body and a disposition to the mortification of the flesh, which again had little or no basis in Jesus' teachings. With original sin there arose too questions about the freedom of the will and the necessity of divine grace to escape damnation for all eternity—a doctrine that was itself the occasion for intense polemics as some Christian thinkers maintained that, in the final analysis, all would be saved. These developments, which reflected a widespread anxiety over sin and salvation that accompanied the emergence of Christianity as the dominant religion in the Roman Empire, are, as I have said, beyond the scope of this book. Here, I wish only to show that these problems were debated within the context of conceptions of sin that had moved some distance from the way sin was understood in the Tanakh and the Gospels.

Let us begin, then, with the story of the paralytic. I argued in the previous chapter that there was no sound basis for attributing the man's disability to specific sins he had committed earlier. We recall that Jesus instructed the man, who had been brought to him for healing by friends, to take up his pallet and walk, and further declared that his sins were forgiven. When the scribes and the Pharisees challenge him for blaspheming, Jesus replies, "Which is easier, to say, 'Your sins are forgiven you,' or to say, 'Stand up and walk?'" (Luke 5:23). Jerome, in his *Commentary on Matthew* (on verse 9.5), offers the following explication:

> The difference between saying and doing is great. Only he who forgave them could have known whether the paralytic's sins had been forgiven. But the words: "Rise and walk" are something that both he who got up and those who saw him rise could prove to be true. There is then a bodily miracle that proves the truth of the spiritual miracle. Yet the same power is needed to forgive the faults both of the body and of the soul. It is also given to us to understand that most bodily weaknesses happen on account of sins. This is perhaps why the sins are forgiven first, so that when the causes of the weakness have been taken away, wholeness might be re-established.[11]

Jerome sees clearly that the miracle of the healing is the visible sign of Jesus' powers, and he takes it that it is intended to persuade the others that he likewise has the capacity to forgive sins, since both derive from the same divine source. The miracles are the basis for confidence in Jesus. Jerome takes it for granted, however, that the man's prior sins were the cause of his ailment. These are presumably particular or personal sins, since he does not refer here to an inherent state of sinfulness, perhaps because of the plural, *hamartiai* (rendered as *peccata* in Jerome's commentary). Jerome refrains here from speculating further, as some modern commentators have done (quoted in Chapter 3), as to what those sins might have been.

Irenaeus, in his treatise *Against Heresies* (second century), wrote in connection with the healing of the paralytic: "Now the commandment was given to man by the word. For Adam, it is said, 'heard the voice of the lord God.' Rightly then does his word [that is, Jesus] say to man, 'Thy sins are forgiven thee;' he, the same against whom we had sinned in the beginning, grants forgiveness of sins in the end" (5.17.1). Irenaeus continues: "By this work of his he confounded the unbelievers, and showed that he is himself the voice of God, by which man received commandments, which he broke, and became a sinner; for the paralysis followed as a consequence of sins" (5.17.2). John Chrysostom, a contemporary of Jerome writing in Greek, comments on the same passage (*Commentary on Matthew*, vv. 9:5–6):

> Now what he says is like this: Which seems to you easier, to bind up a disorganized body, or to undo the sins of a soul? It is quite manifest: to bind up a body. For by how much a soul is better than a body, by so much is the doing away of sins a greater work than this. But because the one is unseen, the other in sight, I throw in that which, although an inferior thing, is yet more open to sense, so that the greater also and the unseen may thereby receive its proof. Thus by his works, he anticipates even now the revelation of what had been said by John, that he takes away the sins of the world.

Once again, the emphasis on the perceptible impact of Jesus' wonder-working is seen to serve as evidence of his divinity, and hence his ability to wipe away sins—presumably those committed by the paralytic prior to falling ill.[12] So too, Gregory of Nazianzus, commenting on John's version of the episode, comments: "you were raised up from your bed, or rather you took up your bed, and publicly acknowledged the benefit. Do not again be thrown upon your bed by sinning, in the evil rest of a body paralyzed by its pleasures. But as you now are, so walk, mindful of the command, Behold thou art made whole; sin no more lest a worse thing happen unto thee if thou prove thyself bad after the blessing thou hast received."[13]

Hilary of Poitiers, however, writing in Latin in the mid fourth century and roughly a generation earlier than Jerome, Augustine, or John Chrysostom, takes a different and at first blush opposing view. In his *Commentary on Matthew* (ch. 8:5 rather than 9 in this numeration), Hilary observes:

> Iamque in paralytico gentium universitas offertur medenda et curationis ipsius uerba sunt contuenda. Non dicitur paralytico: "Sanus esto"; non dicitur: "Surge et ambula"; sed dicitur: "*Constans esto, fili, remissa sunt tibi peccata tua*" [Matthew 9:2]. In Adam uno peccata universis gentibus remittuntur ... Hic filius nuncupatur, quia primus Dei opus est, huic remittuntur animae peccata et indulgentia primae transgressionis ex venia est. Non enim paralyticum pecasse aliquid accepimus, cum praesertim alio in loco idem dominus dixerit, caecitatem a nativitate non ex peccato aut proprio aut paterno fuisse contractam [John 9:3]."[14]

I have provided the Latin text because it is difficult, and translations vary. The following is a good approximation:

> Indeed in the paralytic, the totality [*universitas*] of peoples is offered to be healed, and the words themselves of the curing must be considered. It is not said to the paralytic: "be healed;" nor is it said: "get up and walk;" but what is said is: "Be sure [*constans*], my son, your sins have been remitted for you."[15] In the one person, Adam, sins [*peccata*] are remitted for all peoples ... He is called son because he is the first work of God. The sins of the soul are remitted for him and indulgence is granted for the first transgression through pardon [*venia*]. For we do not accept that the paralytic had committed any sin, especially because in another place the Lord said that blindness from birth had been brought about neither by the man's own sin nor from his parent.[16]

Hilary straightforwardly denies that the paralytic's condition was brought about by his own sin, a point he confirms by referring to the passage on the healing of the blind man that we will discuss next. But before turning to that episode, as recounted by John, we may note that Hilary does not ignore the role of sin entirely, but associates it with pardon via a connection between the lame man and Adam. Ellen Scully, in her recent study of Hilary, comments: "In the pericope of the paralytic (Matt. 9:2–8, *In Matthaeum* 8.5), Hilary explains that the paralytic symbolizes Adam, and in him all humanity, who is brought to Jesus to be cured." Scully goes on to observe: "The unity of humanity that Hilary bases in Adam is manifested here in a unity in sin. Hilary's commentary on this pericope depends upon the presupposition of humanity's unity in sin: without this unity, Jesus' healing of the paralytic could in no way symbolize his healing of the sins of all."[17]

Isabella Image makes the point even more emphatically, stating that Hilary "takes the healing of a paralytic (Mt. 9.2–8) to signify how we are healed of Adam's sin." She offers a slightly different translation of the text:

> In the paralytic, all peoples are offered up for healing. In one man, Adam, sin [*peccata*, plural] was passed on [*remittuntur*] to all peoples ... The soul's sins are passed on [*remittuntur*] to this paralytic, and pardon for the first transgression comes when the paralytic is forgiven.
>
> InMt 8.5

Note that the verb *remitto* here (in the passive) is rendered "passed on" rather than "remitted," although this does not accord well with the sense in the passage from Matthew's Gospel, *remissa sunt tibi peccata tua*, which Hilary cites but Image omits in her excerpt. Image goes on to affirm, in agreement with Scully:

> Hilary sharply rejects the interpretation that the paralytic is being healed of his own personal sin. In common with other patristic authors, Hilary takes this passage as illustrating the healing of Adam's sin. It is not clear, however, whether the paralytic is culpable for Adam's actual sin, or merely provides an analogy.[18]

This last reservation is significant, for it involves the question of whether the descendants of Adam are guilty as a result of his sin. We shall return to this question below, in connection with the doctrine of original sin. What is important to note here is that, even if we interpret Hilary to mean that the sin for which Jesus forgave the paralyzed man was the universal sin of mankind, symbolized by Adam, rather than the man's particular sins, this larger sin cannot have been the cause of his infirmity. For the paralytic shared this sin with everyone else, but only he was afflicted. It remains the case, then, that the forgiving of the sin and the healing of the man are two distinct acts, and not related as cause (sin) and effect (paralysis).

Chromatius, the bishop of Aquileia and a contemporary of Jerome, Augustine, and John Chrysostom, also composed a commentary on Matthew (*Tractatus in Matthaeum*). Ellen Scully observes that "Chromatius is even more explicit than Hilary in equating the paralytic with Adam," for, as he writes: "Thus, for the health of the paralytic, that is, of the gentile people, or doubtless of Adam, who is recognized as the origin of the human race."[19]

Cyril of Jerusalem (fourth century) drew a different lesson from the story of the paralytic, as recounted in the Synoptic Gospels. In his catechetical sermon

"Of Faith," he affirmed: "Yea, so much power hath faith, that not the believer only is saved, but some have been saved by others believing. The paralytic in Capernaum was not a believer, but they believed who brought him, and let him down through the tiles: for the sick man's soul shared the sickness of his body. And think not that I accuse him without cause: the Gospel itself says, when Jesus saw, not his faith, but their faith, he saith to the sick of the palsy, Arise! The bearers believed, and the sick of the palsy enjoyed the blessing of the cure" (5.8).[20] The idea of vicarious faith leading to the remission of sins is intriguing, and it may be that Cyril regarded the fault of the paralytic—that is, the sin of which he was absolved—as residing precisely in his lack of faith. If so, it is an interpretation of the episode in line with the argument presented in the previous chapter. Theophylact of Ohrid, the Byzantine bishop of Bulgaria who wrote during the eleventh century, was also struck by the apparent suggestion that it was the faith of the paralytic's friends that was responsible for his cure. Commenting on the phrase, "And Jesus seeing their faith," he wrote: "Either the faith of the men who brought the paralytic, for Jesus often worked a miracle on account of the faith of those who brought the one sick; or, of the paralytic himself." But he reverted to the position that the sins were those of the paralytic himself; on the lemma, "Said to the paralytic, Take courage, child; thy sins be forgiven thee," Theophylact remarked: "Jesus calls him 'child,' either as one of God's creatures, or because he believed. To show that the man's paralysis is a result of his sins, Jesus first forgives him his sins."[21]

If the paralytic's sins were a matter of controversy for interpreters, Jesus' explicit denial that the blind man whom he cured was afflicted because of his sin or that of his parents required a different approach. John Chrysostom, for example, in his homily on the Gospel of John 9:1-2, begins by quoting John's account: "And as Jesus passed by, he saw a man who was blind from his birth. And his disciples asked him, saying, master, who did sin, this man, or his parents, that he was born blind?" Chrysostom then paraphrases and enlivens the exchange: "when they saw him earnestly regarding the man, they asked him, saying, 'Who did sin, this man, or his parents?'" John then comments: "A mistaken question, for how could he sin before he was born? And how, if his parents had sinned, would he have been punished? Whence then came they to put this question?" John then refers back to the episode of the paralytic, and explains: "Before, when he healed the paralytic, he said, 'Behold, thou art made whole, sin no more.' They therefore, having understood that he was palsied on account of sin, said, 'Well, that other was palsied because of his sins; but concerning this man, what would you say? Has he sinned? It is not possible to say so, for he is blind from his birth. Have his parents sinned? Neither can one say this, for the child suffers not punishment for the father.'" Chrysostom takes it for granted that the paralytic suffered his disability because of his personal sins, but is aware that this motive cannot account for the present instance of an innocent man's congenital blindness. He goes on to explain: "As therefore when we see a child evilly treated, we exclaim, 'What can one say of this? What has the child done?' not as asking a question, but as being perplexed, so the disciples spoke here, not so much asking for information, as being in perplexity. What then did Christ say?" Chrysostom's reply, in his comment on verse 3, is ingenious:

> "Neither has this man sinned, nor his parents." This he says not as acquitting them of sins, for he says not simply, "Neither hath this man sinned, nor his parents," but adds, "that he should have been born blind—but that the son of God should be glorified in him." For both this man has sinned and his parents, but his blindness proceeds not from that. And this he said, not signifying that though this man indeed was not in such case, yet that others had been made blind from such a cause, the sins of their parents, since it cannot be that when one sins another should be punished."[22]

The parents have surely sinned, but that is not the reason for their son's blindness, since the sins of the fathers are not visited upon the children, according to Chrysostom. Nor can the infant have sinned, much less prior to birth, though the man himself has sinned. Everyone sins, and their sins may result in one or another affliction; but it does not follow that any given condition is necessarily a consequence of sinning. In certain cases, presumably rare, the ailment may serve another purpose, such as glorifying Jesus through his works. What might the sins of the man and his parents have been? Chrysostom does not say, but we may suppose that they were of the now conventional kind: not lack of confidence in Jesus, since that was not the case with the man, and is moot in regard to his parents, but illicit desires or actions. Jesus, needless to say, shows not the slightest interest in determining what those sins might have been, since he maintained that, prior to his coming, there was no sin.

Augustine takes a roughly similar line to that of John Chrysostom:

> If no man is sinless, were the parents of this blind man without sin? Was he himself either born without original sin, or had he committed none in the course of his lifetime? Because his eyes were closed, had his lusts lost their wakefulness? How many evils are done by the blind? From what evil does an evil mind abstain, even though the eyes are closed? He could not see, but he knew how to think, and perchance to lust after something which his blindness hindered him from attaining, and so still in his heart to be judged by the searcher of hearts. If, then, both his parents had sin, and the man himself had sin, wherefore said the Lord, Neither has this man sinned, nor his parents, but only in respect to the point on which he was questioned, that he was born blind? For his parents had sin; but not by reason of the sin itself did it come about that he was born blind. If, then, it was not through the parents' sin that he was born blind, why was he born blind? Listen to the Master as he teaches. He seeks one who believes, to give him understanding. He himself tells us the reason why that man was born blind: Neither has this man sinned, he says, nor his parents: but that the works of God should be made manifest in him.[23]

The poor blind man had no need to pluck out his eye, since he was capable of lust even without the ability to see. So sin he must have, and sins of the kind that are all too familiar in the writings of the early Christians. Like Chrysostom, however, Augustine is obliged to separate these sins from the immediate cause of the man's blindness, which he ascribes to the divine plan that might make Jesus' powers apparent to all.

Cyril, the archbishop or patriarch of Alexandria, writing in the first half of the fifth century, a generation or so after Augustine and John Chrysostom, takes a different approach. As he writes in his commentary on the Gospel of John:

> The disciples once made enquiry of our saviour concerning one born blind, and said, *Master who did sin, this man or his parents, that he was born blind?* For since it is written in the prophetic Scriptures, of God, that He visits *the iniquity of the fathers upon the children,* the disciples began to imagine that such was the case with this man. What then does Christ say to this? Verily I say to you, *neither hath this man sinned nor his parents, but that the works of God should be made manifest in him.* How then does he exempt them from sin, although not free from blame as to their lives? For being men, they were

surely liable also to faults. But it is manifest and clear that the discourse pertains to the period prior to birth, during which they not yet existing, neither had they sinned, that Christ may be true.

1.9[24]

The blind man and his parents must have sinned, indeed, but only after they were born: a reasonable restriction, except that it might be seen as compromising the idea of original sin, of which conceivably even the unborn may be bearers. Cyril is clearly thinking of personal sins, of which, he is certain, both the man and his parents must be guilty.

We saw in the previous chapter that Jesus's statement, as recorded by John, that the people had no sin before his manifestation on earth was the cause of some perplexity, not to say consternation, among commentators such as Calvin, who sought some manner of getting around the obvious sense of the pronouncement. Most commonly, the strategy was to insist that Jesus meant that, before he came, people were innocent of the sin of disbelief in him or *apistia*, but not of the various other sins that are itemized, as it is supposed, in the Bible. Thus, Augustine explains in one of his lengthy *Epistles* (194.3.9):

> The Lord himself says in the Gospel: "If I had not come and spoken to them, they would have no sin [*peccatum*]. But now they do not have an excuse for their sin" [John 15:22]. Not that those people would have no sin [*peccatum*] who were filled with many other and great sins. Rather, he meant that, if he had not come, they would not have had the sin by which they did not believe him, although they had heard him [*cum audissent eum, non crediderunt in eum*]. He affirms that they do not have that excuse, by which they could say, "We did not hear, therefore we did not believe." Human pride [*superbia*], of course, as if presuming on the strength of free choice [or free will: *liberum arbitrium*], thinks that it is excused, since the fact that it sins [*quod peccat*] seems to be due to ignorance and not to the will [*voluntas*].

26[25]

Augustine clearly takes it that disbelief is indeed a sin, but not the only sin. In this respect, Augustine is entirely consistent with Calvin's interpretation of the passage. But Augustine adds a fateful twist. For the will itself is not sufficient to overcome the sin inherited from Adam and Eve's choice. As he concludes, "No one sets free those sold into subjection to sin from the chains of the jailer except the grace of the redeemer" (6.28). For Augustine, sin is intimately bound up with the will; and yet, the will itself is wholly dependent on God's grace.

So too, in one of his lectures or sermons, Augustine asks: "What, then, does he mean by the words, If I had not come and spoken unto them, they had not had sin?" And he continues:

> Was it that the Jews were without sin before Christ came to them in the flesh? Who, though he were the greatest fool, would say so? But it is some great sin, and not every sin, that he would have to be understood, as it were, under the general designation. For this is the sin wherein all sins are included; and whosoever is free from it, has all his sins forgiven him: and this it is, that they believed not on Christ, who came for the very purpose of enlisting their faith. From this sin, had he not come, they would certainly have been free.
>
> Tractate 89.1

Here we see the source of Calvin's unease with the view of Augustine, of whom he wrote that Augustine "approaches to that opinion," that is, that "there is no other sin but unbelief." It remains true that there were sins other than that of disbelief, of which people were guilty before Christ came; but of course they could not be charged with *apistia*. Yet after Jesus' manifestation on earth, all other sins are somehow included in that of disbelief, presumably without losing their specific natures. Christ's advent, Augustine affirms, is thus "fraught with destruction to unbelievers," but offers "salvation to those that believe." But Augustine does not leave it at that. For, as he notes, Jesus went on to say, "But now they have no excuse for their sin," and he worries that "some may be moved to inquire whether those to whom Christ neither came nor spoke, have an excuse for their sin":

> For if they have not, why is it said here that these had none, on the very ground that he did come and speak to them? And if they have, have they it to the extent of thereby being barred from punishment, or of receiving it in a milder degree? To these inquiries, with the Lord's help and to the best of my capacity, I reply, that such have an excuse, not for every one of their sins, but for this sin of not believing on Christ, inasmuch as He came not and spoke not to them.
>
> Tractate 89.2

Augustine ends up, then, insisting that, despite Jesus' words, the people did have sins, of what we might call the ordinary or personal sort.

Origen, in his commentary on the Gospel of John, took a subtler, not to say over subtle view of the passage:

> But when the Lord himself says [John 15:22], "If I had not come and spoken unto them, they had not had sin; but now they have no cloak for their sin," the only sense we can find in his words is that the Logos himself says that those are not chargeable with sin to whom he (reason) has not fully come, but that those, if they sin, are guilty who, having had part in him, act contrary to the ideas by which he declares his full presence in us. Only when thus read is the saying true: "If I had not come and spoken to them, they had not had sin".
>
> 1.42

Jesus, according to Origen's characteristically allegorical interpretation, stands for Logos, "the word" or "reason," that which was in the beginning, according to the opening sentence of the Gospel of John. Those in whom reason has not yet developed, such as infant children, cannot be said to sin. But those who have reached the age of reason and so have a part in Logos, which is to say, in Jesus, can be called to account. As Origen continues:

> Should the words be applied, as many are of opinion that they should, to the visible Christ, then how is it true that those had no sin to whom he did not come? In that case all who lived before the advent of the Saviour will be free from sin, since Jesus, as seen in flesh, had not yet come. And more—all those to whom he has never been preached will have no sin, and if they have no sin, then it is clear they are not liable to judgment.

Sins, however, may be rightly charged to "every one who passes beyond the age of boyhood," save for those, we may add, who are mentally handicapped. Origen thus concludes that this is the sense of Logos by which Jesus' words in the present passage are to be understood. But what of Jesus' assertion that "All that ever came before me are thieves and robbers, and the sheep did not hear them" (John 10:8)? This pronouncement rests, Origen claims, on a different sense of Logos, familiar from Stoic thought, according to which Logos refers to the consummation of reason, "which takes place only in the perfect."[26] Anyone who falls short of such consummate wisdom—which, according to the Stoics, is pretty much everyone—is thus a sinner.

Cyril of Alexandria, writing after Augustine but in Greek, like Origen, offers yet another perspective, as he wonders about the audience for Jesus' words. As he says, "We may take in two ways the meaning of the words before us." First he assumes that the passage was directed to both Greeks (that is, pagans) and Jews alike. In this case, the point would be that "unless the divine and heavenly message, I mean the Gospel, had come to all that are on the earth ..., their complete ignorance of what is pleasing to God would perhaps have been a strong reason in each case for the pardon of those who are not eager in pursuing virtue." But Cyril dismisses this excuse: "This ignorance of theirs makes them seem worthy of pardon. But whereas the word of the Gospel has been directed to all men, what reason for pardon is there, or with what words should any one address him that judges, when accused after knowledge of the worst crimes?" The alternative assumption is that Jesus was addressing his word to Jews only. But that is even less of a justification. For the Jews had heard Jesus' teaching, and were "in no way ignorant of what he commanded them to think and do." Nevertheless, they will persecute the disciples, "consumed with an unjust hatred against you." Still worse, as a way of exonerating their violence the Jews will cite the books of Moses, and will pretend that Jesus was an opponent of their ancestral laws. But such a claim is merely self-interested hypocrisy. Paraphrasing Jesus' words, Cyril writes:

> if I had not come and set forth commands superior to the Law given by Moses; if I had not fulfilled it by many words, showing that ... the hour had come in which the truth itself should shine forth; if I had not shown this from the Law itself, saying in the clearest language, *If you believed Moses, you would believe me; for he wrote of me*; if I had not made it clear that my word harmonized with the testimonies of the prophets, and that the power of my presence had already been predicted and proclaimed, then they would have had reasonable grounds for their madness against me and you. Since nothing has been left out, but everything that was essential has been said, the reason which they have devised to cover the nakedness of their sin is vain.[27]

The Jews' own Bible points the way to faith in Jesus, yet they sin not only in failing to trust in Jesus but in their active persecution of him and his followers, as well as in the commission of other crimes, like gentiles generally.

In all three passages from the Gospels that we have examined so far, there is a tension between interpretations of sin, whether of the paralytic, the blind men, or all who preceded or who denied Jesus, as consisting in specific acts of the sort prohibited by the Commandments and other legislation, and a state of sinfulness inherent in the fallen condition of mankind. It is unanimously agreed among Christian writers that Adam and Eve sinned by eating the forbidden fruit of the tree of the knowledge of good and evil. We noted in Chapter 2 that Irenaeus (late second century) argued that Adam was created with a childlike mind, and we considered the possible implications of this view for the question of whether Adam and Eve's offense constituted a sin (as we mentioned, the Hebrew word for sin does not occur in this episode). We noted too that in the so-called *Life of Adam and Eve*, of uncertain date but probably composed within a century of the death of Jesus, there is a powerful emphasis on Eve's responsibility for the fall and on her passionate confession of her sin. Indeed, Ephrem the Syrian, in his *Commentary on Genesis* 2:23.3, speculates that "if Adam and Eve had sought to repent after they had transgressed the commandment, even though they would not have regained that which they had possessed before their transgression of the commandment, they would have escaped from the curses that were decreed on the earth and upon them."[28] Confession, however, as we observed in Chapter 3, is almost entirely absent in the Gospels; it is only John the Baptist who is said to couple repentance (or conversion) with confession, since once Jesus has appeared, the remission of sin comes to depend entirely on trust in him. How different, then, is the role of confession in the Church Fathers. Ambrose, for example, intones:

> Let us not blush to confess our sins. Behold how free he was who could say, I feared not the multitude of the people; that I should not confess my sin in the sight of all [Job 31:33]. For he that confesses his sin is released from servitude, and the just accuses himself in the beginning of his speech [Proverbs 18:17]. Not only the free but the just man also; but justice is in liberty and liberty in confession, for as soon as a man shall confess he is absolved. Lastly, I said I will confess my sins unto the Lord, and so you forgave the wickedness of my sin [Psalms 32:6]. The delay of absolution depends on confessing, the remission of sins follows closely on confession. He therefore is wise who confesses; he is free whose sin [*peccatum*] is remitted, for he contracts now no debt of sin.[29] Farewell: love me as indeed you do, for I also love you.[30]

The sins that bear confessing are particular offenses, committed by individuals who belong to the church and aspire to lead a better life. One does not confess to original sin, however much one may lament that one is heir to Adam's offense. How do personal sins, as they are regarded by the Church Fathers, relate to the more generalized sinfulness of humanity, inherited in one form or another from Adam's original transgression? The matter was intensely debated, and various views emerged.

If people simply imitate the offense of the first couple, then sin is a matter of will, and presumably subject to the control of human beings themselves, to the extent that they can achieve virtue, without the intervention of divine grace. This was the doctrine of Pelagius, at least according to his detractors, who took it to be inspired in part by Stoicism, with its ideal of the perfect sage. In his early writings, which he later renounced in his *Retractions*, Augustine followed the Stoics in affirming that sin is any deed done wrongly, but the sage, who follows reason, does not sin (*De utilitate credendi* 12.27).[31] As he writes: "For everything that is done, if it be not rightly done, is a sin [*nam omne factum, si recte factum non est, peccatum est*], nor can that be rightly done at all which does not proceed from right reason. Further, right reason is virtue itself. But to whom of men is virtue at hand, save to the mind of the wise? Therefore the wise man alone does not sin [*non peccat*]." Later, however, above all in the context of his polemics against Pelagius, Augustine adopted the more radical view that Adam's sin itself is inherited and thus congenital, not merely a consequence of mankind's mortal nature. As he states: "The whole human race was in the first man, and it [death] was to pass from him through the woman into his progeny" (*City of God* 13.3).[32] If mortality, as the consequence of Adam and Eve's insubordination, entails the corruption of the will along with the body, then absolution depends entirely on God's grace. As Augustine writes:

> They can surely say that the forgiveness of sins [*remissio peccatorum*] is a grace [*gratia*] that is not given because of any preceding merits. For what good merit can sinners [*peccatores*] have? It remains ... that we not attribute faith [*fides*] itself to human choice [or will: *arbitrium*], which they extol, nor to any preceding merits, because any good merits there are proceed from faith, but rather that we admit that it is a gratuitous gift of God, if we have in mind true grace, that is, without any merits.
> Augustine *Epistle* 194.3.9[33]

Faith, which is indispensable to salvation, is not within our power but depends wholly on grace or God's gift. Human will or choice is illusory.

As we have observed more than once, the crucial passage in the New Testament on which the doctrine of original sin rests is Paul's letter to the Romans 5:12: "Therefore, just as sin came into the world through one man, and death came through sin, and so death spread to all because all have sinned." Augustine based his interpretation of this passage on Ambrosiaster's commentary, which relied on the Old Latin Version (*Vetus Latina*) of the Bible; this translation preceded that by Jerome (commonly known as the Vulgate) and was regarded by Julian of Eclanum, a follower of Pelagius writing in the first half of the fifth century, and others as faulty.[34] Ambrosiaster comments on the verse in question: "All sinned in Adam as in a lump. Once he was corrupted by sin, those he begat were all born under sin."[35] The word *massa*, "lump" or "mass of dough," corresponding to the Greek φύραμα, does not occur in the passage in question. Ambrosiaster imported it from 11:16: "if the part of the dough offered as first fruits is holy, then the whole batch is holy; if the root is holy, so are the branches," but he altered the image to express rather the way the part can corrupt the whole. Ambrosiaster himself did not hold that sin as such was transmitted, but only that "What is passed down from Adam to all humanity is simply the tendency of the body to decay"; human beings retain freedom of choice or the will.[36]

Cyril of Alexandria (first half of the fifth century) affirms: "Because of the disobedience of one (that is, of Adam), the many became sinners; not because they transgressed together with Adam (for they were not there) but because they are of his nature, which entered under the dominion of sin" (*Commentary on Romans* 5.18). Adam's descendants "are corruptible as the issue of a corruptible source. It is in this sense that we are heirs of Adam's curse" (*Doctrinal Questions and Answers*, 6).

As an innate condition rather than a specific act, sin came to be seen as the metaphysical state of estrangement from God. Thus Gregory of Nyssa writes: "Now sin is nothing else than alienation from God, who is the true and only life. Accordingly the first man lived many hundred years after his disobedience, and yet God lied not when he said, 'In the day that you eat thereof you shall surely die.' For by the fact of his alienation from the true life, the sentence of death was ratified against him that self-same day: and after this, at a much later time, there followed also the bodily death of Adam" (*Against Eunomius* 2.13).

If sin is congenital, baptizing infants becomes a matter of urgency, since they are in a state of sin, even though they have committed no personal sins.

Clement of Alexandria maintained that "the sins committed before faith [that is, before baptism] are forgiven by the Lord, not that they may be undone, but as if they had not been done. 'But not all,' says Basilides, 'but only sins involuntary and in ignorance, are forgiven;' as would be the case were it a man, and not God, that conferred such a boon" (*Stromateis* 4:24). Clement argues further that God has granted, "in the case of those who, though in faith, fall into any transgression, a second repentance" (*Stromateis* 2.13). This view was anathema to Tertullian, who insisted in his treatise on baptism that "we enter into the bath once only, once only are our offenses [*delicta*] washed away, because these ought not to be repeated" (*On Baptism* 15.3). Tertullian thus advocated deferring baptism until one has "become competent to know Christ" (*On Baptism* 18). John Chrysostom sets out the argument in greater detail, with reference to several of the passages we have considered so far:

> Our fathers held baptism to be just the proper curb upon evil concupiscence, and a powerful lesson for teaching to be sober-minded even in a time of delights … Many, after they have received [baptism], immediately have returned to their former vomit, and have become more wicked, and drawn upon themselves a more severe punishment. Having been delivered from their former sins, they have more grievously provoked the judge, since, having been delivered from so great a disease, still they did not learn sobriety. But that has happened them, which Christ threatened to the paralytic man, saying, "Behold you are made whole: sin no more, lest a worse thing come unto you" [John 5:14], and which he also predicted of the Jews, that the last state shall be worse than the first [Matthew 12:45]. For, he says, showing that by their ingratitude they should bring upon them the worst of evils, "if I had not come, and spoken unto them, they had not had sin" [John 15:22]. Thus, the guilt of sins committed after these benefits is doubled and quadrupled. And the Laver of Baptism helps not a whit to procure for us a milder punishment.

John then specifies the kinds of sins that must be avoided:

> A man has gotten grievous sins by committing murder or adultery, or some other crime: these were remitted through baptism. For there is no sin, no impiety, which does not yield and give place to this gift; for the grace is divine. A man has again committed adultery and murder: the former adultery is indeed done away, the murder forgiven, and not brought up again

to his charge, for the gifts and calling of God are without repentance [Romans 11:29]. But for those committed after baptism he suffers a punishment as great as he would if both the former sins were brought up again, and many worse than these. For the guilt is no longer simply equal, but doubled and tripled.

John Chrysostom *Homily 1 on Acts* 1:1–2[37]

Chrysostom's discussion could serve as a warning to postpone baptism, at least until one was reasonably sure of not backsliding afterwards and committing the same sins that had been washed away by the spiritual immersion. But the sins that Chrysostom has in mind are clearly personal in nature. The case is different if the infant emerges from the womb bearing the curse of original sin. On the one hand, the Cappadocian clergy did not see how a newborn infant could be deemed guilty of sin. Thus Gregory of Nazianzus maintained, in his oration *On Holy Baptism* (*Oration* 40:23), that unbaptized infants "will be neither glorified nor punished by the righteous Judge, as unsealed and yet not wicked, but persons who have suffered rather than done wrong." Gregory of Nyssa, in turn, in his essay *On Infants' Early Deaths*, affirmed that since "the innocent babe has no such plague before its soul's eyes obscuring its measure of light and so it continues to exist in that natural life, it does not need the soundness which comes from purgation, because it never admitted the plague into its soul at all."

Augustine, however, was the scourge of those who doubted the sinfulness of the infant fresh from the womb. In his treatise, *On the Merits and Forgiveness of Sins, and on the Baptism of Infants*, Augustine takes aim at those who suppose that the sin of Adam "has not been transmitted from the first man to other persons by natural descent, but by imitation." As a consequence, they "refuse to believe that in infants original sin is remitted through baptism, for they contend that no such original sin exists at all in people by their birth" (1.9). Such misguided people, which is to say, the followers of Pelagius, "say that the reason why infants are baptized is that they may have the remission of the sin which they have themselves committed in their life, not what they have derived from Adam" (1.22). But since the sin of which the infant must be cleaned is that of Adam, transmitted genetically, then it follows that if "the infant departs from the present life after he has received baptism, the guilt in which he was involved by original sin being done away, he shall be made perfect in that light of truth" (1.25). Augustine crisply summarizes the debate by noting "the important difference existing between such of them as maintain that infants are absolutely pure and free from all sin, whether original or actual; and those who suppose that so soon as born infants have contracted actual sins of their own, from which they need cleansing by baptism" (1.64).[38] Again, in his treatise, *The Grace of Christ, and on Original Sin*, Augustine challenges the Pelagians, who, he alleges, approve of infant baptism and yet "persist in holding and urging their opinion that the carnal generation is not held guilty of man's first sin, although they seem to allow infants to be baptized for the remission of sins." Augustine continues the attack on Caelestius, the principal disciple of Pelagius, for affirming that "Adam's sin injured only Adam himself, and not the human race, and that infants at their birth are in the same state that Adam was in before his transgression" (2.2).

If the all-embracing, indeed the unique sin after the advent of Jesus is a failure to believe in his divinity, despite the evidence of his miracles, then infants are indeed innocent. To be sure, they have not had the opportunity to commit personal or particular offenses, but neither are they able either to trust or distrust Jesus, since they are too young to understand what that means. They would decide when they came of age. But what if they died before they acquired reason—that is, the *logos* with which Origen identified Jesus? Jesus does not say, but it is reasonable to suppose that those incapable of receiving his message were among those who "had no sin."

The doctrine of original sin and the corruption of the will had as corollaries the debate over whether salvation is predetermined and thus whether God is responsible for evil in the world. Clement of Alexandria, for example, states firmly: "in no respect is God the author of evil. But since free choice and inclination originate sins, and a mistaken judgment sometimes prevails, from which, since it is ignorance and stupidity, we do not take pains to recede, punishments are rightly inflicted" (*Stromateis* 1.17; cf. 4:13, arguing against Valentinian). To those who cite Isaiah's statement, "I form the light, and create darkness: I make peace, and create evil: I the Lord do all these things" (Isaiah 45:7) in support of the idea that God is responsible for evil, Tertullian objects:

> They take a word whose one form reduces to confusion and ambiguity two kinds of evils (because both offenses [*delicta*] and punishments [*supplicia*] are called evils [*mala*]) . . . We, on the contrary, distinguish between the two

meanings of the word in question and by separating evils of guilt [*mala culpae*] from evils of penalty [*mala poenae*], we assign to each of the two classes its own author: the devil as the author of the evils of sin and guilt [*peccati et culpae*] and God as the creator of evils of penalty [*poenae*] ... Of the latter class of evils which are compatible with justice, God is therefore avowedly the creator.

Against Marcion 2.14[39]

We note again the easy slippage in terminology, in which *peccatum* is equated with *delictum*.

The condemnation of astrology too might serve to affirm the role of will in the commission of sin. Thus Methodius (late second century), a critic of Origen, writes: "For of all evils the greatest which is implanted in many is that which refers the causes of sins to the motions of the stars, and says that our life is guided by the necessities of fate, as those say who study the stars, with much insolence."[40] A further issue was whether Jesus sinned in his mortal form; thus the fifth-century theologian Theodoret asserts: "the Lord was without sin, made in his human nature of incorruptible wood, that is to say, of the Virgin and the Holy Ghost" (*On the Immutable*, Dialogue 1 between Eranistes and Orthodoxus).[41]

Anxiety over inherited or innate sin, combined with the growth of monasticism, led to an increasing emphasis on penitential practices, which took the form of continual self-recrimination and remorse. Justin Martyr advises: "If, indeed, you repent of your sins, and recognize him to be Christ, and observe his commandments, then … remission of sins shall be yours" (*Dialogue with Trypho*, ch. 95). Even in the afterlife, "the greatest torments are assigned to the believer," who feels shame for sins committed after baptism (Clement of Alexandria, *Stromateis* 6:14). Centuries later, John Chrysostom declares: "one must mourn and weep and suffer, not only for one or two days, but one's entire life" (*On Compunction* 1.9 = 4.7.408 Migne). So too, Theodoret (*Festal Letter* 38, for Easter) writes: "the brightness of the feast is dimmed, and lamentation and wailing are mingled with our psalmody. Such sorrows does sin bring forth. It is sin which has filled our life with pangs." The body becomes the particular locus of sin and the seat of concupiscence, above all with regard to sex, which in turn leads to a stress on virginity and suspicion of the desires of the flesh. These must be controlled by ascetic exercises such as fasting and extreme self-discipline in the face of ever-present temptation, well beyond anything intimated in the Gospels or the epistles of Paul.[42] Thus Clement of Alexandria counsels: "it is never right for a just person to put off chastity (*sôphrosunê*). For, see, this corruptible substance (*to phtharton touto*) will put on incorruptibility (*aphtharsia*), when the insatiableness of desire, which runs into licentiousness (*aselgeia*), having been educated by self-control (*enkrateia*) and ceasing to love corruption, surrenders the human being to eternal chastity" (*Paidagogos* 2.10, 230P).

Even thoughts are dangerous. Tertullian affirms: "sins not of deed only, but of will too, are to be shunned" (*On Repentance* 3). Augustine, more systematically, makes the thought or suggestion the first stage of sin, followed by pleasure in the thought and, finally, consent to perform the act (*Commentary on the Sermon on the Mount* 1.12.24–39; cf. *Commentary on Genesis against the Manicheans* 2.14.21).[43] The distinction between tendency or impulse and assent goes back to the Stoic conception of pre-emotions or *propatheiai*. Seneca explained that some reactions, such as vertigo when looking down from heights, blushing at obscene language, and growing pale at terrifying events such as a storm at sea, are involuntary reactions to which even the sage is susceptible and do not involve assent. Hence, they are not emotions in the strict sense of the word, but "preliminary beginnings of emotions" (*principia proludentia adfectibus*, *On Anger* 2.2.6). Jerome, in his *Commentary on Ezekiel* (18:1–2 = *PL* 25.168-69), refers explicitly to the Stoic theory: "thus God in no way punishes the first and second stimuli of thoughts, which the Greeks call *propatheiai*; no human being can be without these. But he does so only if someone has refused to correct by repentance the thoughts he decided to enact or the things he actually did."[44] The Stoic thesis that we are responsible not for automatic responses but only for those actions to which we give our assent granted Christian thinkers some leeway in regard to the sinfulness of even instinctive reactions.

To restrain the tendency to sin, the torments in the afterlife to which sinners were consigned were depicted in vivid terms, and a debate raged over whether punishment and damnation would last for all eternity, without hope of deliverance, or were rather intended ultimately to redeem the sinner, with the result that all, in the end, would be saved. The latter position was sometimes associated with the doctrine, endorsed by Origen and Gregory of Nyssa, of apocatastasis, which holds that after the end of time the universe will return to its original, prelapsarian condition. Thus Origen writes: "We think, indeed, that the goodness of God, through his Christ, may recall all his creatures to one end, even his enemies being conquered and subdued" (*De principiis* 1.6.1). Gregory of Nyssa was still more emphatic, including among those who will ultimately be redeemed even Lucifer himself (*De Anima et Resurrectione*, PG 56.100–01; *Oratio catechetica* 26; cf. also Origen, *De principiis* 3.6.3). But even those who believed in universal salvation allowed that the threat of eternal damnation was useful for discouraging sin (cf. Origen *De principiis* 1.3.5–6; Gregory of Nazianzus, *Moral Poems* col. 663.2 Migne; Evagrius *On Teachers and Disciples* lines 25–26).[45] Some maintained that it was possible for the living, through their prayers, to alleviate or reduce the torments of those consigned to hell. Thus, Tertullian explains that a dutiful widow prays for the soul of her deceased husband; she "requests refreshment for him meanwhile, and begs to join him in the first resurrection; and she offers sacrifices on the anniversaries of his falling asleep" (*On Monogamy* 10 = 2.942 Migne).[46] Arnobius of Sicca (mid third to early fourth centuries) exclaimed against the persecutors of Christians under the reign of Diocletian: "For why, indeed, have our writings deserved to be given to the flames? our meetings to be cruelly broken up, in which prayer is made to the Supreme God, peace and pardon are asked for all in authority, for soldiers, kings, friends, enemies, for those still in life, and those freed from the bondage of the flesh [*adhuc vitam degentibus et resolutis corporum vinctione*]?"[47] There is a suggestion of the efficacy of post-mortem prayer in *The Passion of Perpetua and Felicitas*, in which Perpetua prays, while in prison, for her younger brother, who died in boyhood:

> A few days after, while we were all praying, suddenly in the midst of the prayer I uttered a word and named Dinocrates; and I was amazed because he had never come into my mind save then; and I sorrowed, remembering his fate. And straightway I knew that I was worthy, and that I ought to ask for him. And I began to pray for him long, and to groan unto the Lord ... I was confident I should ease his travail; and I prayed for him every day till we passed over into the camp prison ... And I prayed for him day and night with groans and tears, that he might be given me.
>
> 7[48]

However, a strong position on eternal damnation, such as Augustine advocated, left room neither for reform via punishment and repentance in the afterlife nor intercession after death by survivors' prayers or the invocation of saints.

A contrary concern to lessen the terror associated with sin is evident in the distinction between forgivable and unforgivable sins, inspired by the language of mortal and non-mortal sins in 1 John 5:16–17. Irenaeus observes: "With respect to those actions, again, on which the Scriptures pass no censure, but which are simply set down, we ought not to become accusers, for we are not more exact than God, nor can we be superior to our Master" (*Against Heresies* 4.31). Tertullian, in turn, remarks: "We agree that the causes of repentance are sins. These we divide into two issues: some will be remissible, some irremissible: in accordance wherewith it will be doubtful to no one that some deserve chastisement, some condemnation. Every sin is dischargeable either by pardon or else by penalty: by pardon as the result of chastisement, by penalty as the result of condemnation" (*On Modesty* 2).[49]

The division between capital and venial sins was later formalized by Cassian, who, following Evagrius, identified eight deadly sins (Cassian *Conferences* 5; *Monastic Institutes* Books 5–12); these were reduced by Gregory the Great to the more familiar seven (pride, avarice, envy, wrath, lust, gluttony, and sloth or acedia, *Moralia in Iob*). Lust and gluttony are characteristic vices of the body, and greed, envy, and anger were commonly viewed in antiquity as negative passions. Pride (*hubris*, *superbia*), understood in the sense of arrogance, was never a positive value, but with Christianity it came to be seen as the opposite of the new virtue of humility. Finally, acedia, loosely rendered as despondency (*tristitia*) or sloth, was a kind of "weariness or distress of heart," to which anchorites in particular were susceptible (Cassian *Institutes* 10.1); it has no parallel in classical or Biblical inventories of vices or sins, and its connection with monkish spiritual disciplines is clear.

We have come a long way from Jesus' simple but radical polarization of sin and faith or trust in him, the one leading to damnation (whether eternal or not is unclear), the other to forgiveness.[50] From this perspective, sin simply was the absence of faith, the stubborn refusal to recognize Jesus' divinity and the new dispensation that his advent on earth represented, despite the manifest evidence of his powers. This was the message that the writers of the Gospels sought to convey, and I believe that it was broadly true to the way Jesus must have preached. Jesus' narrow focus on *pistis* and *apistia* or lack of faith excluded a concern with specific offenses, of the sort that are commonly regarded today as sins; when adultery or murder or the like were mentioned, they were described as evils or trespasses rather than as *hamartiai*, the term reserved for the new sense of sin. The Hebrew Bible had already provided something of a precedent for this limitation, since sin there was associated particularly with abandoning the God of the covenant and chasing after other—that is, foreign—gods. But this exclusion of personal or particular offenses from the charged category of sin was not well suited to serving as a basis for controlling the comportment of Christians in everyday life. Jesus might have rescued a woman who had committed adultery from being murdered by a mob and sent her off with the casual injunction to sin no more, but surely she must at some time confess her misbehavior and do penance, if her fault was to be pardoned. Already in the Bible there are hints of a widening of the use of the term sin. With the early Christian thinkers, however, the Greek and Latin terms for sin are extended to cover a wide range of delicts, and the careful terminological discrimination found in the Bible is progressively blurred.

At the same time, and perhaps for similar reasons, there occurred a generalization of the notion of sinfulness, which was now interpreted as a fallen state, initiated by the disobedience of Adam and Eve and passed down, in one or another fashion, to all their descendants. A newborn infant could scarcely be charged with having committed individual sins, and those who maintained that human beings were born innocent might regard the avoidance of sin as wholly within our power. Such was the Pelagian view, and that of others who were ultimately branded as heretics in the early church. But if sin was inherited from the originators of the fall, then all were in state of sin even as they emerged from the womb. Faith, now conceived more broadly as credence in various doctrines of the Church along with belief in Christ's divinity, remained crucial to earning forgiveness and redemption. But faith itself was no longer strictly voluntary, given mankind's fallen state, in which even the will was corrupted; rather, faith depended entirely on God's charity or grace. New questions of moral freedom were raised, causing doubt even in the most devoted about the possibility of salvation—and with this, despair itself came to be regarded as a sin. Perpetual tears and self-mortification were evidence of genuine repentance, and nevertheless insufficient in themselves to guarantee forgiveness.

Under this new regime, fear of sinning was instilled and augmented by a dread of punishment in the afterlife. In addition to the terrifying nature of the torments, the doctrine won out, at least in the Western Church, that the suffering of sinners after death was eternal, with no possibility of alleviation or remission. Sin became a source of mortal terror, with every slip a possible sign of damnation. All this was, as we have seen, a far cry from that confidence in Jesus, inspired by his miracles, which, in the Gospels, earned the healing of the body and the remission of sin.

The Christians were not alone in reinterpreting biblical conceptions of sin. Jewish thinkers too were responding to the accounts of sin in the Hebrew Bible, and they introduced new conceptions as well. Nor were the two traditions developing in isolation from one another. Philo of Alexandria, who died at around the time that Christ was crucified, was a crucial link between exegesis of the Hebrew Bible and Christians such as Clement and Origen, themselves Alexandrians, who applied Philo's methods to what they regarded as the Old Testament as well as the New.

Philo did not propound a systematic interpretation of sin. The verb *hamartanein* often simply means "to err," for example by trusting too much in the senses (*hamartanein*, *On the Cherubim* 65; cf. *diamartanein*, *On the Cherubim* 70). Very common in Philo is the formula *ouk an tis eipôn hamartoi*...,"one would not be wrong in saying..." (*Posterity of Cain* 58). The verb can convey moral error, as at *Posterity of Cain* 86, where Philo speaks of those who natter on about virtue and wisdom but in their plans and actions in their own lives are found to go thoroughly astray (*diamartanontes*). Even here, though, the sense is not quite that of "sin." Philo maintains that a tendency to err is innate in human beings. In the *Life of Moses*, Philo comments on Moses' sacrifice of a heifer and two lambs. He sacrifices the first of these, Philo explains, "for the remission of sins [*aphesis hamartêmatôn*], intimating that to sin is congenital with everything born, however good it may be, inasmuch as it came to birth. Therefore it is necessary that God be propitiated in its behalf by means of prayers and sacrifices, that he may not be provoked to chastise it" (2.29.147).[51] The deepest manifestation of sin is the rejection of the creator in favor of his creation. Hence Philo's emphasis on the sin of idol worship, consistent with the primary emphasis in the Tanakh; this, he exclaims, is even worse than revering astral bodies. As he writes in *On the Decalogue* (66):

> those who are ministers and servants of the sun, and of the moon, and of all the host of heaven, or of it in all its integrity or of its principal parts, are in

grievous error. How can they fail to be, when they honor the subjects instead of the prince? But still they sin less grievously than the others, who have fashioned stocks, and stones, and silver, and gold, and similar materials according to their own pleasure, making images, and statues, and all kinds of other things wrought by the hand ... For they have cut away the most beautiful support of the soul, namely the proper conception of the ever-living God.

66–67[52]

Philo would, of course, have found plenty of support in the Septuagint for associating sin above all with idolatry, as we saw in Chapter 2.

Writing under the influence of classical Platonism and Stoicism, Philo was especially concerned with the freedom of the will, or better, intention in relation to wrongdoing; for this reason, Philo reasons, Adam's offense is less than Cain's. Philo asks, "Why, in the genealogy of Adam, Moses no longer mentions Cain, but only Seth [Genesis 5:3]?" Philo answers that "It can neither be lawful to enumerate a wicked and sinful murderer." Rather,

> he must be cast out like dung ... And on this account the sacred historian neither points him out as the successor of his father who had been formed out of the dust, nor as the head of succeeding generations. But he distributes both these characteristics to him who was without pollution, and names Seth, who is a drinker of water, as having been watered by his father, and as begetting hope in his own increase and progress. On this account it is not inconsiderately and foolishly that he says that he was born according to the form and appearance of his father, to the reproof of his elder brother, who, on account of the foulness of the murder which he had committed, has nothing in him resembling his father, either in body or soul".
>
> *On Genesis* 1.81

As Philo writes elsewhere, "God banished Adam; but Cain went forth from his presence of his own accord." Philo explains:

> Moses is here showing to us the manner of each sort of absence from God, both the voluntary and the involuntary sort. But the involuntary sort as not existing in consequence of any intention on our part, will subsequently have such a remedy applied to it as the case admits of ... But the voluntary flight from God, as one that has taken place by deliberate purpose and intention, will await on irremediable punishment in all eternity. For as good deeds that

are done in consequence of forethought and design are better than unintentional ones, so also among offences [*hamartêmasi*] those that are undesigned are of less heinousness than those that are premeditated.

> *On the Posterity of Cain* 10–11; cf. *On the Special Laws* 1.227; *On the Decalogue* 141

Philo was, of course, writing in Greek, and it is generally agreed that he had at best a superficial knowledge of Hebrew, and more likely none at all. If we turn briefly now to the Hebrew tradition, as represented by the collection of commentaries called the Talmud, the emphases in relation to sin are somewhat different.

At the heart of the Day of Atonement (Yom Kippur) is repentance. The Mishnah, the earliest part of the Talmud dating to the first two centuries before Christ, states that "penitence procures atonement for lighter transgressions ... In the case of severer transgressions it suspends [the divine punishment] until the Day of Atonement comes to procure atonement."[53] But there are exceptions to the efficacy of repentance. First of all, the Mishnah states, "If one says, 'I shall sin and the Day of Atonement will procure atonement for me,' the Day of Atonement procures for him no atonement. For transgressions as between man and the Omnipresent the Day of Atonement procures atonement, but for transgressions as between man and his fellow the Day of Atonement does not procure any atonement, until he has pacified his fellow" (Eighth Mishnah of the Mishnah Yoma, cited in Talmud Yoma 86b). This is a crucial distinction: reconciliation with one's fellow human beings is distinct from forgiveness of sins, which only God can grant. The second exception is the desecration of God's name, for which there is no atonement save death (86a); the view is reminiscent of Jesus' statement that sins against the Holy Spirit are unforgivable (Matthew 12:31–32; Mark 3:28; Luke 12:10). Rabbi Meir is also adduced for the idea that "the entire world is forgiven on account of one individual who repents" (ibid.).

There is indeed some disagreement over terminology in this section. For example, the incompatibility between "stumbling," which seems accidental, and "iniquity," meaning an intentional offense, is discussed in relation to Hosea 14:2: "Return, Israel, to the Lord your God, for you have stumbled in your iniquity." In general, however, the terms for transgression, iniquity, and sin are treated as interchangeable, reflecting the assortment of biblical passages invoked as witnesses.[54] Given that the Mishnah and subsequent commentaries served as the legal code of the Jews, it is not surprising that, apart from the requirements for atonement and forgiveness, the focus is largely on specific misdeeds. Sins in the narrower sense of *ḥaṭa'*, as it is employed in the Tanakh, are included along with crimes, ritual errors, award of damages, and other prescriptions and violations of the law.

The Talmud records a debate over the meanings of the principal biblical terms for misdeeds: *ḥaṭa'* (חטא), *'awon* (עָוֹן), and *pesha'* (פֶּשַׁע). Earlier authorities, including the celebrated Rabbi Meir, had argued that one confesses *'awon, pesha'*, and *ḥaṭa'* (עָוֹן, פֶּשַׁע, and חטא), in that order, rendered as "I have done wrong, I have transgressed (or rebelled), I have sinned," citing Leviticus 16.21 and Exodus 34:7 (Babylonian Talmud Yoma 36b; cf. Tosefta Yoma 2.1). But later rabbis changed the order to *ḥaṭa', 'awon*, and *pesha'* (חטא 'עָוֹן, פֶּשַׁע), on the grounds that "wrongs" are deliberate misdeeds and "transgressions" are acts of rebellion, whereas "sins" are inadvertent errors, citing Leviticus 4:2: "When anyone sins unintentionally and does what is forbidden in any of the Lord's commands." On this interpretation, *ḥaṭa'* is the lightest of offenses, and confession progresses to intentional wrongdoing and, last and most egregious, outright rebellion (cf. Daniel 9:5: "We have sinned, and have committed iniquity, and have done wickedly, and have rebelled"). The Talmud affirms that the opinion of the many outweighs that of the individual (Rabbi Meir), and so rejects his view. The controversy reveals the ingenuity of the commentators but takes no account of the uses of the terms over the extent of the Tanakh, or the particular application of *ḥaṭa'* to idolatry.

There is no conception of original sin in the Jewish tradition. All sins are personal, and are to be atoned for individually. One may transgress involuntarily, and make suitable expiation, but the significant offenses are deliberate, as Philo maintained. The absence of original sin, however, did not preclude discussions over whether human beings had freewill or, on the contrary, all human acts were foreseen by God and, in one or another way, predetermined. The Jewish historian Josephus, who fought against the Romans but later became an adviser to the emperor Titus, pauses in the midst of a narrative of the conflict between Jonathan Maccabaeus and Demetrius II Nicator to explain what he describes as three distinct Jewish views of freewill:

> At this time there were three sects among the Jews, who had different opinions concerning human actions; the one was called the sect of the

Pharisees, another the sect of the Sadducees, and the other the sect of the Essenes. Now for the Pharisees, they say that some actions, but not all, are the work of fate, and some of them are in our own power, and that they are liable to fate, but are not caused by fate. But the sect of the Essenes affirm that fate governs all things, and that nothing befalls men but what is according to its determination. And for the Sadducees, they take away fate, and say there is no such thing, and that the events of human affairs are not at its disposal, but they suppose that all our actions are in our own power, so that we are ourselves the causes of what is good and receive what is evil from our own folly.

Jewish Antiquities 13.5.9[55]

Josephus' account was undoubtedly influenced by controversies about determinism in the Greek philosophical schools, such as the Stoics, who favored determinism, and the Epicureans, who did not. The Bible itself gives little support to ideas of predestination, but the Qumran scrolls indicate that the notion was accepted in such ascetic communities, though not in so strict a form as to exclude human choice.[56]

In relation to the law, the distinction between voluntary and involuntary offenses is obviously significant and the Talmud accordingly takes up the subject of freedom of the human will, while struggling with the problem of God's foreknowledge. Thus the famous sentence of Rabbi Akiva: "Everything is foreseen, but freedom of choice is given" (*Pirkei Avot* [*Sayings of the Fathers*] 3:15). In the Gemara, that part of the Talmud that consists of commentaries on the Mishnah, the tractate called Niddah deals primarily with issues involving menstruation. However, in the Tosefta, a kind of supplement to the Mishnah, there is expressed the view that, whereas a person's physical characteristics are preordained, one's moral character and spiritual orientation are matters of free choice (Niddah 16b). The rabbis debated energetically passages such as this: "Answer me, Lord, answer me, that this people will know that you are the Lord, God, and you have turned their hearts backward" (1 Kings 18:37), from which it might be inferred that "God caused Israel to sin" (Talmud Tractate Berakhot 31b). More aphoristically, Rabbi Ḥanina is quoted as saying: "Everything is in the hands of Heaven, except for fear of Heaven" (Talmud Tractate Berakhot 33b).[57] And in the Tractate Bava Basra, in a discussion of Job's suffering, the rabbis consider Job's cry: "You created the garden of Eden, and you created

Gehenna; and you created righteous people and You created wicked people; who can restrain you?" (16a). Does this not suggest that people are born good or bad, and hence have no control over whether or not they sin? The answer given is that human beings are indeed born with evil inclinations, but with the help of the Torah they are capable of overcoming them. It must be understood, however, that these comments are almost incidental, embedded as they are in discussions of technical interpretations of biblical passages and injunctions. We may note that a similar ambivalence toward astrology is also evident in the Talmud (Shabbat 53b; Babba Kamma 2b).

Within the rabbinical tradition, especially in the school of Ishmael, tensions in the will might be expressed as a rivalry between good and evil desires (*yetser*, יֵצֶר, plural *yetserim*), with the latter sometimes assuming the dimensions of a demonic force. This conception was inspired in part by apparent personifications of sin in the Tanakh, e.g. "sin (חטאת) is crouching at the door; its desire is for you" (Genesis 4:7; quoted in the Sifre to Deuteronomy 45).[58] It is possible, though difficult, to resist or overcome the evil *yetser* through study of the Torah, and thereby to increase the power of righteous *yetser* or will.

The Wikipedia article on "Jewish Views on Sin" affirms that "Judaism regards the violation of any of the 613 commandments as a sin."[59] It goes on to report that there are several Hebrew words for "sin," in addition to *haṭa'*, "each with its own specific meaning." Thus *pesha'* is parsed as "trespass," and defined as "a sin done out of rebelliousness," and other terms are rendered as "transgression" and "iniquity," the latter defined as "a sin done out of moral failing." There are, of course, many wicked acts that the Hebrew Bible condemns, even beyond contravening any of the 613 commandments. But the primacy of the word *haṭa'*, and its highly focused usage in the Tanakh, point to a development in the relationship between human and divine that is distinct from the simple violation of sacred laws. It is this sense of sin that renders it different from anything found in the ambient Greco-Roman culture. Neither *haṭa'* in the Tanakh nor *hamartia* in the Gospels ever lost its fundamental association with forgiveness on the part of God, whether as a result of repentance or of faith, a theme that is absent in the pagan tradition. But the authors of the Talmud, like the Christian exegetes, widened the scope of sin to cover a variety of offenses other than the pursuit of foreign gods or a lack of confidence in Jesus. With this came the danger that the concept of sin grew fuzzy—not less threatening, not less deadly, but embracing offenses punishable by God generally. The purpose of this book has not been to legislate how we use the word "sin," but to recover an original and innovative sense of sin that emerged within Judaism and Christianity, different as these were. It was here that a specific religious sense of sin emerged, endowing it with that aura that, for all the colloquial connotations that the word may bear, still marks it as a transcendental concept.

A Final Word

If "sin" sounds like a special term, not merely elevated in diction but signifying something specific to the Judeo-Christian tradition, that is because it is one, in both the Hebrew Bible and, in a different way, in the Gospels. But just why it is special, and how it differs from ideas of wrongdoing in the circumambient Greek and Roman world, has been obscured by layers of interpretation which are adumbrated even in later books of the New Testament, but become dominant in early exegetical literature, both the Talmud and the writings of the Church Fathers. Sin in the Bible does not refer simply to terrible crimes or even to violations of divine law. Rather, it is inextricably connected to forgiveness; it is a fault that seeks God's mercy. In the Tanakh, sin consists in the abrogation of the covenant with God, for which the Jewish people must atone so as to restore the relationship. In the New Testament, sin is the failure to trust in Jesus as the son of God, to realize the conversion or change of heart that the advent of the Messiah requires. In both Hebrew and Greek, a special term was appropriated to represent these distinctive ideas. I have sought to recover these biblical meanings by focusing on those words, as opposed to general terms for iniquity or evil. The biblical idea of sin survives, to be sure, in ancient commentary and modern sensibility; however, it is embedded in other, broader ideas of sin that cloud its unique nature. Hence the definitions of sin popular today, which capture some aspects but fail to distinguish the biblical sense from others that apply equally to classical Greek and Roman culture.

It will be evident to readers that this is not a book of theology. No doubt, the meanings of sin that I believe I have identified in the Hebrew Bible and the New Testament have important theological implications, but I have not sought to explore them in detail. We may say that this book is rather an exercise in philology, a study of words. To reverse the famous dictum of the elder Cato, *verbum tene, res sequetur* ("grasp the word, the subject will follow"). If I am right that *ḥaṭaʾ* (אטח) in the Tanakh and *hamartia* (ἁμαρτία) in the New Testament bear a special sense and testify to a crucial inflection of the idea of sin, then this book will have achieved its purpose.

Notes

Chapter 1

1. Krötke, Wolf et al. 1998–2007, s.v. Sünde: "der Bruch des Gottesverhältnisses durch den Menschen."
2. Fuhrer 2013: 177: "Die deutsche Begriff 'Sünde'... – wie die entsprechenden Begriffe in anderen modernen westeuropäischen Sprachen—bezeichnet eine verwerfliche Tat, mit der ein Mensch wissentlich einem göttlichen Gesetz oder Gebot zuwiderhandelt und sich also von Gott abwendet."
3. Löhr 1994: 135: "Sünde ist *per se* Sünde gegen Gott."
4. Trans. Murray 1919.
5. Trans. Murray 1924. The revised edition, edited by William F. Wyatt, substitutes "folly" for "sin."
6. Trans. Jebb 1900, modified.
7. For discussion, see Fletcher 2008; Beushausen 2008.
8. On the entire passage in Xenophon, and Socrates' positive doctrine, see Johnson 2003.
9. *Rhetoric* 1.13.2, cited by Jebb in his commentary on Sophocles' *Oedipus the King* 865 (Jebb 1887); compare also verses 863–71. Cf. Euripides fr. 853.1–2 Nauck/Kannicht, where however the common laws are those of the Greeks rather than of all mankind: τρεῖς εἰσὶν ἀρεταὶ τὰς χρεών σ' ἀσκεῖν, τέκνον, / θεούς τε τιμᾶν τούς τε φύσαντας γονῆς νόμους τε κοινοὺς Ἑλλάδος; also Euripides *Heraclidae* 1010.
10. Trans. Mynott 2013.
11. Trans. Bury 1926.
12. We may compare a fragment of the *Roman Antiquities*, composed by the historian and critic Dionysius of Halicarnassus who wrote during the reign of the Emperor Augustus: "One more political incident I shall relate, says Dionysius, deserving of praise on the part of all men, from which it will be clear to the Greeks how great was the hatred of wrongdoing felt in Rome at that time and how implacable the anger against those who transgressed the universal laws of human nature" (16.4.1–2, trans. Cary 1950). The example concerns one Gaius Laetorius, who attempted to rape a handsome youth; he was condemned to death.
13. Uglow (2019: 52) writes: "Early modern jurists represented humanity as bound by a universal law of nature, discernible by reason rather than divine revelation. Once

one had accepted that there were principles of natural justice and rules, 'established,' according to Sir William Blackstone, 'by universal consent among the civilized inhabitants of the world,' then nations who broke, or did not know, these universal principles could be labeled barbarians and treated as such—often with unblinking ferocity." The quotation is from Blackstone 1765–70, Book 4, Chapter 5. The classical sources do not make this distinction between "universal" laws that obtain among some peoples and not others.
14 For an overview of linguistic relativism, see Kay and Kempton 1984; Swoyer 2010. For criticism, see McWhorter 2014.
15 Jeremiah 2012: 12.
16 See Carbon and Pirenne-Delforge 2012; Carbon and Pirenne-Delforge 2017; Podella and Rüpke 2006.
17 Trans. Adams 1868, slightly modified.
18 See Bendlin 2007; the list is on p. 181; the quotation is from p. 183. I have omitted the sources of the citations, which are, respectively: *Monumenta Asiae Minoris Antiquae* 6.288; *Journal of Hellenic Studies* 10 (1889) 217 no. 1; *Supplementum Epigraphicum Graecum* 6.251; and *SEG* 38.1237.
19 F. Sokolowski 1969 = *LSCG* 139 (*Inscriptiones Graecae* 12.1 789), cited in Blidstein 2017: 20–1. The phrase "not to have knowledge of dreadful things" (μηδὲν αὐτοῖς δεινὸν συνειδότας) may be better rendered as "be conscious of," or even "have a guilty conscience for."
20 See Petrovic and Petrovic 2016.
21 Parker 1983. Cf. Eck 2012; Meinel 2015; Carbon and Peels-Matthey 2018.
22 *LSCG* 124.10.
23 Aeschylus *Eumenides*, 276–91, trans. Smyth 1926.
24 See Osteen 2002; Carla and Gori 2014; Konstan 2018a: 95–100.
25 See Harris 2015.
26 Blidstein 2017: 26.
27 Cf. Graf and Johnston 2013: 157.
28 Apuleius *Metamorphoses* 11.23–24, trans. Kline 2013.
29 Herrero de Jáuregui 2010: 19–20.
30 Ibid., p. 27.
31 Trans. Sarah Iles Johnston, in Graf and Johnston 2013: 66.
32 Ibid., p. 68.
33 Ibid., p.120.
34 Bernabé and Jiménez San Cristóbal 2008: 76; cf. pp. 107–8: "In view of these texts, the most logical approach is to think that under the mention of impious actions there lies a reference to the dismemberment of Dionysus at the hands of the Titans, the central myth of Orphism and a version of the origin of man, which,

like others, includes a doctrine of 'antecedent sin.'" Edmonds (2013: 296–390) casts doubt on modern reconstructions of the Zagreus myth.

35 Meisner 2018: 250; cf. Herrero de Jáuregui 2010: 336; Gagné 2013: 451–60.
36 See Tzifopoulos 2010; Bernabé 2004, 2005, 2007. That the gold leaves testify not so much to a myth of redemption as to a claim by the initiate to descent from the gods, and hence divine status, see McClay forthcoming.
37 E.g., Schnabel 2003. For further discussion, see Chaniotis 2004a; Hoz 1999; Rostad 2002; Malay and Petzl 2017; Konstan 2010: 87–90.
38 These are drawn from Rostad 2006, Appendix B; the translations are Rostad's, very slightly modified.
39 Petzl 1994 #4 (= *SEG* 38: 1229); date AD 200/201.
40 Petzl 1994: #5 (= *SEG* 38: 1237); date AD 235/236.
41 See Chaniotis 2004b: 5: "At first sight the procedure seems to concern only the sinner and the divinity, without the interference of any authority, whether secular or sacred. Things are not, however, as simple as that. To begin with, an interference of priests can be recognized in the recording of the confession: in many texts … we notice a change of the subject of the verb—from the third to the first person; this may be due to the fact that a priest recorded the confession, possibly made by an illiterate person."
42 Petzl 1994: #6 (= *SEG* 39: 1279); date AD 238/2399.
43 Petzl 1994: #10 (= *SEG* 28: 914); date AD 194/195.
44 Petzl 1994: #22 (= *SEG* 37: 1737); date = AD 215/216. For a study of the images represented on the stelae, see Hughes 2017: 151–86, the chapter, "Punishing Bodies: The Lydian and Phrygian 'Propitiatory' Stelai, Second–Third Centuries AD." Hughes suggests that the imagery on the stelae "demonstrates an understanding of human transgression and divine punishment as things that could be transmitted between members of the kinship group, and even spread to animals. This same belief had been conceptualised in earlier Greek myth and religion as *miasma*, with myths such as those of Atreus and Oedipus providing powerful mythological examples of how the repercussions of a wrongdoing could ripple over many generations without weakening. The major role that kinship links play in the transmission of wrongdoings and punishments can help us understand why many of the transgressive parties are shown making reparations to the gods in the presence of their families" (p. 180). I am not entirely convinced that the contagiousness of pollution is demonstrated by mentions of kin in these inscriptions.
45 Petzl 1994: #107; date second or third century AD.
46 Rostad 2006: 240.
47 Petzl 1994: #55 (= *SEG* 39: 1278); date AD 160/161.

48 For detailed discussion, see Konstan 2018b.
49 Sorabji 2104: 11–36.
50 Ibid., p. 14.
51 Ibid., p. 195, n. 2.
52 West 1987: 210.
53 Rodgers 1969: 252.
54 For further discussion, see Konstan 2016.
55 Trans. Rouse 1924.
56 On the Epicurean view of the gods, see Spinelli and Verde 2020. For an overview of the notion of sin in Latin texts, see Lamberights 2014a, 2014b.
57 The passage is from the treatise *On Choices and Avoidances*, probably composed by Philodemus, col. XII; I take the translation from Indelli and Tsouna-McKirahan 1995: 106. For Philodemus as the author, see pp. 66–70.
58 For a more detailed discussion of this and related passages, see Konstan 2019b.
59 Fuhrer 2013: 177.
60 In Petronius' *Satyrica*, Encolpius confesses (in verse!) to having done wrong, though, as he insists, it was a minor infraction: "I come unstained with sad blood, I have not laid hands on temples like an impious enemy, but when I was poor and worn down with want I committed a crime, though not with my whole body. When someone who is poor offends [*peccat*], he is less guilty [*minor reus*]. With this prayer I beg you, unburden my mind, pardon a lesser offence." The tone is that of extenuating an offense rather than expressing remorse. He promises, when his affairs have improved, to sacrifice a goat and a pig, and pour wine at the altars. As Justine Potts (2019: 27) observes, in Greek and Roman texts, "the function of confession [is] foremost an act of appeasement rather than revelation of self-authored guilt." Appeals for the mercy of the emperor or other plenipotentiary might be accompanied by confession, often partial or with extenuating circumstances; cf. Cicero *Pro Ligurio* 31; Potts, pp. 205–30.
61 Trans. Evelyn-White 1914.
62 There is an analogous instance of divine offense and retribution against both gods and mortals in the *Homeric Hymn to Demeter*.

Chapter 2

1 On the two accounts and their subsequent interpretation, see Corley 2016.
2 Trans. Roberts and Rambaut 1885, in Schaff 1978.
3 Irenaeus' source for this information is lost. Clement of Alexandria, in his *Stromateis* (3.12), and Origen (*On Prayer* 24) report that Tatian composed a work

on the early chapters of Genesis, which was among those declared heretical, and this is a likely place.

4 See Tromp 2005; Jonge and Tromp 1997; and cf. Greenblatt 2017: 67–73. Greenblatt remarks: "The Life of Adam and Eve provided the elaboration of the sparse Genesis account that many people craved" (p. 73); also Konstan 2017.

5 Mark Boda (2009: 32) argues that in Genesis, "Sin spoils the idyllic conditions of the garden created by God for fellowship with humanity … Throughout Genesis 1–11, sin is described as violating God's command (chaps. 2–3), disobeying God's creation mandate to fill the earth (Genesis 11) and exercise dominion (Genesis 3), seeking to become like God (Genesis 3), and murdering (Genesis 4, 9:46)." Boda treats terms for sin and evil generally as equivalent; cf., for example, p. 31 on Genesis 50:16–17, 20 (Joseph forgiving his brothers).

6 For full discussion of the various contexts for sin in the Tanakh, see Knierim (1965), who notes: "Von allen Begriffen, mit denen im Alten Testament die Sache der 'Sünde' zu Ausdruck gebracht wird, ist die Wurzel חטא am häufigsten verwendet" (p. 19); cf. Kiefer 2017.

7 The association of offenses of various kinds with pollution and consequent purification lies outside the scope of this chapter; for a thorough discussion, see Büchler 1967: 212–461.

8 The Hebrew text is difficult, since the feminine word for sin is modified by a masculine participle.

9 For example, Boda 2009: 19, 23; Tremellius' Renaissance Latin version has *remissio*. The Septuagint here has a different text, and so comparison is impossible. For discussion, see Brayford 2007: 253–4.

10 For discussion of the episode and a different interpretation, see Spanier 1992; cf. Cox and Ackerman 2012: 29–34. Sin, however, is not mentioned in this connection.

11 Smith (1911: 526) affirms more broadly: "A large number of Old Testament passages show that a sin is anything which puts a man in the wrong with reference to another man, which offends him. Pharaoh's butler and baker offend their master, and are put into prison. Laban pursues Jacob and reminds him that he is able to do him an injury," etc. Smith argues further that "Offenses against the divinity are regarded from the same point of view with offenses against men" (p. 527). For Smith, the specific notion of sin comes later: "It is clear … that at some point in history the idea that sin is transgression of a divine command comes in. It is probable that this view became prominent only after the establishment of the monarchy" (p. 528). I am suggesting that even in these ostensibly earlier instances ("early" in the narrative, not the time of composition of the Bible), the notion of an infraction of God's will is evident.

12 Brayford (2007: 404) comments simply: "Having intercourse with another man's wife would be adultery and thus a sin against God"; I am trying rather to tease out the significance of the double expression, "wickedness and sin." Weinberger (1997: 147) offers the radical suggestion that "Joseph's incarceration is punishment for the sin of rejecting mutual attraction and sexual intimacy in favour of loyalty to a slavemaster." But that would not be Joseph's own sense of the word for "sin."

13 Snaith (1965: 73) argues "that the difference between the two terms is that the sin-offering is concerned with unwitting offences whilst the guilt offering is concerned with offences where damage has been done and loss incurred, which in most cases can be assessed. But the confusion is still there." Levavi Feinstein (2017: 15, n. 20) remarks that "Hebrew חַטָּאת" is "sometimes translated 'sin offering,'" but notes that it is "used for the purgation of ritual pollution as well as sin." Watts (2015: 89) states: "The sin offering atones for inadvertent offenses while the guilt offering atones for mistaken acts of sacrilege. Flagrant sins of both kinds cannot be atoned for (Num. 15.26–31), but can be brought within the reach of cultic atonement by confession and, where possible, restitution."

14 Krašovec 1999: 445.

15 Cf. Baruch 6:2, in the so-called "Letter of Jeremiah": "Because of the sins which you have committed before God, you will be taken to Babylon as captives by Nebuchadnezzar, king of the Babylonians."

16 According to 2 Chronicles 33:12–19, after being taken captive Manasseh repents of his sin (ḥaṭaʾ) and trespasses: "And he took away the foreign gods and the idol from the house of the Lord, and all the altars that he had built on the mountain of the house of the Lord and in Jerusalem, and he threw them outside of the city. He also restored the altar of the Lord and offered upon it sacrifices of peace offerings and of thanksgiving; and he commanded Judah to serve the Lord the God of Israel. Nevertheless the people still sacrificed at the high places, but only to the Lord their God" (33:15–17).

17 Cf. 1 Esdras 6:15–16: "But when our fathers sinned against the Lord of Israel who is in heaven, and provoked him, he gave them over into the hands of Nebuchadnezzar king of Babylon, king of the Chaldeans; and they pulled down the house, and burned it, and carried the people away captive to Babylon." So too, Ezra laments: "For our sins have risen higher than our heads, and our mistakes have mounted up to heaven from the times of our fathers, and we are in great sin to this day. And because of our sins and the sins of our fathers we with our brethren and our kings and our priests were given over to the kings of the earth, to the sword and captivity and plundering, in shame until this day" (1 Esdras 8:75–77). At 2 Esdras, Ezra protests: "Are the deeds of Babylon better than those of Zion? Or has another nation known thee besides Israel?" (3:31–32), and asks the

Lord: "Now therefore weigh in a balance our iniquities and those of the inhabitants of the world; and so it will be found which way the turn of the scale will incline. When have the inhabitants of the earth not sinned in thy sight? Or what nation has kept thy commandments so well?" (3:34–35).

18 Mary Douglas (1994) sees Ezra's exclusiveness as inconsistent with the greater openness to outsiders in the Pentateuch. For further discussion, see Epstein 1968; Hayes 1999; Olyan 2004; Japhet 2007.

19 Cf. the much later text called Sirach or Ecclesiasticus 2:11, written originally in Hebrew but not accepted as part of the Tanakh: "For the Lord is compassionate and merciful; he forgives sins and saves in time of affliction." So too, the pillaging of the temple by Antiochus is attributed to the sins of the Israelites (2 Maccabees 5:17–18, written in Greek; cf. 7:18, 12:42–45; 3 Maccabees 2:13).

20 Griswold 2007: 50; see also Konstan 2010.

21 For the rare exceptions when a confession, almost always partial and hedged round with defenses, might earn clemency, see Potts 2019: 108–14 *et passim*.

22 Dover 1974: 156.

23 For fuller discussion, see Konstan 2018c. On biblical analogues in Heliodorus' novel, see Konstan 2004–5.

24 See further Konstan 2001.

25 Psalm 11:5–7; cf. 14:4, 17:13–14: "Arise, O Lord! confront them, overthrow them! Deliver my life from the wicked by thy sword, from men by thy hand, O Lord, from men whose portion in life is of the world."

26 We may recall that Ezekiel affirms that sin is not transmitted from one generation to the next; if a father sins, it is wrong that his offspring be punished (18:4; cf. Deuteronomy 24:16 but contrast Exodus 20:5).

27 Cf. Psalms 54, 56, 58, 64, 73, 94, 140, 141, etc., all contrasting the righteous with the wicked and the oppressors of Israel and expressing the hope for deliverance.

28 The ever-gloomy Ecclesiastes preaches broadly that sinners fare ill (2:26, 7:26, 8:12, 9:2).

29 Compare Zephaniah's harsh judgment, e.g. at 1:17: "I will bring distress on men, so that they shall walk like the blind, because they have sinned against the Lord; their blood shall be poured out like dust, and their flesh like dung"; the prophecy ends, however, on a note of hope (3:14–20). Cf. Lamentations 1:8 on the sins of Jerusalem.

30 On the punishment of sins, cf. Jeremiah 5:25; 8:14; 14:7, 10; 16:10, 18; 18:23; 19:1, 3; 30:14–15; 40:3; 44:23; Lamentations 4:13, 5:7, 5:16.

31 Cf. Jeremiah 15:13 with 15:19; 33:8: "I will cleanse them from all the guilt of their sin against me, and I will forgive all the guilt of their sin and rebellion against me"; 36:3: "It may be that the house of Judah will hear all the evil which I intend to do

to them, so that every one may turn from his evil way, and that I may forgive their iniquity and their sin"; 50:7, 14 with 50:20: "In those days and in that time, says the Lord, iniquity shall be sought in Israel, and there shall be none; and sin in Judah, and none shall be found; for I will pardon those whom I leave as a remnant."

32 On confession bringing forgiveness, cf. also Micah 7:9, 19: "He will again have compassion upon us, he will tread our iniquities under foot. Thou wilt cast all our sins into the depths of the sea"; Zechariah 13:1: "On that day there shall be a fountain opened for the house of David and the inhabitants of Jerusalem to cleanse them from sin and uncleanness"; cf. the non-canonical "Prayer of Manasseh" (composed originally in Greek) 1:11–14.

33 Cf. 1 John 1:9–10: "If we confess our sins, he is faithful and just, and will forgive our sins and cleanse us from all unrighteousness. If we say we have not sinned, we make him a liar, and his word is not in us"; 2 Esdras 16:53: "Let no sinner say that he has not sinned; for God will burn coals of fire on the head of him who says, 'I have not sinned before God and his glory'" (cf. 16:63–66). Cf. Lamentations 3:39–42: "Why should a living man complain, a man, about the punishment of his sins? Let us test and examine our ways, and return to the Lord! Let us lift up our hearts and hands to God in heaven: 'We have transgressed and rebelled, and thou hast not forgiven.'"

34 Contrast Lambert 2016: 51–68, on the relationship between confession and penitence, esp. p. 61: "Confession not only establishes a general fact of culpability; it articulates the exact sin (or sins) responsible for that state, preparing each to be removed through the operation of the cult." At Ezekiel 18:4 particular acts are listed as sins (cf. 18:14, 19); but this is something of an exception to the rule.

35 Cf. Wisdom (or The Wisdom of Solomon) 15:12–17; this is a late text, composed originally in Greek, and not part of the Tanakh.

36 Cf. Amos 5:12 on Israel's sins and transgressions, also 9:7; Micah 1:5, 13; 3:8).

37 The sins of the Canaanites are mentioned in Wisdom 12:11, a late text composed originally in Greek.

38 Again, we must bear in mind that the books of the prophets are composed primarily in verse, where the parallelism within each couplet invites and indeed requires extensive synonymy; hence the frequent pairings of sin with terms for iniquity, evil, and the rest.

39 For cultic associations, including possible allusions to Tammuz, Baal, and Marduk, as well as royal substitution, see KyeSang Ha (2009), with ample bibliography.

Chapter 3

1. Cf. Guzik 2005: ad loc.: "In a way, it was 'harder' to heal the man than to forgive his sins, because forgiveness is invisible—no one could verify at that moment the man was forgiven before God. Yet it could be instantly verified whether or not the man could walk. Jesus is willing to put Himself to the test."
2. Cf. Barclay 1975: ad loc.: "The Jews integrally connected sin and suffering. They argued that if a man was suffering he must have sinned. That is in fact the argument that Job's friends produced. 'Who,' demanded Eliphaz the Temanite, 'that was innocent ever perished?' (Job 4:7). The Rabbis had a saying, 'There is no sick man healed of his sickness until all his sins have been forgiven him.'" Barclay observes that such a connection is characteristic of certain "primitive peoples," but he adds: "We do not make the close connection that the Jews did, but any Jew would have agreed that forgiveness of sins was a prior condition of cure. It may well be, however, that there is more than this in this story. The Jews made this connection between illness and sin, and it may well be that, in this case, the man's conscience agreed. And it may well be that that consciousness of sin had actually produced the paralysis. The power of mind, especially the sub-conscious mind, over the body is an amazing thing."
3. Barnes 1884: 43. So too, Henry (1708–10) affirms of Jesus: "He could not have cured the disease, which was the effect, if he could not have taken away the sin, which was the cause."
4. On the connection between miracles and belief (*pistis*) in traditional miracle stories (*thaumata, mirabilia*) like those recounted by Phlegon of Tralles in his Περὶ θαυμασίων or "On Wonderrs," see Walsh 2021: 149-55. The difference between such narratives and the Gospel accounts lies in the element of forgiveness that caps the miracles and the demand for belief.
5. Cf. the definition of faith in *The Oxford Dictionary*: "Strong belief in God or in the doctrines of a religion, based on spiritual apprehension rather than proof." So too, *Dictionary.com* offers the definition: "belief that is not based on proof . . ., belief in God or in the doctrines or teachings of religion" and "a system of religious belief"; "a strongly held belief or theory." The dictionaries also give: "complete trust or confidence in someone or something"; "confidence or trust in a person or thing"; and "the obligation of loyalty or fidelity to a person, promise, engagement, etc.; fidelity to one's promise, oath, allegiance, etc." The latter two definitions correspond broadly to the meanings of the classical terms *pistis* and *fides*.
6. See Morgan 2015: 12–13, citing Augustine, *De trinitate* 13.2.5.
7. P. 76.1197C in the *Patrologia Latina*, trans. Bhattacharji 2001: 92.

8 Compare, however, Paul's claim in Romans 8:24–25: "For in hope we were saved. Now hope that is seen is not hope. For who hopes for what is seen? But if we hope for what we do not see, we wait for it with patience."
9 Morgan 2015: 428; but Morgan (pp. 440–1) allows that 1 John 5.4–5 may anticipate later connotations: "For whatever is born of God overcomes the world; and this is the victory that overcomes the world, our faith. Who is it that overcomes the world but he who believes that Jesus is the Son of God?" Notice the conjunction "that."
10 Compare John 11:21–27 on Martha's faith in Jesus:

> [21] Martha said to Jesus, "Lord, if you had been here, my brother would not have died. [22] But even now I know that God will give you whatever you ask of him." [23] Jesus said to her, "Your brother will rise again." [24] Martha said to him, "I know that he will rise again in the resurrection on the last day." [25] Jesus said to her, "I am the resurrection and the life. Whoever believes in me [*ho pisteuôn eis eme*], even though they die, will live, [26] and everyone who lives and believes in me will never die. Do you believe this [*pisteueis touto*]?" [27] She said to him, "Yes, Lord, I believe that [*pepisteuka hoti*] you are the Messiah, the Son of God, the one coming into the world."

This is one of the passages in which the verb for believing (here in the perfect tense) is accompanied by the conjunction "that." But the core idea is that Martha believes in Jesus (*eis eme*), which is to say, in his divinity; from this salvation follows.

11 *Revised Standard Version of the Bible* 1989, 1993.
12 For a partial correction of emphasis, looking primarily to healings rather than other manifestations of wonder-working, see Wallis 2020. Wallis' socio-political analysis of the nature of the diseases and their miraculous cures is not directly germane to the present argument.
13 France (2007: 107–8) writes: "John's followers as a whole confessed their sins when they were baptized, the proper response to John's call for repentance (v. 2) . . . He avoids Mark's statement that the baptism was 'for the forgiveness of sins,' perhaps because he wants to stress that such forgiveness is the prerogative of Jesus (9:6) and especially derives from the cross (26:28)." But repentance and confession for the forgiveness of sins is a regular motif in the Hebrew Bible, to which John, in his call to the people, is conforming. It will be for Jesus to forgive sins not by virtue of confession—no one confesses to him—but by trust in his divine mission, inspired by the manifest evidence of his miracles.
14 In classical Greek, a character confesses (*homologein*) to having done wrong (*adikein*, Euripides fr. 265); cf. Alexis *Athis* fr. 27, etc.; it is rare in the Septuagint (twelve times in all), while the noun *homologia* occurs seven times. The compound

form, *exomologeisthai*, first appears in Hellenistic texts, usually in the sense of acknowledging a debt or some other agreement or contract. It is the term for confessing (or praising) in the Septuagint, where it occurs 137 times, though only rarely in connection with sins (explicitly at Daniel 9:20). Cf. Tertullian *On Repentance* 9.2: "*exomologesis* is that by which we confess our offense [*delictum*] to the Lord." The Septuagint employs *exagoreuein*, literally, "to speak out," with "sin" as object (e.g., Leviticus 5:5: καὶ ἐξαγορεύσει τὴν ἁμαρτίαν περὶ ὧν ἡμάρτηκεν κατ' αὐτῆς; cf. Leviticus 26:40; Numbers 5:7; Plutarch *Moralia* 168D). At Leviticus 16:21, Aaron is ordered to reveal the iniquities and sins of the Israelites. For discussion, see Potts 2019: 31–50.

15 The Latin *confessio* too is used of praise, though Augustine says that in his time this sense was less familiar than that of confession of guilt (*Commentary on Psalms* 138.1).

16 As Kruse (2000: 68) observes, "Confession of sin is not a theme that is found often in the NT." Apart from Matthew 3:6, Mark 1:15, and John 1:9, it is found "in James 5:16, where, in the context of praying for the sick, people are urged to confess their sins and pray for each other that they may be healed. People in Ephesus confessed their 'evil deeds' and burned their magical books during the ministry of Paul in that city (Acts 19:18)." On Paul's wonder-working, see Eyl 2019, especially chapter 4, "A Taxonomy of Paul's Wonderworking."

17 McKnight (2011: 218) states: "What is clear is that James 5:15b reveals a very common connection made in the ancient world: sickness derives from sinfulness." McKnight relates the passage to *The Testaments of the Twelve Patriarchs* (Reuben 1:6–7, Zebulon 5, and Gad 5:9–11), as well as passages in the Talmud, and adds: "The same connection is found in the New Testament. Jesus said as he healed a paralyzed man, "Son, your sins are forgiven," and this implies that the paralysis was the result of sin." As we have seen, this is by no means a necessary interpretation of the episode of the paralyzed man, nor is it here in James. McKnight also affirms that "This confession of sins to one another was not a substitute for confession to God" (p. 220). This is true; but neither does it lead to the remission of sin.

18 See Danker 2000: s.v., def. 4. Cf. Yarbrough 2008: 63: "Among NT writers more generally, the verb ὁμολογέω can mean to affirm plainly and honestly (Matt. 7:23), to promise or fulfill a promise (Matt. 14:7; Acts 7:17), to admit or concede (Acts 24:14), and to acknowledge (Matt. 10:32; Acts 23:8)."

19 Kruse 2000: 35.

20 Cf. Yarbrough 2008: 62: "Instead of denying sin, John commends owning up to it (1:9). Old Testament passages clearly prescribe this practice"; Yarbrough cites Proverbs 28:13; Psalms 32:5 and 51; 2 Samuel 12:13; 2 Chronicles 32:26; Job 42:6;

Ezra 9:6–15; Nehemiah 1:6, etc.). He adds: "Old Testament writers seem to have confession to God foremost in mind."

21 Carroll 2012: 177.
22 Ibid., p. 180.
23 Haenchen (1984: 28) comments: "This 'I am' (ἐγώ εἰμι) sounds mysterious and is intended to sound mysterious. The Christian reader knows that Jesus is the Son of God and the Son of man. But how are the Jews to know that? They can only ask: 'Who are you then?'" There is presumably an echo of Exodus 3:14, "I am that I am" (אֶהְיֶה אֲשֶׁר אֶהְיֶה), rendered in the Septuagint as ἐγώ εἰμι ὁ ὤν (cf. the Vulgate: *si enim non credideritis quia ego sum*). The verb εἰμι can mean "exist"; the meaning would then be, "believe that I exist," that is, Jesus as the Messiah. Conceivably too, the expression might mean, "believe what [ὅ τι] I am," that is, God's son.
24 Wasserman 2008: 409–10. Cf. Wasserman 2007: 794–95.
25 Wasserman 2007: 800. Paul's notion of the law is related complexly to his conception of Mosaic law; cf. Romans 8:2: "For the law of the Spirit of life in Christ Jesus has set you free from the law of sin and of death"; also Romans 7:23 and 15:56, Galatians 1:4.
26 So too, the truth that frees one from bondage to sin (John 8:31–37) is just the fact that Jesus is the son of God (cf. John 16:13–14); it is in this that one must have confidence.
27 Taking τῶν ἀλισγημάτων in apposition with τῶν εἰδώλων καὶ τῆς πορνείας καὶ τοῦ πνικτοῦ καὶ τοῦ αἵματος; more commonly, the sentence is translated "abstain only from things polluted by idols and from fornication and from whatever has been strangled and from blood" (NSRV).
28 Cf. Mark 11:25–26: "Whenever you stand praying, forgive, if you have anything against anyone; so that your Father in heaven may also forgive you your trespasses. But if you do not forgive, neither will your Father in heaven forgive your trespasses [*paraptômata*]" (the second sentence is missing in some manuscripts).
29 Ἐνδύσασθε οὖν ὡς ἐκλεκτοὶ τοῦ θεοῦ, ἅγιοι καὶ ἠγαπημένοι, σπλάγχνα οἰκτιρμοῦ, χρηστότητα, ταπεινοφροσύνην, πραΰτητα, μακροθυμίαν, ἀνεχόμενοι ἀλλήλων καὶ χαριζόμενοι ἑαυτοῖς ἐάν τις πρός τινα ἔχῃ μομφήν· καθὼς καὶ ὁ κύριος ἐχαρίσατο ὑμῖν οὕτως καὶ ὑμεῖς. Anderson (2009) treats sin exclusively as a debt that can be paid by alms-giving, as evidenced by metaphors. Lam (2016) examines various metaphors for sin, including burden, accounting, path, stain, etc.
30 Nestle and Aland (2012), for example, in their edition of the New Testament maintain that they are an interpolation. Ramelli (2008), who provides a full discussion of the textual question, points to the correspondence between this appeal and the passage in Acts, in which Peter declares (3:17): "And now, brethren, I know that you acted in ignorance [*kata agnoian*], as did also your rulers." It may

be that, rather than interpolated, the words were expurgated by scribes who objected to what they imagined to be a potential exculpation of those who condemned Jesus to death.

31 Abelard 1995: 24 (section 112 of the treatise).
32 For full discussion, see Konstan 2018b.
33 Hart 2017.
34 Many more versions can be cited. Swedish Bibeln eller den Heliga Skrift has "predikade bättringens," but the Nya Levande Bibeln offers "han predikade att alla skulle vända sig till Gud." At Luke 3:3, the Russian version of the Bible in common use has ПОКАЯНИЕ, that is, "repentance."
35 See, for example, Hooker (1991), who translates "repentance for the forgiveness of sins" in the lemma, but notes: "The Greek word for repentance (*metanoia*) means literally 'a change of mind.' Although in popular usage it often has a sense of regret for what is past, it is generally used in a more positive way in the New Testament, implying a deliberate turning, or conversion, to God" (p. 37). So too, Maier (1991: 127) renders Luke 3:3 as "Die Taufe der Umkehr zur Vergebung der Sünden," but observes: "Das deutsche Wort 'Bußtaufe' reicht also nicht ganz aus, weil es den Ton zu stark auf die Abkehr legt und die entschlossene Hinkehr zu wenig zum Ausdruck bringt. Besser ist es, von einer 'Umkehrtaufe' oder "Bekehrungstaufe' zu sprechen" (p. 128). Of the lexica, for example, Coenen and Haacker (1997: 230–8) have an entry under the combined lemma, "Buße/Bekehrung," that is, "Repentance/Conversion," and remark in passing that Buße and Bekehrung "sind im Kern identisch" ("are essentially identical," p. 237). There is the same combined lemma in Léon-Dufour (1964: 91–7), but the comment is added: "Wenn Jesus die Bekehrung fordert, so spielt er in keiner Weise auf die Bußliturgien an" ("When Jesus calls for conversion, he does not in any way allude to the penitential liturgies," p. 96).
36 Arndt and Gingrich 1979.
37 So Nave (2002: 121) remarks: "Like the translators of the Hebrew Bible, Paul conveys the idea that sorrow lies at the heart of repentance."
38 Contra Nave 2002: 122: "It appears that for Paul, *metamelomai* represents nothing more than regret." So too, Peace (1999: 351) states: "The sense of *metamelomai* is that one regrets a past deed but does not decide necessarily never to do it again. *Metanoeô* is the stronger word and the one that bears upon the process of conversion." For Peace, the words do not differ in "the classical and Old Testament contexts," but in the New Testament they "cease to have identical meanings."
39 In this, I disagree, for example, with Torrance (2013: 51), who states: "the use of the present imperative form of the verb μετανοέω in Mt 3.2, 4.17 and Mk 1.15 evokes a sense of repentance as ongoing, a permanent 'state' into which the disciples of Jesus are called to enter."

40 Calvin 1949: 86–7. Cf. the comment of Barnes 1884: "This is evidently to be understood of the particular sin of persecuting and rejecting him. Of this he was speaking; and though, if he had not come, they would have been guilty of many other sins, yet of this, their great crowning sin, they would not have been guilty."
41 Calvin 1949: 87.
42 Cf. 2 Esdras 7:116–18: "it would have been better if the earth had not produced Adam, or else, when it had produced him, had restrained him from sinning. For what good is it to all that they live in sorrow now and expect punishment after death? O Adam, what have you done? For though it was you who sinned, the fall was not yours alone, but ours also who are your descendants"; this book, included among the apocrypha in most traditions, most likely dates to the second century AD.
43 Contrast Dunn 1988: 276: "παράβασις obviously = sin accounted."
44 For the association of sin with the flesh and its desires, see also Ephesians 2:3, and for that between fornication and sin, 1 Corinthians 6:18; cf. 1 Corinthians 7:28 and 36, 15:34; 2 Corinthians 12:21; 2 Peter 2:14. For sins and *epithumiai* ("desires," "lusts"), cf. 2 Timothy 3:6.

Chapter 4

1 Cooper 2005: 281. For the Latin text, see Locher 1972; Gori 1986.
2 Cooper 2005: n. 148. The reference is to Luther's Commentary on St. Paul's Epistle to the Galatians, translation in Dillenberger 1962: 58. Luther's crisp formula reads: "glaubstu, so hastu, so glaubstu nit, so hastu nit."
3 Trans. Bray 2009: 3.
4 Trans. Plumer 2003: 153.
5 Trans. Plumer 2003: 215; quoted also in the previous chapter.
6 Cf. Plumer 2003: 214–15; the Latin reads: *aliud est enim non peccare, aliud non habere peccatum. Nam in quo peccatum non regnat, non peccat, id est qui non oboedit desideriis eius, in quo autem non existunt omnino ista desideria, non solum non peccat, sed etiam non habet peccatum. Quod etiam si ex multis partibus in ista uita possit effici, ex omni tamen parte nonnisi in resurrectione carnis atque commutatione sperandum est.*
7 In the following chapter, *delinquere* (the verb corresponding to *delictum*) is paired with *peccare*: *conscientiae tuae latebras intuere, immo, quia nullus iam delinquendi metus vel pudor est, et sic peccatur quasi magis per ipsa peccata placeatur* ("look into the hiding-places of your own conscience. Nay, since now there is not even any fear or shame of erring [*delinquendi*], and you sin [*peccatur*] as though it were

rather by your sins [*peccata*] themselves that you were pleased …"). Cf. *Treatise* 10: *On Jealousy and Envy*, 14.

8 For the references, see Lamberights 2014a: 591–95.

9 *Contra Faustum Manichaeum*, 22.27 (*PL* 42.418); cf. Thomas Aquinas, *Summa Theologica* I–II q71 a6. Cf. 6.9.1 on the figurative meaning of the prohibitions in the Hebrew Bible: "To mix linen garments with purple, or to wear a garment of mixed linen and wool, was formerly a sin [*peccatum*]; now it is not a sin. But to live intemperately, and to wish to mix styles of different sorts, as when a woman devoted to religion wears the ornaments of married women, or when one who has not abstained from marriage dresses like a virgin, is wholly sin."

10 1.19, pp. 458–9. Trans. Fremantle 1893.

11 Trans. Scheck 2008: 106.

12 Cf. Theophylact, commenting on Matthew 9:3–5: "And, behold, certain of the scribes said within themselves, This man blasphemeth. And Jesus knowing their thoughts said, Wherefore think ye evil in your hearts? For which is easier to say, Thy sins be forgiven thee; or to say, Arise, and walk?": "By knowing their thoughts, Jesus shows that He is God. He rebukes them by saying, 'You think that I am blaspheming by promising to forgive sins, which is a great thing, and that I resort to this because it is something which can not be verified. But by healing the body, I shall guarantee that the soul has been healed as well. By doing the lesser deed, though it appears to be more difficult, I shall also confirm the remission of sins, which is indeed something great even though it appears easier to you since it is not visible to the eye.'"

13 Oration 40, *Oration on Holy Baptism* 33, on John's version (preached in Constantinople on January 6, 381), trans. Brown and Swallow 1894: 372.

14 *Commentary on Matthew* 8.5 (SC 254 198.1–6, 7–10).

15 The Greek here is θάρσει, "take courage" or "take heart"; the Latin *constans* is best understood in the sense of "be firm," or more colloquially, "steady on."

16 My translation (except for the final sentence) is based on Scully 2015: 140, with modifications. For a different version, see Williams 2012: 110.

17 Scully 2015: 140.

18 Image 2017: 83. Cf. p. 157: "the healing of the paralytic in Matthew is explicitly a cipher for the removal of original sin; the healing includes forgiveness, resurrection, and the entry into paradise, but does not mention baptism."

19 "*Pro huius ergo paralytici salute id est populi gentilis, uel certe Adae qui auctor humani generis esse cognoscitur*" (*Tractatus* 44.4 = *CCL* 9A 414.78–80), quoted by Scully 2015: 140, n. 13. For the translation, see also Scheck 2018. Image too (2017: 83, n. 3) cites Chromatius and also Irenaeus *Against Heresies* 5.17.1–3, but as we saw above, Irenaeus speaks rather of the paralytic's personal sins.

20 Trans. Gifford 2007: 31.
21 Trans. Stade 1992.
22 Homily 56, trans. Schaff 1978: 394–5.
23 *Tractate* 44.1.3, trans. Gibb 1888.
24 Book 1, ch. 9, trans. Pusey 1874/1885.
25 Trans. Teske 2004: 299–300, modified.
26 Trans. Menzies 1896.
27 Trans. Pusey 1874/1885.
28 Trans. Louth and Conti 2001: 85.
29 *mora ergo absolutionis in confitendo est, confessionem sequitur peccatorum remissio. Sapiens est igitur qui confitetur, liber cui peccatum dimissum est, nulla iam trahens aera peccati.*
30 Letters, vol. 2.7.45, to Simplicianus, trans. Walford 1881: 249–50.
31 See Colish 1990: 214.
32 Cf. *On the Merits and Forgiveness of Sins*, 1.9; *Contra Julianum*.
33 Trans. Teske 2004: 292.
34 On Julian, see Brown 2000: 383–99. Bray (1994: 430) observes: "The Ambrosiaster is especially noteworthy because he was the first to use the faulty, Old Latin translation of Romans 5:12, on which Augustine was later to base his teaching about inherited guilt. The original text says that 'death passed to all men, because all men have sinned.' The Greek for 'because' is the compound conjunction *eph' hoi*, which the Ambrosiaster read as *in quo*, 'in whom' and which he interpreted as a reference to Adam. This then seemed to offer Biblical evidence for the belief that all mankind shared in the act, and therefore in the guilt, of Adam's sin" (p. 43). See also Bonner 1968; Toews 2013: 73–89. Also useful are Stickelbroeck 2007 and Hauke 2007. Hauke refers especially to Messalianism, a sect, also called Euchites, who believed that by prayer one could achieve union with God. For the Latin *peccatum*, see Lamberights 2014a, b, s.vv. "peccatum" and "peccatum originale."
35 Trans. Bruyn 2017: xcii and ad loc.
36 For Augustine's transition from the idea of free will to determinism, see Wilson 2018, in particular p. 262 on Augustine's use of φύραμα.
37 Trans. Walker et al. 1889. Cf. Brattston 1991.
38 Trans. Holmes and Warfield 1867.
39 Trans. Evans 1972, modified.
40 *The Banquet of the Ten Virgins*, Discourse 8, "Thecla," ch. 13, "The Seven Crowns of the Beast," etc., trans. Clark 2012.
41 On the idea of a sinless Jesus in the New Testament, see Siker 2015.
42 On the shift in sexual attitudes from classical Rome to Christianity, see Harper 2016.

43 Augustine's source for this account was probably Aulus Gellius, *Attic Nights* 19.1.15–19: "The mental visions, which the philosophers call φαντασίαι or 'phantasies,' by which a person's mind on the very first appearance of an object is impelled to the perception of the object, are neither voluntary nor controlled by the will, but through a certain power of their own they force their recognition upon people. But the expressions of assent, which they call συγκαταθέσεις, by which these visions are recognized, are voluntary and subject to people's will. Therefore, when some terrifying sound, either from heaven or from a falling building or as a sudden announcement of some danger, or anything else of that kind occurs, even the mind of a sage must necessarily be disturbed, must shrink and feel alarm, not from a preconceived idea of any danger, but from certain swift and unexpected attacks which forestall the power of the mind and of reason. Presently, however, the sage does not approve 'such phantasies,' that is to say, such terrifying mental visions, that is, does not consent to them [οὐ συγκατατίθεται]), but he rejects and scorns them, nor does he see in them anything that ought to excite fear. And they say that there is this difference between the mind of a fool and that of a sage."

44 *Deus igitur primos et secundos stimulos cogitationum, quas Graeci προπάθειαις vocant, sine quibus nullus hominum esse potest, nequaquam punit; sed si cogitata quis facere decreverit, aut ipsa quae fecerit, noluerit corrigere paenitentia.* For discussion, see Visintainer 1962: 97. Cf. Sorabji 2000: 472–84. On *propatheiai*, see Graver 2007: 85–108.

45 See Ramelli 2013: 154, 178, 238–9; as she writes, "Fear of punishment is a pedagogical strategy, for Hilary just as for Origen" (p. 239).

46 Trans. Thelwall 1885.

47 Arnobius, *Adversus Gentes* 4.36 (5.1076 Migne), trans. Bryce and Campbell 1871: 218.

48 Trans. Shewring 1931.

49 Trans. Holmes and Thelwall 2017.

50 On the question of eternal damnation, see Ramelli and Konstan 2007.

51 Philo of Alexandria, *On the Life of Moses,* Book II, trans. Yonge 1855. Cf. Baudry 2000: 115–35.

52 Cf. 70; see also Radice 2000: 86. But Philo also hesitated at times, perhaps for practical reasons, to attack pagan worship directly; thus in the *Life of Moses* he writes: "For the world as we know it is full of idols of wood and stone, and suchlike images. We must refrain from speaking insultingly of these, in order that no one of the disciples of Moses may ever become accustomed at all to treat the appellation of God with disrespect" (2.205).

53 On the complex "category-formation" of sin, repentance, and atonement in the rabbinical tradition, see Neusner 2005: 299–317.

54 On Hebrew terms for evil, see Lyu 2011: 24–9.
55 Trans. Whiston 1859.
56 See Merrill 1975.
57 Trans. Steinsaltz 2012.
58 Cf. Rosen-Zvi 2011: 21.
59 *Wikipedia* 2021.

References

Abelard, Peter (1995), *Ethical Writings: His* Ethics *or "Know Yourself" and His Dialogue between a Philosopher, a Jew and a Christian*, trans. Paul Vincent Spade, with an introduction by Marilyn McCord Adams, Indianapolis, IN: Hackett Publishing.

Adams, Charles Darwin, trans. (1868), *The Genuine Works of Hippocrates*, New York: Dover.

Anderson, Gary A. (2009), *Sin: A History*, New Haven, CT: Yale University Press.

Arndt, William F. and F. Wilbur Gingrich (1979), *Greek-English Lexicon of the New Testament and Other Early Christian Literature*, 2nd ed., Chicago, IL: University of Chicago Press.

Barclay, William (1975), *The Daily Study Bible: The Gospel of Mark*, Philadelphia, PA: Westminster Press. Available online: https://www.dannychesnut.com/Bible/Barclay/Gospel%20of%20Mark.htm (accessed April 15, 2019).

Barnes, Albert (1884), *Notes on the New Testament*, London: Blackie.

Baudry, Gérard-Henri (2000), *Le péché dit originel*, Paris: Beauchesne.

Bendlin, Andreas (2007), "Purity and Pollution," in Daniel Ogden, ed., *A Companion to Greek Religion*, 178–89, Malden, MA: Blackwell.

Bernabé, Alberto and Ana Isabel Jiménez San Cristóbal (2008), *Instructions for the Netherworld: The Orphic Gold Tablets*, trans. Michael Chase, Leiden: Brill.

Bernabé, Albertus, ed. (2004, 2005, 2007), *Poetae Epici Graeci*, Pars II: *Orphicorum et Orphicis similium testimonia et fragmenta*, Munich: K.G. Saur.

Beushausen, Katrin (2008), "Dangerous Fracture: Undermining the Order of the Law in Sophocles's *Antigone*," *Mosaic: An Interdisciplinary Critical Journal* 4: 15–30.

Bhattacharji, Santha (2001), *Reading the Gospels with Gregory the Great: Homilies on the Gospels, 21–26*, Petersham, MA: St. Bede's Publications.

Blackstone, William (1765–70), *Commentaries on the Laws of England*, Oxford: Clarendon Press.

Blidstein, Moshe (2017), *Purity, Community, and Ritual in Early Christian Literature*, Oxford: Oxford University Press.

Boda, Mark J. (2009), *A Severe Mercy: Sin and its Remedy in the Old Testament*, Winona Lake, IN: Eisenbrauns.

Bonner, Gerald (1968), *Augustine on Romans 5, 12*, Berlin: Akademie-Verlag.

Brattston, David (1991), "The Forgiveness of Post-Baptismal Sin in Ancient Christianity," *Churchman* 105: 332–49.

Bray, Gerald L. (1994), "Original Sin in Patristic Thought," *Churchman* 108: 37–47.

Bray, Gerald L., trans. (2009), *Ambrosiaster: Commentaries on Galatians – Philemon*, Downers Grove, IL: Intervarsity Press.

Brayford, Susan, ed. (2007), *Genesis*, Septuagint Commentary Series, Leiden: Brill.

Brown, Charles Gordon and James Edward Swallow, trans. (1894), Gregory of Nazianzus, *Orations*, in *Nicene and Post-Nicene Fathers of the Christian Church*, 2nd series, vol. 7, Oxford: James Parker.

Brown, Peter (2000), *Augustine of Hippo: A Biography*, 2nd ed., Berkeley, CA: University of California Press.

Bruyn, Theodore S. de, trans. (2017), *Ambrosiaster's Commentary on the Pauline Epistles: Romans*, Atlanta, GA: SBL Press.

Bryce, Hamilton and Hugh Campbell, trans. (1871), *The Seven Books of Arnobius Adversus Gentes*, Edinburgh: T&T Clark.

Büchler, Adolf (1967), *Studies in Sin and Atonement in the Rabbinic Literature of the First Century*, New York: Ktav Publishing.

Bury, R. G., trans. (1926), *Plato: Laws*, Loeb Classical Library, vol. 11, Cambridge, MA: Harvard University Press (reprinted 1968).

Calvin, John (1949), *Commentary on the Gospel According to John*, vol. 2, trans. William Pringle, Grand Rapids, MI: Wm. B. Eerdmans.

Carbon, Jan-Mathieu and Vinciane Pirenne-Delforge (2012), "Beyond Greek 'Sacred Laws,'" *Kernos* 25: 163–82.

Carbon, Jan-Mathieu and Vinciane Pirenne-Delforge (2017), "Codifying 'Sacred Laws' in Ancient Greece," in Dominique Jaillard and Christophe Nihan, eds., *Writing Laws in Antiquity/L'écriture du droit dans l'Antiquité*, 141–57, Wiesbaden: Harrassowitz Verlag.

Carbon, Jan-Mathieu and Saskia Peels-Matthey, eds. (2018), *Purity and Purification in the Ancient Greek World: Texts, Rituals, and Norms*, Kernos Supplement 32, Liège: Presses Universitaires de Liège.

Carla, Filippo and Maja Gori (2014), "Introduction," in Filippo Carla and Maja Gori, eds., *Gift Giving and the "Embedded" Economy in the Ancient World*, 7–49, Heidelberg: Universitätsverlag Winter.

Carroll, John T. (2012), *Luke: A Commentary. The New Testament Library*, Louisville, KY: Westminster John Knox Press.

Cary, Earnest (1950), *The Roman Antiquities of Dionysius of Halicarnassus*, vol. 7, Cambridge, MA: Harvard University Press.

Chaniotis, Angelos (2004a), "Von Ehre, Schande und kleinen Verbrechen unter Nachbarn: Konfliktbewältigung und Götterjustiz in Gemeinden des antiken

Anatolien," in Frank R. Pfetsch, ed. *Konflikt*, 233–54 (Heidelberger Jahrbücher #4), Berlin: Springer.

Chaniotis, Angelos (2004b), "Under the Watchful Eyes of the Gods: Divine Justice in Hellenistic and Roman Asia Minor," in Stephen Colvin, ed., *The Greco-Roman East: Politics, Culture, Society*, 1–43, Cambridge: Cambridge University Press.

Clark, William Robinson (2012), *The Sacred Writings of Methodius*, Altenmünster: Jazzybee Verlag Jürgen Beck.

Coenen, Lotha and Klaus Haacker, eds. (1997), *Theologische Begriffslexikon zum Neuen Testament*, Neubearbeitete Ausgabe, Band I, Wuppertal: R. Brockhaus Verlag.

Colish, Marcia L. (1990), *The Stoic Tradition from Antiquity to the Early Middle Ages*, vol. 2: *Stoicism in Christian Latin Thought through the Sixth Century*, 2nd ed., Leiden: Brill.

Cooper, Stephen Andrew, trans. (2005), *Marius Victorinus' Commentary on Galatians*, Oxford: Oxford University Press.

Corley, Jeremy (2016), "Divine Creation and Human Mortality from Genesis to Ben Sira," *Irish Theological Quarterly* 81: 343–61.

Cox, Benjamin D. and Susan Ackerman (2012), "Micah's Teraphim," *Journal of Hebrew Scriptures* 12: 1–37.

Danker, Frederick W., ed. (2000), *A Greek-English Lexicon of the New Testament and Other Early Christian Literature* (*BDAG*), 3rd ed., Chicago, IL: University of Chicago Press.

Dictionary.com. Available online: http://dictionary.reference.com/browse/faith (accessed February 21, 2016).

Dillenberger, John, ed. (1962), *Martin Luther: Selections from his Writings*, New York: Random House.

Douglas, Mary (1994), "The Stranger in the Bible," *European Journal of Sociology/ Archives Européennes de Sociologie* 35: 283–98.

Dover, Kenneth J. (1974), *Greek Popular Morality in the Time of Plato and Aristotle*, Oxford: Blackwell.

Dunn, James D. G. (1988), *Romans 1–8*, Dallas, TX: Word Books.

Eck, Bernard (2012), *La mort rouge: homicide, guerre et souillure en Grèce ancienne*, Paris: Les Belles Lettres.

Edmonds, Radcliffe G., III (2013), *Redefining Ancient Orphism: A Study in Greek Religion*, Cambridge: Cambridge University Press.

Epstein, Louis M. (1968), *Marriage Laws in the Bible and the Talmud*, Cambridge: Cambridge University Press.

Evans, Ernest, trans. (1972), *Tertullian Adversus Marcionem, Books 1–3*, Oxford: Clarendon Press.

Evelyn-White, Hugh G. (1914), *Hesiod, the Homeric Hymns and Homerica*, Cambridge, MA: Harvard University Press.

Eyl, Jennifer (2019), *Signs, Wonders, and Gifts: Divination in the Letters of Paul*, Oxford: Oxford University Press.

Fletcher, Judith (2008), "Citing the Law in Sophocles' *Antigone*," *Mosaic: An Interdisciplinary Critical Journal* 4: 79–96.

France, R. T. (2007), *The Gospel of Matthew: The New International Commentary on the New Testament*, Grand Rapids, MI: Wm. B. Eerdmans.

Fredriksen, Paula (2012), *Sin: The Early History of an Idea*, Princeton, NJ: Princeton University Press.

Fremantle, W. H., trans. (1893), *The Principal Works of St. Jerome*, in *A Select Library of Nicene and Post-Nicene Fathers of the Christian Church*, vol. 6, Oxford: James Parker.

Fuhrer, Therese (2013), "Kann der Mensch ohne Fehler sein? Augustin über die 'Sünde,'" in Hans-Günther Nesselrath and Florian Wilk, eds., *Gut und Böse in Mensch und Welt: Philosophische und religiöse Konzeptionen vom Alten Orient bis zum frühen Islam*, 177–91, Tübingen: Mohr Siebeck.

Gagné, Renaud (2013), *Ancestral Fault in Ancient Greece*, Cambridge: Cambridge University Press.

Gibb, John, trans. (1888), "Augustine, Tractates on the Gospel of John," in Philip Schaff, ed., *Nicene and Post-Nicene Fathers*, 1st series, vol. 7, Buffalo, NY: Christian Literature Publishing.

Gifford, Edwin Hamilton, trans. (2007 [1893]), *The Catechetical Lectures of S. Cyril, Archbishop of Jerusalem*, in Philip Schaff and Rev. Henry Wallace, eds., *Nicene and Post-Nicene Fathers*, 2nd series, vol. 7, New York: Cosimo Classics.

Gori, Franco, ed. and trans. (1986), *Marii Victorini opera pars II: opera exegetica*, Vienna: Hoelder-Pichler-Tempsky.

Graf, Fritz and Sarah Iles Johnston (2013), *Ritual Texts for the Afterlife: Orpheus and the Bacchic Gold Tablets*, 2nd ed., London: Routledge.

Graver, Margaret (2007), *Stoicism and Emotion*, Chicago, IL: University of Chicago Press.

Greenblatt, Stephen (2017), *The Rise and Fall of Adam and Eve*, New York: W.W. Norton.

Griswold, Charles (2007), *Forgiveness: A Philosophical Exploration*, Cambridge: Cambridge University Press.

Guzik, David (2005), *Mark: Verse by Verse Commentary*, Goleta, CA: Enduring Word Media. Available online: https://enduringword.com/bible-commentary/mark-2/ (accessed April 15, 2019).

Ha, KyeSang (2009), "Cultic Allusions in the Suffering Servant Poem (Isaiah 52:13–53:12)," PhD dissertation, Andrews University, Berrien Springs, MI. Available online: https://digitalcommons.andrews.edu/dissertations/1637 (accessed May 24, 2021).

Haenchen, Ernst (1984), *John 2: A Commentary on the Gospel of John, Chapters 7–21*, Minneapolis, MN: Augsburg Fortress.

Harper, Kyle (2016), *From Shame to Sin: The Christian Transformation of Sexual Morality in Late Antiquity*, Cambridge, MA: Harvard University Press.

Harris, Edward M. (2015), "The Family, the Community, and Murder: The Role of Pollution in Athenian Homicide Law," in Clifford Ando and Jörg Rüpke, eds., *Public and Private in Ancient Mediterranean Law and Religion*, 11–33, Berlin: De Gruyter.

Hart, David Bentley (2017), *The New Testament: A Translation*, New Haven, CT: Yale University Press.

Hauke, Manfred (2007), *Urstand, Fall und Erbsünde in der nachaugustinischen Ära bis zum Beginn der Scholastik: Die griechische Theologie*, in *Handbuch der Dogmengeschichte*, Band 2, Fasz. 3a, 2 Teil, Freiburg: Herder.

Hayes, Christine (1999), "Intermarriage and Impurity in Ancient Jewish Sources," *Harvard Theological Review* 92: 3–36.

Henry, Matthew (1708–10), *An Exposition on the Old and New Testament*, London: William and James Stratford. Available online: https://www.biblestudytools.com/commentaries/matthew-henry-complete/mark/2.html (accessed April 15, 2019).

Herrero de Jáuregui, Miguel (2010), *Orphism and Christianity in Late Antiquity*, Berlin: De Gruyter.

Holmes, Peter and Benjamin B. Warfield, trans. (1867), *Augustine: On the Merits and Forgiveness of Sins, and on the Baptism of Infants*, in Philip Schaff, ed., *The Early Church Fathers and Other Works*, Edinburgh: Wm. B. Eerdmans.

Holmes, Peter and Sidney Thelwall, trans. (2017), *The Sacred Writings of Tertullian*, vol. 2, Loschberg: Jazzybee Verlag.

Hooker, Morna D. (1991), *A Commentary on the Gospel According to St Mark*, London: A & C Black.

Hoz, María Paz de (1999), *Die lydischen Kulte im Lichte der griechischen Inschriften*, Asia Minor Studien 36, Bonn: Verlag Dr. Rudolf Habelt.

Hughes, Jessica (2017), *Votive Body Parts in Greek and Roman Religion*, Cambridge: Cambridge University Press.

Image, Isabella (2017), *The Human Condition in Hilary of Poitiers: The Will and Original Sin between Origen and Augustine*, Oxford: Oxford University Press.

Indelli, Giovanni and Voula Tsouna-McKirahan, eds. (1995), *On Choices and Avoidances*, Naples: Bibliopolis.

Japhet, Sara (2007), "The Expulsion of the Foreign Women (Ezra 9–10): The Legal Basis, Precedents, and Consequences for the Definition of Jewish Identity," in

Friedhelm Hartenstein and Michael Pietsch, eds., *Sieben Augen auf Einem Stein (Sach 3,9): Studien zur Literatur des Zweiten Tempels: Festschrift für Ina Willi-Plein zum 65. Geburtstag*, 141–61, Göttingen: Vandenhoeck & Ruprecht.

Jebb, Richard C., ed. (1887) *The Oedipus Tyrannus of Sophocles*, Cambridge: Cambridge University Press.

Jebb, Richard C., ed. (1900), *Sophocles: The Plays and Fragments*, part III: *The Antigone*, Cambridge: Cambridge University Press.

Jeremiah, Edward T. (2012), *The Emergence of Reflexivity in Greek Language and Thought: From Homer to Plato and Beyond*, Leiden: Brill.

Johnson, David M. (2003) "Xenophon's Socrates on Law and Justice," *Ancient Philosophy* 23: 255–81.

Jonge, Marinus de and Johannes Tromp (1997), *The Life of Adam and Eve and Related Literature*, Sheffield: Academic Press.

Kay, Paul and Willett Kempton (1984), "What Is the Sapir-Whorf Hypothesis?," *American Anthropologist* (n.s.) 86: 65–79.

Kiefer, Jörn (2017), "Sünde/Sünder (AT)," in Michaela Bauks, Klaus Koenen, and Stefan Alkier, eds., *Das wissenschaftliche Bibellexikon im Internet* (http://www.wibilex.de). Available online: https://www.bibelwissenschaft.de/stichwort/31970 (accessed August 27, 2018).

King James Version Dictionary. Available online: https://av1611.com/kjbp/kjv-dictionary/sin.html (accessed May 24, 2021).

Kline, Anthony S. (2013), Apuleius *Metamorphoses*. Available online: https://www.poetryintranslation.com/PITBR/Latin/TheGoldenAssXI.php#anchor_Toc353982295 (accessed May 24, 2021).

Knierim, Rolf P. (1965), *Die Hauptbegriffe für Sünde im Alten Testament*, Gütersloh: Gerd Mohn.

Konstan, David (2001), *Pity Transformed*, London: Duckworth.

Konstan, David (2004–5), "Travel in Heliodorus: Homecoming or Voyage to a Promised Land?," *Classica – Revista Brasileira de Estudos Clássicos* 17/18: 185–92.

Konstan, David (2010), *Before Forgiveness: The Origins of a Moral Ideal*, Cambridge: Cambridge University Press.

Konstan, David (2016), "Did Orestes Have a Conscience? Another Look at *Sunesis* in Euripides' *Orestes*," in Poulheria Kyriakou and Antonios Rengakos, eds., *Wisdom and Folly in Euripides*, 229–40, Berlin: De Gruyter.

Konstan, David (2017), "Sin: The Prehistory," *Scandinavian Journal of Byzantine and Modern Greek Studies* 3: 125–40.

Konstan, David (2018a), *In the Orbit of Love: Affection in Ancient Greece and Rome*, Oxford: Oxford University Press.

Konstan, David (2018b), "Reue," in *Reallexikon für Antike und Christentum*, vol. 28, columns 1216–42, Stuttgart: Anton Hiersemann.
Konstan, David (2018c), "Pity vs. Forgiveness in Pagan and Judaeo-Christian Narratives," in Marília Futre Pinheiro, David Konstan, and Bruce MacQueen, eds., *Crossroads in the Ancient Novel*, 305–14, Berlin: De Gruyter.
Konstan, David (2019a), "Jesus' Sense of Sin," in Janet E. Spittler, ed., *The Narrative Self in Early Christianity: Essays in Honor of Judith Perkins*, 121–32 (Writings from the Greco-Roman World Supplement #15), Atlanta, GA: Society for Biblical Literature Press.
Konstan, David (2019b), "Lucretius and the Conscience of an Epicurean," *Politeia* 1 (2): 68–80.
Konstan, David (2021), "Sünde," in *Reallexikon für Antike und Christentum*, Bonn: Franz Joseph Dölger-Institut.
Krašovec, Jože (1999), *Reward, Punishment, and Forgiveness: The Thinking and Beliefs of Ancient Israel in the Light of Greek and Modern Views*, Leiden: E.J. Brill.
Krötke, Wolf, Klaus Hock, Alexandra Grund, Rainer Metzner, Heinrich Holze, et al. (1998–2007), "Sünde/Schuld und Vergebung," in Hans Dieter Betz, ed., *Religion in Geschichte und Gegenwart*, 4th ed., Leiden: E.J. Brill. Available online: http://dx.doi.org/10.1163/2405-8262_rgg4_COM_025015 (accessed December 5, 2018).
Kruse, Colin G. (2000), *The Letters of John: The Pillar New Testament Commentary*, Grand Rapids, MI: Wm. B. Eerdmans.
Lam, Joseph (2016), *Patterns of Sin in the Hebrew Bible: Metaphor, Culture, and the Making of a Religious Concept*, Oxford: Oxford University Press.
Lamberights, Mathijs (2014a), "peccatum," in Robert Dodaro, Cornelius Mayer, and Christof Müller, eds., *Augustinus Lexikon*, vol. 4, 581–99, Basel: Schwabe.
Lamberights Mathijs (2014b), "peccatum originale," in Robert Dodaro, Cornelius Mayer, and Christof Müller, eds., *Augustinus Lexikon*, vol. 4, 599–615, Basel: Schwabe.
Lambert, David A. (2016), *How Repentance Became Biblical: Judaism, Christianity, and the Interpretation of Scripture*, Oxford: Oxford University Press.
Léon-Dufour, Xavier (1964), *Wörterbuch zur biblischen Botschaft*, Freiburg: Herder.
Levavi Feinstein, Eve (2017), *Sexual Pollution in the Hebrew Bible*, Oxford: Oxford University Press.
Liddell, Henry George, Robert Scott, Henry Stuart Jones, and Roderick McKenzie, eds. (1966), *A Greek–English Lexicon*, 9th ed., Oxford: Oxford University Press.
Locher, Albrecht, ed. (1972), *Marii Victorini Afri commentarii in epistulas Pauli ad Galatas, ad Philippenses, ad Ephesios*, Leipzig: Teubner.
Löhr, Hermut (1994), *Umkehr und Sünde im Hebräerbrief*, Berlin: De Gruyter.
Louth, Andrew and Marco Conti, trans. (2001), *Ancient Christian Commentary on Scripture: Old Testament*, vol. 1, *Genesis 1–11*, Downers Grove, IL: InterVarsity Press.

Lyu, Eun-Geol (2011), *Sünde und Rechtfertigung bei Paulus: eine exegetische Untersuchung zum paulinischen Sündenverständnis aus soteriologischer Sicht*, Tübingen: Mohr Siebeck.

Maier, Gerhard (1991), *Lukas-Evangelium*, 1 Teil, Neuhausen: Hänssler-Verlag.

Malay, Hasan and Georg Petzl (2017), *New Religious Texts from Lydia*, Vienna: Verlag der Österreichischen Akademie der Wissenschaften.

McClay, Mark F. (forthcoming), "'You Fell into Milk': Symbols and Narratives of Kinship in Bacchic Mysteries," *Classical Antiquity*.

McKnight, Scot (2011), *The Letter of James: New International Commentary on the New Testament*, Grand Rapids, MI: Wm. B. Eerdmans.

McWhorter, John H. (2014), *The Language Hoax: Why the World Looks the Same in Any Language*, New York: Oxford University Press.

Meinel, Fabian (2015), *Pollution and Crisis in Greek Tragedy*, Cambridge: Cambridge University Press.

Meisner, Dwayne A. (2018), *Orphic Tradition and the Birth of the Gods*, Oxford: Oxford University Press.

Menzies, Allan, trans. (1896), Origen, *Commentary on the Gospel of John*, in Ante-Nicene Fathers, vol. 9, Buffalo, NY: Christian Literature Publishing. Revised and edited for New Advent by Kevin Knight. Available online: https://www.newadvent.org/fathers/101501.htm (accessed September 25, 2019).

Merriam-Webster.com Dictionary. Available online: https://www.merriam-webster.com/dictionary/sin (accessed May 24, 2021).

Merrill, Eugene H. (1975), *Qumran and Predestination: A Theological Study of the Thanksgiving Hymns*, Leiden: E.J. Brill.

Morgan, Teresa (2015), *Roman Faith and Christian Faith: Pistis and Fides in the Early Roman Empire and Early Churches*, Oxford: Oxford University Press.

Murray, A. T. (1919), *The Odyssey*, revised by George E. Dimock, Cambridge, MA: Harvard University Press.

Murray, A. T. (1924), *The Iliad*, revised by William F. Wyatt, Cambridge, MA: Harvard University Press.

Mynott, Jeremy, trans. (2013), *Thucydides: The War of the Peloponnesians and the Athenians*, Cambridge: Cambridge University Press.

Nave, Guy D., Jr. (2002), *The Role and Function of Repentance in Luke-Acts*, Atlanta, GA: Society of Biblical Literature.

Nestle, Eberhard and Kurt Aland, eds. (2012), *Novum Testamentum Graece*, 28th ed., Stuttgart: Deutsche Bibelgesellschaft.

Neusner, Jacob (2005), *Rabbinic Categories: Construction and Comparison*, Leiden: E.J. Brill.

Olyan, Saul (2004), "Purity Ideology in Ezra-Nehemiah as a Tool to Reconstitute the Community," *Journal for the Study of Judaism* 35: 1–16.
Osteen, Mark (2002), "Gift or Commodity," in Mark Osteen, ed., *The Question of the Gift: Essays across Disciplines*, 229–47, London: Routledge.
Oxford English Dictionary.com. Available online: https://www.lexico.com/en/definition/sin (accessed May 24, 2021).
Parker, Robert C. T. (1983), *Miasma: Pollution and Purification in Early Greek Religion*, Oxford: Oxford University Press.
Peace, R. V. (1999), *Conversion in the New Testament: Paul and the Twelve*, Grand Rapids, MI: Wm. B. Eerdmans.
Petrovic, Andrej and Ivana Petrovic (2016), *Inner Purity and Pollution in Greek Religion*, vol. 1: *Early Greek Religion*, Oxford: Oxford University Press.
Petzl, Georg (1994), *Die Beichtinschriften Westkleinasiens* (Epigraphica Anatolica #22), Bonn: Habelt.
Plumer, Eric, ed. and trans. (2003), *Augustine's Commentary on Galatians: Introduction, Text, Translation, and Notes*, Oxford: Oxford University Press.
Podella, Thomas and Jörg Rüpke (2006), "Ecclesiastical/Religious Law"/"Sakralrecht," in Hubert Cancik, Helmuth Schneider, and Manfred Landfester, eds., *Der Neue Pauly*, Leiden: E.J. Brill. Available online: http://dx.doi.org/10.1163/1574-9347_dnp_e1027750 (accessed March 2, 2019).
Potts, Justine (2019), "Confession in the Greco-Roman World: A Social and Cultural History," PhD dissertation, Oxford University, Oxford.
Pusey, P. E., trans. (1874/1885), *Cyril of Alexandria, Commentary on John*, 2 vols., London: Walter Smith.
Radice, Roberto (2000), *Allegoria e paradigmi etici in Filone di Alessandria: Commentario al Legum allegoriae*, Milan: Vita e Pensiero.
Ramelli, Ilaria (2008), "Review of Griswold 2007: *Forgiveness: A Philosophical Exploration*", *Rivista di Filosofia Neo-scolastica* 100: 658–62.
Ramelli, Ilaria (2013), *The Christian Doctrine of Apokatastasis: A Critical Assessment from the New Testament to Eriugena*, Leiden: E.J. Brill.
Ramelli, Ilaria and David Konstan (2007), *Terms for Eternity:* Aiônios *and* aïdios *in Classical and Christian Texts*, Piscataway, NJ: Gorgias Press.
Revised Standard Version of the Bible Catholic Edition (*RSVCE*) (1989, 1993), Washington DC: National Council of the Churches of Christ. Available online: https://www.biblegateway.com/passage/?search=Matthew+8&version=RSVCE (accessed April 18, 2019).
Roberts, Alexander and William Rambaut (1885), "Irenaeus Against Heresies," in Alexander Roberts, James Donaldson, and A. Cleveland Coxe, eds., *Ante-Nicene*

Fathers, vol. 1, Buffalo, NY: Christian Literature Publishing. Available online: https://www.newadvent.org/fathers/0103.htm (accessed May 24, 2021).

Rodgers, V. A. (1969), "Σύνεσις and the Expression of Conscience," *Greek, Roman, and Byzantine Studies* 10: 241–54.

Rodríguez Adrados, Francisco, ed. (1980–), *Diccionario Griego-Español*, Madrid: Instituto "Antonio de Nebrija." Available online: http://dge.cchs.csic.es/xdge (accessed May 24, 2021).

Rosen-Zvi, Ishay (2011), *Demonic Desires: Yetzer Hara and the Problem of Evil in Late Antiquity*, Philadelphia, PA: University of Pennsylvania Press.

Rostad, Aslak (2002), "Confession or Reconciliation? The Narrative Structure of the Lydian and Phrygian 'Confession Inscriptions,'" *Symbolae Osloenses* 77: 145–64.

Rostad, Aslak (2006), "Human Transgression – Divine Retribution: A Study of Religious Transgressions and Punishments in Greek Cultic Regulations and Lydian-Phrygian Reconciliation Inscriptions," PhD dissertation, University of Bergen, Bergen.

Rouse, W. H. D., trans. (1924), *Lucretius: On the Nature of Things*, revised by Martin F. Smith, Cambridge MA: Harvard University Press.

Schaff, Philip (1978), *The Homilies of St. John Chrysostom on the Gospel of St. John* (Post-Nicene Fathers, series 1, vol. 14), Grand Rapids, MI: Christian Classics Ethereal Library.

Scheck, Thomas B., trans. (2008), *St. Jerome: Commentary on Matthew*, Washington, DC: Catholic University of America Press.

Scheck, Thomas P., trans. (2018), *Chromatius of Aquileia: Sermons and Tractates on Matthew*, New York: Newman Press.

Schnabel, Eckhard J. (2003), "Divine Tyranny and Public Humiliation: A Suggestion for the Interpretation of the Lydian and Phrygian Confession Inscriptions," *Novum Testamentum* 45: 160–88.

Scully, Ellen (2015), *Physicalist Soteriology in Hilary of Poitiers*, Leiden: E.J. Brill.

Shewring, W. H., trans. (1931), *The Passion of Perpetua and Felicity*, London: Sheed & Ward.

Siker, Jeffrey S. (2015), *Jesus, Sin, and Perfection in Early Christianity*, New York: Cambridge University Press.

Smith, Henry Preserved (1911), "The Hebrew View of Sin," *American Journal of Theology* 15: 525–45.

Smyth, Herbert Weir (1926), *Aeschylus* Eumenides, revised by Cynthia Bannon, further revised by Gregory Nagy, Cambridge, MA: Harvard University Press. Available online: https://chs.harvard.edu/CHS/article/display/5298 (accessed May 24, 2021).

Snaith, N. H. (1965), "The Sin-Offering and the Guilt-Offering," *Vetus Testamentum* 15: 73–80.

Sokolowski, Franciszek (1969), *Lois sacrées des cités grecques*, Paris: E. de Boccard.

Sorabji, Richard (2000), *Emotion and Peace of Mind: From Stoic Agitation to Christian Temptation*, Oxford: Oxford University Press.

Sorabji, Richard (2014), *Moral Conscience through the Ages: Fifth Century BCE to the Present*, Chicago, IL: University of Chicago Press.

Spanier, Ktziah (1992), "Rachel's Theft of the Teraphim: Her Struggle for Family Primacy," *Vetus Testamentum* 42: 404–12.

Spinelli, Emidio and Francesco Verde (2020), "Epicurean Theology," in Phillip Mitsis, ed., *The Oxford Handbook of Epicurus and Epicureanism*, 94–117, Oxford: Oxford University Press.

Stade, Christopher, trans. (1992), *Theophylact of Ohrid: The Explanation of the Holy Gospel according to St. Matthew*, House Spring, MO: Chrysostom Press.

Steinsaltz, Adin Even-Israel, trans. (2012), *Koren Talmud Bavli*, Jerusalem: Koren. Available online: https://www.sefaria.org/Berakhot.33b.23?lang=bi&with=all&lang2=en (accessed September 29, 2019).

Stickelbroeck, Michael (2007), *Urstand, Fall und Erbsünde in der nachaugustinischen Ära bis zum Beginn der Scholastik: Die lateinische Theologie*, in *Handbuch der Dogmengeschichte*, Band 2, Fasz. 3a, 3 Teil, Freiburg: Herder.

Swoyer, Chris (2010), "Relativism," in Edward N. Zalta, ed., *The Stanford Encyclopedia of Philosophy*. Available online: http://plato.stanford.edu/archives/win2010/entries/relativism (accessed November 5, 2019).

Teske, Willard J., trans. (2004), *The Works of Saint Augustine: A Translation for the 21st Century*, vol. II.3, *Letters 156–210*, Hyde Park, NY: New City Press.

Thelwall, S., trans. (1885), *Tertullian: On Monogamy*, in *Ante-Nicene Fathers*, vol. 4, Buffalo, NY: Christian Literature Publishing. Edited for New Advent by Kevin Knight. Available online: http://www.newadvent.org/fathers/0406.htm (accessed May 25, 2021).

Thomas, Keith (2018), *In Pursuit of Civility: Manners and Civilization in Early Modern England*, Waltham, MA: Brandeis University Press.

Toews, John E. (2013), *The Story of Original Sin*, Cambridge: James Clarke.

Torrance, Alexis (2013), *Repentance in Late Antiquity: Eastern Asceticism and the Framing of the Christian Life c. 400–650 CE*, Oxford: Oxford University Press.

Tromp, Johannes (2005), *The Life of Adam and Eve in Greek: A Critical Edition*, Leiden: E.J. Brill.

Tzifopoulos, Yannis Z. (2010), *"Paradise Earned": The Bacchic-Orphic Gold Lamellae of Crete* (Center for Hellenic Studies, Hellenic Series #23), Cambridge, MA: Harvard University Press. Available online: http://www.hup.harvard.edu/catalog/TZIPAR.html (accessed May 24, 2021).

Uglow, Jenny (2019), "Civility and Its Discontents: Review of Keith Thomas, *In Pursuit of Civility: Manners and Civilization in Early Modern England*", *The New York Review* 68 (13): 51–3.

Visintainer, Severino (1962), *La dottrina del peccato in S. Girolamo*, Rome: Libreria Editrice dell'Università Gregoriana.

Walford, H., trans. (1881), *The Letters of Ambrose, Bishop of Milan*, Oxford: James Parker.

Walker, J., J. Sheppard, and H. Browne, trans. (1889), John Chrysostom, *Homilies*, revised by George B. Stevens, in Philip Schaff, ed., *Nicene and Post-Nicene Fathers*, First series, vol. 11, Buffalo, NY: Christian Literature Publishing. Revised and edited for New Advent by Kevin Knight. Available online: http://www.newadvent.org/fathers/210101.htm (accessed September 26, 2019).

Wallis, Ian G. (2020), *The Galilean Wonderworker: Reassessing Jesus' Reputation for Healing and Exorcism*, Eugene, OR: Cascade.

Walsh, Robyn Faith (2021), *The Origins of Early Christian Literature: Contextualizing the New Testament within Greco-Roman Literary Culture*, Cambridge: Cambridge University Press.

Wasserman, Emma (2007), "The Death of the Soul in Romans 7," *Journal of Biblical Literature* 126: 793–816.

Wasserman, Emma (2008), "Paul among the Philosophers: The Case of Sin in Romans 6–8," *Journal for the Study of the New Testament* 30: 387–415.

Watts, James W. (2015), "The Historical and Literary Contexts of the Sin and Guilt Offerings," in Francis Landy, Leigh M. Trevaskis, and Bryan D. Bibb, eds., *Text, Time, and Temple: Literary, Historical and Ritual Studies in Leviticus*, 85–93, Sheffield: Sheffield Phoenix Press.

Weinberger, Theodore (1997), "'And Joseph Slept with Potiphar's Wife': A Re-reading," *Literature and Theology* 11: 145–51.

West, Martin L., ed. (1987), *Euripides Orestes*, Warminster: Aris & Phillips.

Whiston, William, trans. (1859), *The Works of Josephus, with a Life*, vol. 2, Philadelphia, PA: Lindsay & Blakiston.

Wikipedia (2021), "Jewish Views on Sin." Available online: https://en.wikipedia.org/wiki/Jewish_views_on_sin (accessed September 29, 2019).

Williams, D. H., trans. (2012), *St. Hilary of Poitiers, Commentary on Matthew*, Washington, DC: Catholic University of America Press.

Wilson, Kenneth M. (2018), *Augustine's Conversion from Traditional Free Choice to "Non-free Free Will": A Comprehensive Methodology*, Tübingen: Mohr Siebeck.

Yarbrough, Robert W. (2008), *1, 2, and 3 John: Baker Exegetical Commentary on the New Testament*, Grand Rapids, MI: Baker Academic.

Yonge, C. D., trans. (1855), *Philo of Alexandria, On the Life of Moses,* Book II, in *The Works of Philo Judaeus*, vol. 3, London: H.G. Bohn.

Index

Abelard, Peter
    on ignorance and sin 106
Abimelech
    and Sarah 39–40
Achan 44
Adam and Eve 33–6
    Life of 35–6
    on Adam's sin 142–5
    Ephrem the Syrian on 140
    Philo on 152–3
adulterous woman (in John) 101
Aegisthus (slayer of Agamemnon) 2–4, 6–7
Aeschylus, *Oresteia* 7–8, 15–17
afterlife, punishment in 147–8
Ambrose, on confession 140
Ambrosiaster
    on faith 124
    on original sin 142
ametameletos (unregretted) 113
anomia (lawlessness) 99
Antigone 9–10
aphienai (forgive, remit) 104
apistia (lack of faith) 95, 114
    Augustine on 136–8
    of Hebrews, according to Paul 116
    not the only sin 124
    Origen on 138
Apocatastasis (return to original condition) 147–8
Apuleius, Metamorphoses 17–18
Aristophanes, *Frogs* 17
Aristotle
    on *hamartia* 12–13
    on ignorance and pardon 106
    on unwritten law 10
Arnobius of Sicca, on prayer for the deceased 148
astrology 146
atasthalia (madness, sin) 3
Atonement, Day of 153

Augustine
    on the blind man 135
    on faith 85
        absence of not the only sin 124
    on grace 141
    on having sin (vs. sinning) 125
    on infants and sin 144–5
    on no sin before Jesus 136–8
    on sin, definition 126–7
    on thoughts as first stage to sin 147
    on the wise do not sin 141

baptism
    and remission of sin 125–6
    sins committed before 142–5
    unbaptized infants 144
Bible, multiple sources xi-xii
Blackstone, William 162 n.13
Blind man
    in John 94–5
        Augustine on 135
        Cyril of Alexandria on 135–6
        John Chrysostom on 133–4
    in Matthew 89–90

Caananite woman's faith 93
Caelestius (disciple of Pelagius), on Adam's sin 145
Calvin, John, on unbelief as the only sin 114
capital sins 149
Cassian, on capital sins 149
centurion, faith of (in Matthew) 87
Chariton, *Callirhoe* 62
chastity 146–7
Chromatius (bishop of Aquileia), on paralyzed man 132
Cicero, on confession of guilt 61
Clement of Alexandria
    on chastity 147
    definition of sin 126

evil, God's responsibility for 145
on repentance 146
on sins committed after baptism
   (second repentance) 143
confession
   Ambrose on 140
   Cicero on 61
   to one's fellows 98
   and forgiveness 59–60, 98–9
   in Greece and Rome 61
   not in Greek novels 61–3
   in Hebrew Bible 43–4
   and John the Baptist 99–100
   in the New Testament 96–8
   and the Prophets 70
   in Psalms 66–7
   refusal of 70–1
confession inscriptions (in Lydia and
   Phrygia) 22–5
confidence, faith as 86–90
conscience 26–31
conversion, vs. repentance 107–13
Cyprian of Carthage
   on forgiveness of sins 108
   on offenses (*delicta*) 126
Cyril of Alexandria
   on the blind man 135–6
   on no sin before Jesus 139
   on original sin 142
Cyril of Jerusalem, on paralyzed man
   132–3

Daniel 70, 72
David
   and Saul 46–7
   and Uriah's wife (Bathsheba) 47–8
demons, casting out of 90, 92
Dionysius of Halicarnassus, on universal
   law 161 n.12
Dionysus, and Orphism 21–2

Eden 33–6
eleos (pity, mercy) 61
Eli, sons of 45
Elijah, and miracles 73
Encratites 37
Ephrem the Syrian, on Adam and Eve
   140
eternity of punishment 147–8

eukhê (prayer) 98
   of faith 98
Euripides, *Orestes*, on conscience 27–8
Eve, repentance in *Life of Adam and Eve* 36
Evil
   God's responsibility for 145–6
   Talmud on 155–6
   terms for
      Greek 103–5
      Hebrew 37, 65, 72, 154
exomologeisthai (confess, profess) 96–8
Ezekiel 69–71
Ezra, and intermarriage 57–8

faith
   Augustine on 85
   of the blind
      in John 94–5
      in Matthew 89–90
   of centurion 87
   as confidence in Jesus 86–90
   definitions of 84–5
   of the disciples (when Jesus walks on
      water) 93–3
   and forgiveness 100–2
   and grace 141
   and healing 77–83, 86–90
   of Hebrews, according to Paul 116
   lack of 95, 114
      Augustine on 136–8
   and miracles 81–96
   in the New Testament 85–90
   non-rational 85
   and the paralyzed man 82–3
   Pope Gregory on 85
   prayer of 98
   propositional (belief that) 85–6
   and resurrection 115–16
   and sin 72, 75, 102, 107, 111
   as trust in Jesus 86–90, 118
fides (faith) 85
   see also faith
freewill
   and sin 145–6
   Talmud on 155–6
forgivable sins 149
forgiveness
   of brother 105, 108
   and confession 59–60, 98–9

of debts 104
definitions of 60
denied 105–6
by disciples of Jesus 108
and faith 100–2
God's 48, 78, 104
in Greece and Rome 61
of the ignorant 106–7
Jesus' power of 78
and Psalms 68
and sin 100–1
terms for 120–1

Gellius, Aulus on pre-emotions 177 n.43
Gospel writers' mission 118
grace 119
    Augustine on 141
    of faith 124
Gregory (Pope)
    on capital sins 149
    on faith 85
Gregory of Nazianzus
    on the paralyzed man 130
    on unbaptized infants 144
Gregory of Nyssa
    on apocatastasis 148
    on sin as estrangement from God 142
    on unbaptized infants 144
guilt offerings 42–3

hamartêma (sin) 13
hamartia (sin) 4–5, 96
    loose uses of 119–20
    in Paul 102
haṭa' (sin) 36–7
    of Cain 38
    and commandments 41
    in the Hebrew Bible (summary) 73
    and idolatry 41–3
    and non-Israelites 59, 72
    of Sodom and Gomorra 38–9
    Talmud on 154
healing
    of the blind 89–90, 94–5
    and faith 77–83, 86–90
    of ruler's daughter (in Matthew) 88–9
Heliodorus, *Aethiopica* 63
hemorrhaging woman (in Mark) 86–7
Hesiod on Prometheus 32

Hilary of Poitiers on paralyzed man 130–2
Hippocrates, *On the Sacred Disease* 13
Homer
    Iliad 5–6
    Odyssey 2–4, 6–7
homologein (confess, profess) 96–8
Hosea 72

idolatry
    and Israelites 41–3, 53, 56
    in Israel and Judea 48–55
    among non-Israelites, not a sin 52–3, 56
    Philo of Alexandria on 151–2
    and the Prophets 71–2
ignorance and forgiveness 106–7
infants, sinfulness of 144–5
intermarriage and sin 44
    in Ezra 57–8
Irenaeus
    on Adam and Eve's childlike nature 140
    on Adam's salvation 35
    on forgivable sins 149
    on paralyzed man 130
Isaiah 69–73
    and the suffering servant 72–3
Israel (northern kingdom) 48–52
    conquered by Assyrians 52

Jacob and Laban 39–40
Jeremiah 70
Jeroboam 48–9
Jerome
    on paralyzed man 129–30
    on pre-emotions 147
    on sins not all equal 127
    translation of Bible (Vulgate) 127
Jesus
    casting out of demons 90, 92
    forgiveness of sins 78
    miracles 78–9
    and the Sabbath 92
    no sin before 81
        Augustine on 136–8
        Cyril of Alexandria on 139
        Origen on 138
    sinless 146
Job 63–5

John the Baptist
  confession and repentance 99–100, 107, 110–11
  in prison 91
John Chrysostom
  on the blind man 133–4
  on God's forgiveness 78
  on paralyzed man 130
  on repentance 146
  on sins committed after baptism 143–4
Joseph and Potiphar's wife 40–1
Josephus on predestination 154–5
Judah (southern kingdom) 49, 51–2, 54–5
  and Ezekiel 69
  and Isaiah 69, 71
  and Nebuchadnezzar 55
Judas 105–6
Judgment of Paris 5–6
Julian of Eclanum (disciple of Pelagius) 142
Justin Martyr
  on baptism 125–6
  on repentance 146
  on sins 125

Laban 39–40
lack of faith (as only sin) 95, 114
  Augustine on 136–8
  of Hebrews, according to Paul 116
  not the only sin 95, 124
  Origen on 138
law
  sacred 13–15
  and sin (according to Paul) 116–17
  universal 11, 161 n.12
  unwritten 9–11
lawlessness and sin 99
Life of Adam and Eve 35–6, 140
Lucretius
  on conscience 29–31
  on law 31
Luther, Martin on faith 123

Manasseh 54–5
Martha, faith in Jesus 170 n.10
mercy 61
metameleia (regret, conversion) 25, 28, 111–13
  contrasted with *metanoia* 112–13

metanoia (repentance, conversion) 107–14
  contrasted with *metameleia* 112–13
Methodius on astrology 146
miasma 15–17
Micah 72
miracles
  and calming of the winds (in Matthew) 88
  and faith 81–96
  and healing 77–83, 86–90
  in the Hebrew Bible 73
  of Jesus 78–9
  of the loaves and fish 92–3
  of Paul 97–8
  of resurrection 115–16
  walking on water 92–3
Mishnah on Yom Kippur 153
mortal and non-mortal sins 120, 149
murder and pollution in Athens 16
mystery cults 17–19

Nebuchadnezzar 55
Nehemiah and walls of Jerusalem 58–9
nomos (law, custom) 9–11
novels, Greek, absence of confession in 61–3

Oedipus and ignorance 106–7
offenses
  as sins 119–20
  vs. sins 103–5
Olympiodorus 21–2
Orestes
  and conscience 27–8
  and pollution 15–17
  and sin 7–8
Origen
  on apocatastasis 148
  on no sin before Jesus (allegory) 138
original sin
  Ambrosiaster on 142
  Augustine on 141–2, 144–5
  not in Judaism 154
  denied by Pelagius 144–5
  and Orphism 21–2
Orphism 20–2

paenitentia (regret, repentance) 26
pagan viii

and death of Jesus 115–16
definitions
    Augustine 126
    Clement of Alexandria 126–7
    modern 1–2
as estrangement from God 142
eternal punishment of 147–8
vs. evil 103–5
and faith 72, 75, 102, 107, 111
hamartia 96
having sin 125
against the Holy Spirit 105
of infants 144–5
inherited from Adam 131–2
not before Jesus' coming 81, 114
    Augustine on 136–8
    Cyril of Alexandria on 139
    Origen on 138
    as lack of faith 95, 114
    not just lack of faith 124
in Latin Vulgate 127
and the law (in Paul) 116–17
and lawlessness 99
loose uses of 119–20
mortal and non-mortal 120, 149
original
    Ambrosiaster on 142
    Augustine on 141–2
    Cyril of Alexandria on 142
    and Orphism 21–2
    and predestination 145–6
    ranking of (in Talmud) 154
    and sickness or debility 79–82, 86–7, 94–5, 129–36
of thoughts 147
tripartite script for x, 43, 59, 111, 120–1
voluntary vs. involuntary (Philo on) 152–3
see also *hamartia, haṭa'*
sinful woman (in Luke) 100–1
sinlessness (of those born of God) 99
sin offerings 42–3
Sodom and Gomorrah 3–4, 38–9

Sophocles
    Antigone 9–10
    Philoctetes 15
Stoicism on pre-emotions 147, 177 n.43
sunesis and conscience 27–8
sungnômê (pardon) 106
sunoida (of conscience) 26–7

Talmud 153–5
    on ranking of sins 154
Tatian denies Adam's salvation 35
teraphim 39–40
Tertullian
    on evil and God 145–6
    on forgivable sins 149
    on prayer for the deceased 148
    on sinning after repentance 126
    on sins committed after baptism 143
    on thoughts as sinful 147
Theodoret
    on Jesus' sinlessness 146
    on repentance 146
Theophylact of Ohrid on paralyzed man 133, 175 n.12
Thomas, Acts of 126
Thomas Aquinas on figurative prohibitions 175 n.9
thoughts as sinful 147
Thucydides on unwritten law 10–11
tripartite script for sin x, 43, 59, 111, 120–1
trust, faith as 86–90

Vetus Latina (Old Latin Version of the Bible) 142
Victorinus, Marius on faith 123
Vulgate 127

Xenophon on unwritten law 10
Xenophon of Ephesus, *Ephesian Tale* 61–2

yetser (desire) 156
Yom Kippur (Day of Atonement) 153

paralyzed man
    Chromatius (bishop of Aquileia) on 132
    Cyril of Jerusalem on 132–3
    Gregory of Nazianzus on 130
    Hilary of Poitiers on 130–2
    Irenaeus on 130
    Jerome on 129–30
    John Chrysostom on 130
    in Luke 79–82
    in Mark 77–9, 82–3
    Theophylact of Ohrid on 133
Paul
    his miracles 97–8
    his mission 119–20
    on the law and sin 116–17
    on the self, 102 117
    on sin 102, 116–17
peccatum (sin) 127
Pelagius
    on free will 141
    on all sins equal 127
    on sins of infants 144
penitential practices 146–7
Perpetua and Felicitas on prayer for the deceased 148
Petronius, *Satyrica* 164 n.60
Philemon (comic poet) on *metanoia* 110
Philo of Alexandria
    on congenital sin 151
    on idolatry 151–2
    on voluntary vs. involuntary sin 152–3
Philoctetes 15
Philodemus on law 31
pistis (faith), 85–90, 111, 118
    see also faith
pity 61
    and desert 63
    God's 105
Plato
    on false prophets 19
    on *hamartia* 12
    on unwritten law 11–13
Plautus and conscience 29
Plutarch on conscience 28
pollution 15–17
Polybius on universal law 11

Potiphar's wife 40–1
prayer 98
    effectiveness for the deceased 148
predestination
    in Judaism 154–5
    and sin 145–6
    in the Talmud 155–6
pre-emotions in Stoicism 147, 177 n.43
Prometheus 32
propatheia (pre-emotion) 147
prophets
    false 19
    Hebrew 69–73
    and idolatry 71–2
Proverbs 69
Psalms 65–8
    and confession 66–7
    and forgiveness 68
punishment
    in the afterlife 147–8
    not eternal 148
purity 15–17

Rachel, theft of *teraphim* 39–40
regret 25–6
remorse 25–6, 30
repentance
    vs. conversion 107–13
    intensification of 146–7
    of Israelites 112
    sinning after 126, 143
resurrection of Jesus 115–16

Sabbath, Jesus' actions on 92
sacred laws (*leges sacrae*) 13–15
salakh (forgiveness), used only of God 48, 78, 104
Samaria 52–3
Samuel and idolatry 45–6
Saul 46–7
Seneca, on pre-emotions 147
skandalon (stumbling block) 104
sickness (or debility)
    and sin 79–82, 86–7, 94–5
    caused by sin 129–36
sin
    and baptism 142–5
    capital vs. venial 149

www.ingramcontent.com/pod-product-compliance
Lightning Source LLC
Chambersburg PA
CBHW051643230426
43669CB00013B/2424